OUT OF ORANGE

OUT OF ORANGE

A Memoir

CLEARY WOLTERS

HarperOne
An Imprint of HarperCollinsPublishers

HarperOne

This is a work of nonfiction. The events and experiences detailed herein are all true and have been faithfully rendered as remembered by the author, to the best of her ability. Many names and personal details have been changed in order to protect the privacy of individuals involved. Though conversations come from the author's keen recollection of them, they are not written to represent word-for-word documentation; rather, they have been retold in a way that evokes the real feeling and meaning of what was said, and in keeping with the true essence of the events.

FIRST EDITION

Designed by Terry McGrath

Library of Congress Cataloging-in-Publication Data
Wolters, Cleary.
Out of orange : a memoir / Cleary Wolters. — First edition.
    pages cm
ISBN 978-0-06-237613-8
1. Wolters, Cleary. 2. Women drug dealers—United States—Biography. 3. Women ex-convicts—United States—Biography. 4. Women prisoners—Connecticut—Danbury—Biography. 5. Drug trade—United States. I. Orange is the new black (Television program) II. Title.
HV5805.W65A3 2015
364.1'77092—dc23
[B]   2015001467

15 16 17 18 19   RRD(H)   10 9 8 7 6 5 4 3 2 1

For Dad

Contents

OUT OF ORANGE

Prologue: Karma

I DEVELOPED A SKILL, where if I want to concentrate on something, anything, and my surroundings are distracting or loud, I can block out the noise and activity surrounding me and focus solely on whatever task needs my attention. It's a very useful skill at times, but it bugs the shit out of my mother when I'm not listening to her. In that case, it's not really a skill; it's a habit. It's not my intention to ignore her. But if we are watching one of our favorite television shows together at the end of a very long day, I might miss the fact that she has been talking to me for a while.

It was in one of these typical end-of-day scenes where she was going on and on about something trivial, like how many lights our neighbor has on tonight compared to any other night or the number of cars that have driven down our road. I was tuned in to a comedy when she clapped to get my attention away from the show and onto her dilemma. Dad's been gone for years, and I don't hear dead people, so I can't really help her resolve their most recent spat. Besides that, I have a hard time imagining Dad making the long trip all the way back from heaven just to discuss the day of Mom's hair appointment.

Mom is a bit senile, and she's a talker. Sometimes I think she loves the sound of her own voice—maybe it helps her hold on to her fading reality. Other times, I think she's just loopy, like when she talks during the climax of a show we are watching, then hushes me during the commercials. As I was saying, this is a typical end-of-day scene with Mom and me. It's over when she falls asleep, usually after I discover her trying to find her bed in the bathroom, or vice versa. That is when I help her to the right room for the right purpose, tuck her in, and go to bed myself.

On this particular night, though, I hadn't gone straight to bed myself. I was about to turn the TV off when a commercial for shampoo or bath soap captured my attention. A cute baby getting a bath in a sink laughed, then the scene changed to an attractive woman in a bubble bath sipping a glass of red wine, then she's naked snuggling with a man in a different tub, and then the same woman stood alone in a shower with water spraying over her face. The woman had been talking about water and her happy places. I had my thumb poised over the power button of my remote when the background music, a softly tinkling piano that matched the happy water theme, ended abruptly.

This was not a shampoo commercial. A loud angry alarm had interrupted the piano, and the haunting sound of a heavy metal door slamming shut gave me goose bumps. The camera zoomed out from a close-up on the showering woman's face to reveal she was in prison, not in a happy place. A scene change later and the same young blond woman popped out of a van fully dressed. She was hugging a familiar pin-striped pillow to her chest and she was in an orange uniform. The narrator of the story said, "My name is Piper Chapman," and I dropped the remote.

The rest of the dialogue and scene changes in the brief commercial came too quickly. I heard, "lesbian lover . . . drug smuggling . . ." Then I saw "Donna" from *That '70s Show* appear a couple of times wearing my glasses. I realized that what I was looking at was a fucking trailer for *my life*—and I don't mean the show being promoted was something I could relate to—I mean, literally, my fucking life.

Piper is my ex-lover and I used to be the drug-smuggling lesbian they were talking about. I stared dumbstruck at my television screen after the commercial for the new Netflix series ended.

I had heard about her book, *Orange Is the New Black*. That was more than two years earlier in the spring, right after I had moved back to my childhood home in Cincinnati from a halfway house also in Cincinnati. Piper's memoir was a surprise then too. I was gardening when my sister, Hester, called me on my cell and told me to turn on NPR immediately. Piper Kerman, my ex-lover and co-defendant, was being interviewed about her then new book. I recall being amazed with what she said in the interview. Hester and I stayed on the phone and cheered through the interview as if her victory was ours. Piper was off paper by then and totally out from under the oppressive system that still had our backs pinned to the wall. Hearing her stand up to that system, fearlessly poking at its faults, had filled me with indescribable joy.

After the talk show, my sister and I came down from our initial euphoria a bit and decided we had better get the book, see if she mentioned us in it, and how. While Piper had the distance and mobility necessary to poke at these bears safely, we did not. My sister and I were still very engaged in the pointless and arbitrary fight for survival and against recidivism that Piper had just described so eloquently on NPR. We still had to navigate life very carefully, making sure our criminal pasts didn't haunt our still very fragile futures. Living on paper can be like living in a house of cards: a gentle breeze can be all it takes to topple everything. You can too easily find yourself in court for an absurd violation and a quick return to prison. It's not really just a simple matter of behaving perfectly.

So while Piper had devoted herself to a great cause, I was still within arm's length of the system she criticized and the people who controlled my fate. I needed to read the book to know just how hard she was poking. I bought Piper's memoir, read it, and relaxed . . . sort of. Piper hadn't used my real name—she'd used Nora. She had also changed my physical description. Even if my PO did know which character I was in her memoir, she really hadn't said much about me that could change my PO's opinion so much that he would react.

There was also my career to consider. While I had disclosed my felonious past to my recruiter, human resources, and my boss before I was hired as a software test analyst, I had never discussed my colorful history with anyone but them. That was two years earlier and I hadn't shared my private life with anyone at work since. A year later it felt deceitful to know them all so well. I didn't lie, I just never offered up any salacious details about my life. My house of cards would fall without my job, so as much as I wanted to share more than cordial banter, I couldn't risk it.

When the book came out, I feared the consequence of my co-workers discovering I was the woman depicted in Piper's bestseller. I hadn't even shared that I was gay at work. If anyone had a problem working with me because of that or my past, what would I do? It had been a miracle getting my career in software development restarted in Cincinnati. A felony conviction in the conservative corporate world of Cincinnati was a deal breaker everywhere else I had applied, and my PO could violate me for being unemployed.

Fortunately, it seemed almost impossible that anyone at work would even read her book, much less make the connection. But that was before Netflix began streaming Piper's story and mine onto every laptop and smart TV in the universe. No, this was an entirely different beast. The stakes were no different than they had been when the book came out two years earlier. If anything, they were higher and my house of cards was even more fragile. Having had a heart attack and open-heart surgery, living without health insurance would be insane, and returning to prison with a heart condition, suicidal.

I wanted to see the trailer again. Maybe I was wrong, maybe it wasn't me being portrayed by Laura Prepon. Maybe the glasses she wore in the commercial were just a coincidence. After all, nothing else about her appearance looked like me. After consulting Google I knew when the show would be available on Netflix. I also confirmed that Laura Prepon *was* playing me, Piper's former lover and the one who had gotten her involved in drug smuggling. But, unlike Nora in the book, this character would be front and center.

I tried to go to sleep that night, but it was pointless. My imagination kept bouncing between extremes, from horrible doomsday scenarios to fantasies of fame.

When I went to a meeting at work the following Monday morning, someone asked, "How was your weekend?" People used to always ask me this, and I would answer but leave out the parts that included anything related to my legal status.

"Uneventful," I responded, smiled, and took my seat at the conference table. I wanted to tell them—tell everyone—what was really happening. But it didn't seem prudent to run through the halls and cubicles at work announcing my good news and revealing all my secrets. So when I learned "Donna" from *That '70s Show* was going to be playing a role based on my life, I kept it under my lid.

I waited with the rest of the world for the release date: July 11, 2013. I told a couple of my close friends at home. They knew about my past, about the book, and now the show. At first they treated it like a great novelty. "Maybe you'll get to meet Laura Prepon," one said. When nobody contacted me from the production, I began to worry. As the date neared, the commercials increased, as did my paranoia. *Was the show going to disclose more than the book had? Was this why they hadn't contacted me?* I knew Piper wouldn't try; she knew I couldn't communicate with her because I was still prohibited from any contact with my co-defendants. But surely someone could have connected with me, if only to assure me not to worry.

I came home from work on the Friday after *Orange Is the New Black* was released, and instead of waiting until Saturday, when my friends and I were supposed to watch it together, I watched the first episode by myself. I couldn't wait.

I had never watched a series on Netflix before and was not yet accustomed to the way a series prompts you to watch episode after episode, back to back. I had figured I would just watch the first one a second time with my friends the next day. But I watched a second one, then another, then another, then . . .

About halfway through the series, I realized I couldn't have watched this with my friends. The experience was too weirdly personal. I would have driven them crazy. It was incredibly unnerving to see how someone I didn't know had interpreted the little tidbits of my life that the show had touched.

I was both disappointed and relieved that almost everything regarding the character of Alex was pure fiction. I never had sex with Piper in prison—we didn't even do our time together. But it got weird as I sat through each episode, trying to figure out what actual reality might have inspired which scene. I loved how well they depicted the life of women in a federal prison camp. It bugged me, though, that they missed huge things like 205s, two-for-ones, and the smoking-ban wars. I was also disappointed that they never sent anyone up the hill to the big house so I could see how they depicted that. But the characters who played prison staff were dead-on. We had a few porn stashes where I served my time, and we had the same nasty guards in admitting and in visiting, the same counselors, and the same evil prison executives.

It all made me wonder what part of Alex's character came from consulting Piper. Why did they choose to make me the product of a poor childhood with no education or marketable skills other than smuggling dope? *Is that what Piper thought of me?* It bothered me that they made Alex's father a failed rock star, a drug addict, and a loser. Then they killed Mom. I had strange emotional reactions to the bizarre mix of reality with fiction. The whole subplot about whether I was *the* snitch who ratted Piper out really pissed me off. They painted a big target on my back for any psychotic ex-felon with a snitch-grudge to scratch and the wherewithal to look up who Alex's character was based on. I'm sure there are plenty of those out there. Maybe only a handful nearby and fewer still that might act on it, but still.

The "rat versus ratted-on" cliché didn't fit our circumstance. It was hardly representative of what happened in real life. If cooperating and pleading guilty were Alex's shortcomings, they were Piper's too. Only one of our many co-defendants had the right to stake a claim to that particular plot of questionably moral high ground, and it wasn't Piper or me.

Somewhere around episode seven my dog barked, growled, and scared the bejesus out of me. She saw something outside, probably a raccoon or a deer. I became keenly aware of the dark woods outside my house. It had been a long time since the inability to see what might be lurking out there in the night scared me. I went around and locked all our doors, checked the windows, and turned on all the outside lights.

By three A.M. I had watched nine out of thirteen episodes. My butt hurt from sitting at my desk in front of my computer for so long. I stopped Netflix before episode ten played. I had smoked every one of the cigarettes that I shouldn't have been smoking. I'd quit smoking less than a year earlier. But I had been sliding lately. I impulsively Googled "the real Alex Vause" hoping to discover nothing, but saw my picture staring back at me in the first results page. I Googled my own name, just as I had done repeatedly for three years, making sure nothing damaging had surfaced. There was my face again, a blurry mug shot from a popular inmate search website. I checked out the site and learned I could have my photo removed for a fee. But that's a scam. You pay them to remove your information and image at one site, and it pops up at five other sites five minutes later with new fees to remove those.

I nervously reached for a cigarette, forgetting my pack was already empty. I crushed the box and threw it, disgusted with myself and irritated that I was actually going to run to the store for another pack, a whole new pack of swear-they-are-my-lasts. But I was a wreck. This was it, the absurd and random glitch that everyone ever on probation fears will cause them to violate. The show was going to be a hit. It was incredible, and I wanted to smoke.

A year earlier, I had lost thirty-five pounds, not just quit smoking. I suppose you could say the heart attack was my wake-up call. I realized I could die waiting for my circumstances to change to begin living again. It had surprised me how quickly I lost the weight, bounced back, and returned to work. It didn't surprise me, though, that I had been slowly regressing, one suicide stick and Coca-Cola after another. It had taken a year, but my brilliant resolve to live a long, healthy, and meaningful life had wilted into a weird, drab apathy.

I knew what was at the root of my bad health and my less-than-peppy disposition. It wasn't the simple depression that doctors warn comes after open-heart surgery or that a pill a day could fix. My shell—which had once acted as a great barrier, a protection for my tender bits, the metaphoric device I had used for so long in the double life I had been leading for twenty years—had become a real physical entity and had gotten heavier with time. Now it was crushing me. Secrets do that.

On my way to the store to buy cigarettes, I felt so alone in the world, and exposed, like people were watching me from their homes as I drove by, saying, "There she is. It's her!" I passed by a cop car and panicked. I was experiencing some strange kind of emotional collapse, not from the mug shot or fear. It was all about Alex Vause and a question that taunted me: *Is that who I am?*

A silver-tailed fox darted out into the road in front of me and I stopped just short of hitting the cute little fellow. He hesitated, trying to decide whether to cross the road or retreat to where he had come from, then stopped in my headlights and stood his ground. He stared at me for a minute like he wanted to fight, then crossed the road and ran off into the dark. I drove on. I went to the gas station, got cigarettes and a Coke, and just started driving again. I cried, banged my hands on the steering wheel, smoked, cried some more, laughed, called my sister and left messages that probably made her worry I had lost my mind, and drove on until I got my answer: no. That wasn't me. Aside from being tall and gorgeous, Alex didn't have a sister and she was missing some vital ingredients: regret, contrition, faith, and hope.

1 The Point of No Return

Hôtel Saint-André des Arts, Paris, France
February 1993

THE COLD, FRESH AIR WOKE ME. The bathroom door opened and Bradley stuck his head out for a moment. He looked disapprovingly over the top of his steamy eyeglasses toward the window that Henry had just opened. Then he retreated and closed the door again. I could hear a police car siren moving away from the hotel. The sirens always sounded to me like they were repeating the phrase "Uh-oh, oh-oh, uh-oh." It usually amused me, but on this particular morning it felt like a melodic warning about my day.

On the antique mahogany desk lay Henry's leather-bound weekly minder with his black Montblanc pen sitting atop the opened notepad. The collection of gallery cards, show invitations, and receipts that had been tossed about the hotel room in yesterday's predeparture hissy fit were neatly stacked or reinserted into the pockets of his black leather valise. The amazing Toshiba laptop computer I wanted for myself was carefully tucked back into its case, and most of the other contents of his valise had also been restored to their meticulous order. In this way, Henry is a classic gay stereotype; the world could be coming to an end, and as long as everything's tidy, it's all good. He was in the middle of the room, seated rigidly upright on a swiveling wooden stool, a mismatched accompaniment to the compact writing desk.

Henry had turned on the desk lamp and looked as though he was meditating in its warm glow, except that his dark brown eyes were wide open and staring directly at me. It was 5:45 A.M. in Paris, time for me to get up and start the day.

Henry had been busy. He had already exercised, showered, shaved, manicured, and packed his bags. His dark hair was still wet and the room was chilly, though he was unaffected. I shivered a little but was glad for the invigoratingly fresh air. Henry sat quietly, breathing slowly. His tanned face was flushed red, even though he was dressed only in his travel underwear: a white silk-knit T-shirt and snug white briefs. I could smell his cologne; it mixed with the lingering odor of espresso and Gauloises cigarettes. Physically, he was not an effeminate man, but he had a grace to his movements and posture that belonged to a ballet dancer.

I was accustomed to seeing him with his hair slicked back, not hanging down over his face. Henry swiveled and turned his back to me to extract something from his suitcase. The tight T-shirt defined his angular shoulders and tiny waist. From the back, he looked like a long, sinewy woman. I noticed his dark gray Armani suit hanging on the door of the armoire as he retrieved something from his bag, then spun back around. A bottle of water and a breakfast tray sat on the table in front of him among a few other items he had set there with the same care surgeons use when arranging their instruments.

Henry turned, facing me again, but his mind was elsewhere. He took a deep breath, reached into a wrinkled brown bag, and extracted a large black capsule-like object about an inch long. He took the capsule, forced it down into the finger of a latex glove, and tied it off with a double knot. Then he gingerly cut the capsule stuffed finger of the glove free with his silver grooming scissors, leaving a little excess rubber at the end. Henry dipped the pinkie-size creation into a bowl of plain yogurt, then put it into his mouth and swallowed it whole. I watched the lump as it moved down his throat, under his Adam's apple, and disappeared beneath his collarbone. He took one deliberate gulp of water, straightened his back, and sat quietly again; then he repeated the entire process. He would do this until he was full. Bradley would do the same, but with just a handful of the heroin-filled breakfast bites.

Bradley emerged from the steamy little bathroom dressed, except for his shoes, socks, and suit jacket. He sat down on the edge of the bed and watched Henry's ritual, like he was a student. But he was really just procrastinating. He couldn't see a thing without his glasses, and he had removed them.

I was impressed with his bravery. Like me, this was his first trip. I wasn't the only novice. Bradley had volunteered to swallow the last of the capsules so none would have to be left behind. For a few trips now other couriers had been chipping away at this last batch of capsules from a stash that needed to be transported back to the United States. That method of transport was being abandoned. Even so, I had learned that men could hold a lot more of these heroine-packed capsules than women could. Henry ate them slowly, probably because if he ate too fast, he might eat too many. If he did that, his system would painfully rebel all the way to our destination, the Blackstone Hotel in Chicago.

Bradley could easily have forgone the extra risk and taken only the heroin-stuffed suit jackets, same as me. I don't think it was greed; he wouldn't make much more money for swallowing this shit, not enough to make it worthwhile. Considering a leak in even one capsule would be enough heroin to kill an elephant instantly, Bradley's motivation had to be something totally irrational. Maybe he was trying to prove to Henry or himself that he wasn't afraid or he was a tough man or something. Maybe he had a crush on Henry. A crush might explain doing something this suicidal. If he didn't have a crush, I decided he should, and Henry should be a model.

Bradley was adorable, too, in his own way. But he looked like a young, blond-haired Mr. Magoo at the moment. He normally wore Coke-bottle-thick glasses that made his blue eyes look much bigger than they were. Without them, he squinted, pretending to watch Henry, still stalling.

Personally, I couldn't have swallowed the capsules, not for all the money in the world. I wanted to gag just watching. I would have bailed like my sister had on her first trip. She hadn't been able to get her first capsule down. In fact, she'd almost choked on it, or so I had recently been told. I would have knocked her the fuck out for even trying such a stupid thing if I had been there. Especially since it wasn't diamonds, as I had been told originally; it was a lethal dose of heroin wrapped in the little package she had tried to swallow.

The new method for transporting and concealing the heroin being utilized made it possible for me to do it. It was now sewn into the lining of men's suit coats. We simply packed the jackets in our luggage with our own clothes and trusted that the tailors were better at concealing the drug scent from drug-sniffing dogs than they were at sewing. The convenience of the drug-stuffed jackets we were carrying made it all too easy to ignore the little voice in my head telling me not to do it and to just keep moving forward and toward home.

Hester, Henry, and Bradley had a little spat the night before. We were clearly getting on one another's nerves and I couldn't wait to get back safe and sound. That discord had evaporated, though, in the morning's tense preparations. I guessed that Hester was still asleep in her and Bradley's room. She was still so angry at me for coming over in the first place, and she had tried every way she could to get me to leave. But I was stubborn. I wouldn't listen to her, not after coming as far as I had already. It was my decision to do this, not anyone else's, and that made lashing out at them pointless. She didn't see it that way.

She had called the invitation for me to join them a betrayal. They said if she was pissed about the money, she could have it. Apparently, someone else would be paid a finder's fee for getting me involved. It made her even angrier that they thought it was the money she was mad about. She had said she didn't want to see me before I left. I really wanted everything to be all right between us before I took off though. But after ranting about how insulted I was that she thought I couldn't do this, I didn't want her to know I was scared. Especially since it was too late to turn back now.

It was so quiet. It felt like we were all getting ready for our own funerals. I don't know, but all the bravado from the night before was gone. We had started getting ready—Henry, Bradley, and then me—and mechanically begun our rituals to prepare for the flight. I kind of got it now, why Henry had us focus so much on rituals. It was soothing and distracting to focus on details, like is my suit wrinkle-free or is my hair just so. Better that than to focus on the stupid shit I was about to do.

Suddenly, I felt a powerful rush of fear run over me like ice water. My heart palpitated and my stomach flipped when it really sank in, exactly, what day it was. Since I had left Chicago, whenever I woke, reality was like a great, but complicated, book I had put down the night before; I had to remember where in the story I was before I could get going again from where I had left off. On a day like this one, it was tempting to leave the book unopened and go back to sleep.

As I had at the precipice of every frightening moment in my life since I was a teenager, I made a mental connection between the fear at hand and a fear I had a lot of practice at calming. I was horribly afraid of heights. My best friend as a kid had been a diver; so in order to share the same summer, I had become a diver too. While some people may be able to obliterate their phobias by facing them once or twice, this didn't work for me. I faced my fear again and again, by diving competitively, but I remained as afraid of heights on my last dive as I was on my first. Instead, I developed into what someone once described as a peevish imp. That is, a person with the compulsion to throw herself off whatever lofty place I approached. Great for diving, not so useful on escalators, Ferris wheels, or mountaintops.

I told myself this was just another controlled and deliberate dive. I would be fine, but not if I freaked out. I took a deep breath. There was a lot I could do to ensure a smooth entry, and focusing on that calmed my racing heart long enough for me to begin the day. I lifted my cozy blanket, sat up, and opened the book again.

For the first time in weeks, the sight of Henry comforted me. Aside from being an experienced drug smuggler, extraordinarily handsome, organized, and tidy, Henry was a control freak. His control over me had begun to feel like a spiked choke chain, but today it felt like a parachute's harness. He was so calm. All I had to do was follow his lead.

I wasn't quite ready for that yet though. I pressed pause, lay back down in the bed, and stared at the ceiling. I started breathing slowly and, one by one, let my imagination eliminate each of the obstacles that might appear in my path that day. I could see myself walking through the airport exit in Chicago without a hitch: nobody overdosing on the plane because the capsules burst in his stomach, no long interrogation with Customs officials doubting my cover story, no delays, no screwups, and everyone getting through—everyone. The end.

I would walk away with the money—ten thousand dollars—enough to fix everything. I would look back on this ridiculous stunt with Hester and we would laugh someday. Who knows? It could end up being a real turning point for me, a new twist on being scared straight. The notion of going home to my parents to regroup and going back to school actually appealed to me at that moment. Shit, joining a convent appealed to me at that moment.

My stomach turned over again at the thought of leaving my little sister behind. Hester was on a later flight, three hours behind ours. Sisters couldn't pretend not to know each other. She would be alone for three hours in Paris, and she wouldn't know my fate till she got to Chicago, to the hotel. Somewhere along the way, Hester had grown up. She was a gorgeous woman now, with auburn colored hair, green eyes, and her own rich history delicately carved into her beauty. But to me, she would always be the little five-year-old with long curly blond hair, crying at the bus stop because I had to abandon her and go to school. The notion of abandoning her in Paris, even for a few hours, tortured me more than the fear of failure.

I chased that image away. I closed my eyes and imagined myself on Main Street in Northampton. I hadn't talked to anyone from there in two months. I knew by now Phillip, my best friend, would be insane with worry and curiosity, but it would all be over this afternoon. By this time tomorrow I would be on my way back east, my sister would be safely deposited at her house in Chicago, and this would all be behind me. What a party it would be, and ten thousand dollars in cash. What did that even look like? Alajeh would be in Africa, where we had left him, and we would be in America, where he would not come. Henry would be gone soon enough too, as soon as he paid me. I would be on the verge of a new life, whatever it was.

I pushed back the suffocating blankets, sat up, and got out of bed. I looked at the manner in which I had packed my nifty little shower bag. The night before, I had cleaned each and every container of lotion and balm that came in the set of skin care products from Madame Calignion. She was the exquisitely refined, middle-aged French beautician at the salon and spa I had gone to a couple of days earlier. I had needed help picking out makeup and applying it. Henry had taken me to the salon and to the madame for my final transformation from a frumpy dyke into a worldly art critic. That was who I would pretend to be that day. Apparently, in Paris you can accomplish that at a spa.

I had arranged my collection of toiletries as neatly as Henry might have. I grabbed a towel and walked to the communal showers down the hall. Our fancy room's little bathroom would be wrecked already and it had bad ventilation. Some of the rooms in our hotel had only a toilet and sink, no shower or bath. For those residents, there was a shared bathroom. I preferred that over the sloppy whiskery mess I knew Bradley had left for me. Besides, the shared showers would be pristine, warm, and dry so early in the morning.

I noted every detail I passed and everything I touched. In the shower, I washed, recounting as many of the items I had passed in my short trip to the bathroom as I could. For each item I remembered, I made up a very brief story about how and why it had affected my business trip abroad in some ridiculous and infinitesimal way. I was cramming my head with new images, stupid mundane facts from Paris instead of Africa, a place U.S. Customs would not know I had traveled. I had been doing this since I'd had my passport replaced in Brussels.

I panicked a little and cut my shower short. I was chronically late to everything. This was not a day I could let time get away from me while I cataloged the bathroom. I dried off, wrapped myself up, and scurried back to the room.

Henry swallowed the last of his capsules, rose, and walked to the opened window. The sun was breaking over the city. The sky behind Notre-Dame was deep blue where it had been black a few minutes earlier. The telltale signs of a new day were popping up everywhere. Below the window, a drunk was being prodded from the sidewalk by a whistling street cleaner and his big green broom. Tables and chairs were being moved back out onto the sidewalk at the café across the narrow street. Henry stood tranquilly staring out at the cathedral and down on the few people already taking their seats outside the café. He didn't move. The wet breeze tossed his hair while he waited for his full stomach to settle.

I was still wrapped in my towel. Henry handed me the thick terry-cloth robe he had used earlier. He had packed my hotel robe away in my luggage. He had once told me that it's a good idea to give the cops something to find, something other than dope. Little hotel knickknacks, towels, and robes were great. Everyone has stolen something from a hotel room at some point in their lives, even Customs agents. Being snared in a miniscule crime like this by a Customs agent was awesome. They would flag us away, certain they had discovered all that was discoverable about us.

I stepped over to the armoire and pulled the chair close to its mirror. I stood there looking at myself. I had this strange sense of unfamiliarity with my own reflection. Behind me, I could see the boys scurrying around the room in an oblivious blur. I took the robe off, still looking for myself in the mirror. Four weeks in Africa, swimming madly to maintain my appetite every day so I could eat the nasty food, and a bout of *Giardia* had left me thinner and in better shape than I had been since I was a teenager. This combined with weeks of Henry's tutelage in Paris, efforts to turn me into a convincing art critic, made it no surprise that I didn't know who was looking back at me in the mirror.

Any modesty that might have existed in this elegant little room with Henry and Bradley had been wiped out by weeks of bathing, shitting, and puking over each other in the shower room we had all shared at Alajeh's compound in Benin, Africa. I continued to inspect myself, moving about in ways that flattered my new physique. I smiled, thinking about seeing Joan, my ex-lover, and potentially watching the tables turn on her—now I would be the one rejecting her. I sat on the chair, facing the mirror, and began putting on my new face.

I gently patted under my eyes some creamy goop Madame Calignion had concocted. It felt cool and smelled of peppermint. Once done, I carefully replaced the small silver cap on the glass bottle. My manicure had made it through the night without getting any dings or scratches. I wanted this preserved for as long as possible. I pulled each item from my toiletry bag with care not to scratch my nails. This amused me for a moment. I remembered watching Henry on the train ride to Belgium, where this adventure had begun. I had watched him put things away in his satchel this carefully. I was acting like Henry.

The person in the mirror seemed isolated. I was surprised and saddened. I looked at the boys and felt the ties that bound us all together. I would not be able to recount any of this to anyone back home. Although I might try to tell interesting stories about where I had been and what I had done, I could never really express what this all felt like, not without being judged. I wondered if that would create a huge gulf between me and almost everyone else, forever.

I finished my face and packed away my toiletry bag. Returning to the armoire and the mirror, I grabbed the three black velvet boxes that contained the jewelry Henry had chosen for me. First, I put on the pearl earrings, then the pearl necklace, and finally the fake diamond ring. It looked real. In my bra, panties, and heels, with the pearls against my tan and my hair up in such a neat bun, I looked like such a lie. Nonetheless, I couldn't stop staring at myself.

This was the first and only complete dress rehearsal I had. Each of the additions to my look or cover story had been an incremental change: a shopping trip here, a facial there, and so on. Putting it all together now, I saw what Henry and I had created and it was truly bizarre. I looked like my mother. I took my pumps off, stopped play-ing in the mirror, and slid into the creamy white hose and my slip. I pulled one of the mirrored armoire doors toward me so that I could see my ass. As I turned the glass, I saw Henry watching me. He had in his outstretched hand a delicate white lace girdle. It didn't look like the girdles my mother wore; it looked more like lacy white bike shorts. I put it on and it made my butt cheeks lift a little. I laughed at myself. This was better. Now I looked like a fucking stripper.

The next hour passed in a whirlwind, like time was speeding up, as the point of no return got closer. All bullshit aside, until we walked through security at the Charles de Gaulle airport, I could still turn around, I could stop the train and get off, consequences be damned. I could call Mom and Dad and tell on us, me and my sister. They would be pissed, after they got up off the floor. When I told them where we were and the mess their precious daughters had gotten themselves into . . . Oh my God! They would faint, shit their ever-loving pants, and fucking kill us when we got home. Mom would probably have us committed to a nunnery or just flat-out committed. I pushed this thought out of my mind. We could get through this. Then it would be over, period, no big drama.

I looked myself over, as did Henry and Bradley, one last time before we all paraded through the hotel and down to the street, where a taxi waited. I was the last into the taxi. I took my seat and the driver closed the door. At one of the café tables, I saw my sister smiling and waving. "Catch you on the flip side!" Hester yelled. She looked calm and happy.

When the taxi pulled up to the curb at the airport, everyone was quiet and calm. Henry paid the cab fare. He was the keeper of money. He had been so the whole trip. He handed me a one-hundred-franc note and Bradley one too. This was where we would all go our separate ways. We would pretend like we didn't know each other until we stepped back into a taxi in Chicago, hopefully, all of us.

"This is it." Henry was right too. This was it, my last chance to bail. He walked away and Bradley followed just a couple of seconds behind him. They both entered the stream of traffic inside the revolving doors.

I had not eaten any heroin-filled capsules; all I had were the jackets packed in my bag. Henry and Bradley had both. Bradley couldn't leave his stomach behind, but I could leave the jackets somewhere and bail. The only thing standing between me and getting home safely was a decision: How did I want to do it? I had one hundred francs in my sweaty little palm, the cost of a phone card. I could buy one in the airport *tabac*, call home, call Hester at the hotel, and what? I could also just fucking get this shit over with. Do the stupid deed, make ten thousand dollars, and deal with my sister and her boyfriend problems later. I couldn't stand out on the curb forever. I would miss my flight. I walked into the airport, past the tobacco shop, and without hesitation right up to the security checkpoint. The feeling was just like walking right up to the end of the high dive, gracefully turning, and stepping back so that only my heels were free and my toes held me there.

When I got to the gate, I saw Henry and he didn't so much as look in my direction. But Bradley caught my eye and gave me a look that said he was about to cry. I looked away from him as if I hadn't noticed the face he'd made.

We boarded the plane and I took my seat, carefully stowing my garment bag full of the heroin-packed jackets in the overhead compartment. I pulled a French language tutorial out of my bag with a pen before taking my seat. I had definitely crossed the line. This was past the point of no return.

I stayed awake the whole flight back. I did the French lessons from front to back. I had bought the book in the O'Hare Airport six weeks earlier, before the trip had begun. I watched a movie, *The Last of the Mohicans*, and cried at the part where one of the sisters throws herself off the waterfall rather than be raped. I studied what I had already written in my fake journal, making new fake entries for each of the days I had been in Paris. By the time they passed out the customs and immigration forms before landing in Chicago, I had created a story for each and every day in Paris, even for the ones I was actually in Africa. My new passport had no stamps indicating my venture to Africa, which was the point of replacing it.

I watched a plane crawl across a map on the screen where the movie had been playing. It approached the Great Lakes and then Chicago. I hurriedly got up out of my seat and grabbed my purse so I could make my way to the bathroom one more time. It amazed me how Bradley and Henry both ignored me every time I passed each of them. I couldn't help but look at them, if only to be sure they were still alive. Henry's face was blank and Bradley's had a pained expression, but aside from that, they were both breathing. I wondered if Bradley was scared or excited. I couldn't figure out which I was. But I couldn't wait to get back to my world and away from this whole mess.

When the plane landed, I was deaf. My ears had not popped yet, but I kind of liked the way everything sounded muffled. It was easier to turn my thoughts inward, back onto what should be playing over in my mind: the musings of Cleary the art collector, critic, and historian, not Cleary the drug-smuggling fool about to ruin her life.

I was surprised when I disembarked the plane. We were all actually being loaded onto a shuttle, a shuttle that could lift up and down and had its doors at the front and back. It was like a big creature that latched onto the plane and opened its big mouth to suck out all the passengers. I opted to stand and hold on to the pole in front of a young man dressed as sharply as I was. He offered me his seat, but I declined. "I can't sit down for another minute." He smiled but kept staring at me like he was interested. That would only happen to Cleary the art collector, not Cleary the frumpy dyke. I could see myself reflected back in the window behind him, and a ball of fear and excitement down in the pit of my stomach tightened again.

The shuttle was full, and it closed its door and then lowered itself down to street level. We zoomed across the tarmac, past a row of huge planes, their butts sticking out from the building. It looked like a bunch of giant birds at a feeding trough. The bus came to a stop in front of one of the buildings and rose up again, pulled forward, and jerked a little before the door opened. My knees were shaky and my heart was racing, but my reflection looked as calm and bored as everyone around me. My garment bag's strap was digging into my shoulder; the pad intended to keep that from happening was twisted and made it more uncomfortable than if it had not been there at all. But it gave me something to focus on.

I had been one of the last few to get on the bus, so I was near the front and one of the first to get off. I walked alongside the handsome young guy who had offered me his seat. He didn't offer to take my bag and carry it for me. That would be funny, I thought. I walked along the same route and kept pace with the crowd. Henry and Bradley were on another bus or busses; they had been seated much farther back in the plane, and there had been three busses waiting to devour passengers disembarking. I felt my hip pocket. My passport and the Customs card I had filled out were there; everyone else had theirs in their hands. I pulled them out and gripped my keys to the kingdom tightly.

We finally came out into a big area full of other passengers, maybe a couple of planeloads, where everyone was splitting up and heading for different lines. Instead of cashiers, like in a grocery store, these lines terminated at a series of booths, each one fitted with a Customs agent. I picked the line where a bunch of twenty-somethings would be right in front of me. If they'd had skateboards flung over their shoulders, it would have matched their outfits and messy grunge hair. The guy directly in front of me had an Amsterdam T-shirt.

Our line crept forward each time I heard the *whomp* of the passports being stamped. The crowd of grungy youngsters in front of me was quiet until one of the guys turned around and said something to one of the girls. He spoke Dutch. I looked at the passports everyone in my line held. They were burgundy. *Holy shit!* I was in the wrong fucking line.

I should have been in line with Americans. I scanned the ten other lines and saw passengers carrying blue passports and light blue Customs cards at the opposite end of the big lobby. I was not able to just hop out of my line and scoot right over. First, I had to negotiate my way back through the waiting people and their bags behind me. Each line was delineated by a barrier, like at a movie theater. I could go under it, were it not for the Customs agents floating around the lobby. Henry had told me that these ones watch for any irregularities, and they randomly pick folks out for a more thorough questioning.

If I left the line where I was, I would pop right into the line of sight of one lady who was standing with her arms crossed, legs parted, blankly staring down all the foreign passengers. I was not supposed to attract attention to myself in any way. *What would Cleary the art snob do in a situation like this?* I asked myself. She would hop the fucking line, the hell with the barrier. I slid under it and stood back up. I had caught the Customs agent's attention. I held up my blue passport, smiled at her, and shook my head, like *Look at me, the big dummy in the wrong line.* Her blank expression cracked, and she smiled and started walking. I turned and walked toward the correct lines, hoping like hell that when I turned around, it was not toward me she had started to move. I picked the shortest line and turned around. *Fuck.*

She was standing up by the booth, waving for me to come to her. I smiled, pointed at myself, like *What? Me?* She nodded, still smiling, and I walked forward. In movies, this is when the hallway stretches out and the star can't seem to reach the end of it. In reality, I was standing in her face in a flash. She motioned for me to head to the booth, turned to the agent in the booth, and said, "She's been over in international." She made a funny face at me, like an exaggerated

Oops. The agent waved me on up to the spot everyone was waiting for, and she walked away.

The guy laughed and said, "It's a madhouse here today." He took my passport and Customs card. "Where are you coming from?" I knew this by heart. Every question he might come up with I had the answer ready to fire back.

"Paris."

"Purpose of your trip?" He asked this while making notes on the blue Customs card.

"Business," I answered as glibly as I could. He looked up, gave me a quick once-over.

"Anything to declare?" His attention was back on my Customs card. This is where I was supposed to list the valuable items I was bringing into the country. Of course, I had not noted the heroin, stuffed in the lining of the jackets I had packed in my garment bag.

"Welcome back. Hand this to the agent on your way out." He slammed a stamp down on the Customs card, made some big squiggly mark on it, and handed it back to me, tucked inside my passport.

I walked toward the exit of the big entry hall, one blue door still flipping closed from the last entrant, and there was now one more agent between me and the end of this fucking trip. I pulled the card out of my passport and handed it to him. He was perched on a tall stool and looked more bored than anything else. He had a stack of cards already amassed in his hand. He reached out, took mine, scanned the front and the back, nodded toward the door, and said nothing.

I walked through the door and into the busy baggage claim area. I didn't have to wait for any luggage; I just had to wait for Henry and Bradley on the curb outside. I made my way to the door, skipping an opportunity to trade my hundred francs for dollars. I would keep this as a souvenir. I got outside and it was bitter cold, but I felt fantastic. I pulled a cigarette out of my purse and lit it, then moved toward the area where people were getting into taxis.

I saw Bradley come out the doors. He spotted me and walked

over, reaching out with two fingers, a give-me-your-cigarette gesture. I handed my lit cigarette over and he took a long drag. "Holy shit!" Smoke and his breath in the cold air came out in two big plumes.

"That was so fucking easy!" I said this to Bradley, under my breath.

"Speak for yourself. Try holding your poop for six hours." He handed me back the cigarette and made a groaning noise. He looked terribly uncomfortable. I was just about to suggest he go on ahead to the hotel when Henry came out the door and headed to the last cab in the line of taxis. We hustled to catch up and practically dove into the backseat of the taxi. Henry was in the front seat, telling the taxi driver he was sorry, but we could not wait in line. He had diarrhea. The driver objected strongly, telling us to get out, then Henry held out two hundred-dollar bills and said please. Henry turned and smiled at us, like a proud father, as soon as the taxi left the curb.

2 Homeward Bound

Northampton, Massachusetts
March 1993

NORTHAMPTON IS A COLLEGE TOWN, a picturesque little village nestled in the Berkshire Mountains of New England in Massachusetts. Think of Norman Rockwell's *Saturday Evening Post* cover images decades ago: simpler times, when kids sat at old soda fountains talking to white-smocked, rosy-cheeked old men—a perfect little town, with clapboard homes and white picket fences. That's Northampton. Just add a lot of lesbians to Rockwell's painting.

I was the only passenger left on the bus when we pulled into the Northampton station at nightfall. The big snowstorm my driver had been racing to beat was already heavy in the air, muffling the quiet night. I surveyed the empty parking lot, recalling the distance to my hotel. I used to live right near the bus station, but back then I'd had my motorcycle to go into town. I hadn't been walking then, and I hadn't been dressed up with bags to lug. Fortunately, I had packed light—just the one bag and my purse. The Tumi bag had tough little rollers, so I decided to make the walk to the hotel. It's not that I had an alternative. There were no taxis around and the pay phone to call one was inside the closed bus station.

I took a deep breath of the cold, clean air and my mind filled with images of hot chocolate, glowing fireplaces, and familiar faces. It was odd not having an actual home to return to, especially with the storm coming. Storms made me want to curl up in bed and cuddle with my kitties or a lover if there was one handy. But I didn't have my cats, Edith and Dum Dum, with me, my love life was in shambles, and I didn't even have a bed yet.

The remnants of a previous storm still littered the sidewalks. Salt and piles of compacted and refrozen slush might make it a difficult walk. There was a shortcut up a steep hill to Main Street. I chose the longer but safer route and avoided wiping out. My Italian leather boots had heels, but they were just a couple of inches high. I wouldn't wipe out on this route, not if I was careful. I loved the way the boots felt—slippery, soft, and pliant inside and out. They weren't particularly warm, but they were cute, and the clack and the crunch they made on the sidewalk sounded expensive to me.

I pulled out the thin leather gloves I had picked up at a boutique in Paris and slid them on. My coat was designed for show. Long, black, and lightweight, it was not intended for snow. I was warm though; I had a surplus of adrenaline and layers. Each layer was thin and slippery—silk, linen, and a wool and silk blend—my coat, a jacket under that, and blouse. I had shopped for two days in Chicago, assembling the outfit, getting my hair and nails done again like I was going to some big formal occasion. It wasn't formal, but it was definitely an occasion. I had made it. Now I just needed to make it to a bathroom before I ruined my fabulous outfit.

There were so many people I wanted to see. But I wanted everything to be perfect when I saw my friends. Just the same, I was impatient. I wanted to run into somebody on my way to the hotel right then, maybe just an acquaintance, just to see if they recognized me. Nobody knew I was coming. I looked totally different, and I had never been able to afford to dress as nicely as I was dressed at the moment. No, my friends would expect a short, dumpy tomboy in tattered jeans and motorcycle boots, if they were expecting me. But they weren't.

I walked by the steamy windows of Spoleto, a restaurant I had worked at before deciding to leave Northampton and move to Chicago two months before. The restaurant was packed, but it was impossible to tell who was in there. I couldn't see who was working. All I could make out through the sweating glass were the general shapes and number of people crowded in, trying to get seated. It was hard to believe it had been only two months since I had left. It had been snowing then too.

The Hotel Northampton felt like the deserted hotel in *The Shining* or any one of Vincent Price's haunted mansions. When I walked into the big empty lobby, there was no one around to greet me, and the only sound came from the wind outside. I supposed they were operating with a skeleton staff, probably because of the expected snowstorm but more likely because nobody visits Northampton at that time of year.

I took the elevator to my floor after checking in. When the elevator door opened, I peeked out, looking in both directions, listening for signs of other guests, before stepping out. It was silent, except for the closing elevator doors behind me. I walked down the carpeted hallway to my room, picking up my pace as I neared my room number. When I closed the door behind me, I felt the hairs rising on the back of my neck. I was totally spooked. I made two quick hops to the bathroom, as if by hopping I was safe from whatever had spooked me. I did my business, and then I turned on every light in the room.

Washing my hands, I was shocked by my reflection. I had seen myself every day through some fast changes, but I was still surprised to see myself in a mirror. My rebellious curls hadn't changed, but my brown hair had gotten lighter, turned golden from all the sun. My face was thin—I had a chin and neck now—and I wore makeup. My black-rimmed glasses were a new look for me too. They looked a little like the glasses my father had worn or that Clark Kent wore when he wasn't being Superman. The glasses made me look intelligent and nerdy. They had taken me some time to appreciate; they were a much bolder look than my old tortoiseshell specs I'd been wearing since high school, but Henry had loved them. The mascara and tan made my eyes look bluer and the whites whiter. The lipstick still looked weird to me.

I suddenly had the urge to remove my makeup. I had been back in Northampton for thirty minutes, and the new me was already starting to crumble. The makeup felt wrong, like a mask or something of my mother's I shouldn't be wearing. I knew that was crazy—some bizarre ass-backward insecurity I had about myself. Most women wear makeup because of their insecurities. I was uncomfortable being pretty, or trying to be. Cute I had no trouble with, but pretty made me squirm. I was a tomboy at heart.

When I was in seventh grade, my father was called into a parent-teacher conference with my school counselor at Anderson Middle School. I had taken to wearing my father's shirts to school. Dad was an office man and a very sharp dresser. I liked his starchy white oxford-cloth shirts and thought they looked cute on me. I had gotten the idea from a Doris Day movie in which she was running around in a similar shirt with no pants on, tan, with her golden hair a mess. I'd thought she looked fantastic. Doris was probably an early crush, the first tingles in my gaydar going off, but that concept wasn't yet part of my consciousness. In any case, I had finally seen something famously worn that I liked, so I felt like a movie star wearing Dad's too-big shirts. If that happened today, my flare for creative expression in my attire would have made me a fashionista, not a deviant in need of reprogramming, but it was 1975.

The counselor attributed my innocent fashion faux pas to something insidious. He wanted my parents to deal with the troubling crisis he saw brewing or remove me from among the perfectly preppy young darlings dressed in Ralph Lauren, Izod, and J. Crew. In his defense, I think he was suffocating in his own gay closet. It wasn't just the shirts that would fix me, and he had to have known that; his swish and lisp hadn't been corrected by his plaid flannel. Perhaps he thought that if he caught it early enough, he could save me from his fate. I don't know, but I was a tomboy. The men's shirts just gave him the circumstance to do what he felt was needed: talk to my father.

The counselor believed it would be in my best interest to start wearing clothes little girls should be wearing and wanted to enlist my father's help in making that happen. Dad disagreed, and in my best interest, enrolled me in a Catholic girls' school. Uniforms made the issue moot. I suspect this swift resolution actually came from my mother. The men's shirt incident just gave her license to do something she had wanted to do since I'd entered first grade.

This was her opportunity to get me into a better place, where I could meet the right boys and make the right friends. Mom hadn't gone to public school. She was a spoiled Southern belle and former mistress of the Birmingham Civic Ballet Company. She'd been raised in a very religious Irish Catholic family in George Wallace's backyard: Birmingham, Alabama. Mom had some very distinctly Southern and snobby notions about how to raise a little girl in the world, and she felt her little girl needed the kind of grooming nuns and priests could provide.

Mom had also been noisily suffering from a troubling void any good Catholic woman of the seventies experienced when they didn't attend Mass every Sunday or make sure their children did. Her daughter's expensive enrollment in a Catholic school alleviated that guilt a little. Church had been taken from Mother's Sundays by my father's refusal to go. Dad didn't try to bar her from going to church on her own, but she would not go without him. If she didn't go, then my sister, Hester; my brother, Gene; and I didn't have to go to church either, or Sunday school.

Dad had been raised a poor farm boy in Kansas, and he had his own rich history with the Catholic Church. Unlike Mom's spoiled upbringing in an otherwise empty nest, he had five younger brothers and sisters with whom he had endured an impoverished existence. He loved his brothers and sisters madly and wouldn't have traded any one of them for anything, but he didn't want to create the same-size litter his parents had been obliged to create. He also wanted to have sex more than a few times in his life.

Ironically, the Catholic Church had paid for his education in the seminary where he had nearly become a priest. His passion for

Christ hadn't matched his passion for sex, and with his thirst for knowledge sated, he had been unable to blindly accept the man-made rules of his church as he had done all his life. He'd chosen a more practical vocation and married Mom in 1960.

In 1975, Dad had stumbled into a final intellectual conflict with the men who ruled the church and had decided that the Catholic Church, as an institution, was insane. It had no place in his life. We stopped going to church when I was in third grade. In any case, the Catholic school choice and the uniform that came with it worked for both my parents in different ways, so I went to Saint Ursula Villa for my eighth grade.

For middle school students, eighth grade is like their senior year—a strange time to be uprooted. I hated the uniform, hated the school, and hated all the pretentious brats I didn't know. Money and affluence make no difference; eighth-graders anywhere are fierce little monsters. They thrive in packs, and I didn't have a pack. Fortunately, it was only eight months before summer arrived and grade school was over. High school turned everyone into new students, not just me. I was advanced to Saint Ursula Academy, an all-girls high school—the perfect place for a young blossoming lesbian, you would think. But no, I left there my senior year. I had to go back to public school, at Anderson High School. I think this lifelong problem with who I was is what accounted for my alarm every time I looked in a mirror and saw who they had always wanted me to be.

Having forgotten about being spooked, I dimmed the lights and looked around my hotel room. All that was missing was a crackling fire, in a fireplace of course. The phone sat in its cradle on the desk, patiently waiting for me to summon it into action. I picked up the receiver, listened for a dial tone, and pressed nine plus the first three numbers for any phone in Northampton. I knew Phillip's number and Joan's by heart but didn't know which to call. I had been waiting so long, dreaming of the moment when I could talk to my best friend or ex-lover again. I set the receiver back into its cradle and rested my head in my palms. I could hear the fast *thump, thump, pa-dump* of my heart. The wind picked up outside and shook my window. I heard light taps on the glass pane. *Damn it!* I didn't want to get stuck in the hotel all by myself, and now the storm had started. I called Phillip. He was my dependable cure for loneliness and a much better impulse than my misguided desire to call Joan.

"Hey. Are you hungry? I'm starved." My cheery invitation was greeted with silence.

"Cleary?" Phillip sounded completely indifferent, not at all surprised by the unexpected reemergence of his vanished, possibly presumed dead friend. He always sounded that way though. "Are you in town?" His voice got just a tiny bit higher at the end of his question. It wasn't enough input for me to determine whether the pitch change meant *I'm going to kill you* or *Yippee, you're all right!* I couldn't be sure how angry Phillip might be at me for ditching him, leaving him almost penniless in Chicago, and not communicating with him as to my whereabouts or well-being. I had told him I would be gone for only a week.

"Yes, it's me. I'm here. Bolognese?" As soon as I said it, my stomach growled. This was the dish I ordered every time I ate at Spoleto, the restaurant where I had worked with Phillip until we had both taken off for Chicago in January.

"I'm broke." Phillip had a hint of irritation in his tone now.

"Come on. I'm buying. It's my apology." I giggled. I'm not one for giggling; it just happened, like a drunken hiccup. I hoped Phillip's forgiveness could be bought for a lot less than a dinner at Spoleto, but it's what I wanted.

"What time?" he asked.

"Now's good." Phillip hung up as soon as I said it. He had horrible phone etiquette and wasn't much more polite face-to-face.

Phillip was my eye-candy sidekick. He had been handsome in the black-and-whites we used to wear at Spoleto. He came across as a mildly snobby Italian, though he was neither snobby nor Italian. The snobbism was an unintentional indifference. The Italian look relied on context; outside of Spoleto he was a generic-brand American. He had dark brown hair and brown eyes, and he was pale, always pale. He carried himself lightly, but he was not effeminate—sort of like a skinny rock star but without the long hair. He actually looked a little like Henry, but looks were all they had in common. Phillip was the straight version, he was an artist, and instead of being the temple of self-control, he drank too much, chain smoked, and did recreational drugs like it was the eighties.

He had recently become my best friend. We had a lot in common. We were both unfashionable scotch drinkers, meat eaters, and cigarette smokers. We had both followed our girlfriends to Northampton from Provincetown; his current girlfriend was an old schoolmate of mine from Boston and a former lesbian I'd had a crush on; Phillip and I worked at the same restaurant, the same shifts; we were both about to graduate from our twentysomethings with nothing to show for it; and we were surrounded by a population of students whose bright futures were practically guaranteed by their pedigree, provenance, or trust funds.

As soon as Phillip hung up the phone, the quiet of my hotel room tried to swallow me. My wild imagination started churning away again, and I was spooked anew. I took the manila envelope full of cash from my Tumi bag and secured it in the room's safe, then prepared myself for a dash to the lobby. I peeped out the eyehole of my door before opening it, opened it, and found the hall was still deserted.

I couldn't keep this secret from everyone, not after everything I had just been through. I had done something so completely out of the ordinary, survived something I thought was amazing, and it was behind me. I was all the way back in Northampton, back in the fold of my friends, and far, far away from my co-conspirators in my drug-smuggling adventure. I could never have told anyone about my trip with my co-conspirators around.

I had fantasized about my return to Northampton the whole way there. Honestly, I had been fantasizing about my return to Northampton since I had left in January. The story line I was returning with had changed quite a bit, but I was still returning victorious. It was just a different kind of victory than I had planned on when

I'd set out for Chicago with Phillip. My bullshit cover story would be fine for most everyone else. But I would tell Phillip the real story. He had been there in Chicago when I got the sudden invitation to meet my soon-to-be brother-in-law and he knew about the rather odd job offer too. He knew what I had run off to do and it wasn't to work as an art critic.

The snow was falling when I left the hotel and it had become much colder. The gas lanterns that flank Main Street had come to life, and halos formed in their light, caught by the falling snow. An inch had already fallen and there was as much as a foot expected. At the moment, it was very close to being a whiteout. I could only see halfway up the hill when I got to the intersection of State and Main, and when I squinted, all I could really see were the lit entries of a few still-open businesses. The buildings themselves had vanished into the murky dark.

I walked out of the cold and damp wind into Spoleto. Once inside, I could see as little of the world outside the picture windows as I had been able to see of the restaurant's interior from the street. But the sweat on the windows that had told of how warm the restaurant would be inside, now that I was inside, told of how very cold it was outside. The world looked bitter, watery, and white. I scanned the main room of Spoleto and the immense rectangular granite bar, which took up a large part of the space. There was no more of the waiting-to-be-seated crowd, and the seats at the bar I liked were open.

I walked to my old barstool, the one I used to take my shifters at when I was done with work, and sat down. Larry, a permanent resident of Northampton and my favorite waiter, was bartending. It took him a moment to realize who had just asked him for a short Dewar's and soda, but as soon as he did, his eyes lit up and he poured my drink. He handed me the scotch and was about to say something.

"Hey." I looked over my shoulder, knowing full well who had whispered it. Joan sat down next to me, looking for a sign that it was all right to remain in the seat. I smiled and she slid the rest of the way onto the stool. "Can I buy you a drink?" she asked and grabbed my hand. I nodded and looked down at her lap, where her hand covered mine. "I'm so sorry." I could swear she actually sighed this.

I felt disgust and deep sadness simultaneously. I remembered the "I'm sorry" from months ago. I had felt completely blindsided. I had been sure that we were in love with each other, very in love with each other, not some one-sided obsession that the ultimate development in our relationship had suggested. It had been the most irrationally timed breakup imaginable. We had gone to Paris together. (This, by the way, had been my first trip overseas, not hers.) Joan had said something. I can't recall exactly what, but it had meant our affair was ending, right there in the City of Love and on the morning I was to fly home. She had planned to stay behind for a few weeks, so I didn't even have time to change her mind. I had hoped when she came back from Paris we would work it out. It seemed crazy that we would not. But by the time she'd come back, she didn't want to see me.

That was months before. I thought, mistakenly, that enough distance, absurdity, and time had passed that the only thing I felt for her would be spite and anger. I was wrong. It wasn't spite or anger I felt as she spoke so alluringly about the trivial developments in her simple, perfect world. She was just so goddamned beautiful! Her watery blue eyes, perfect lips, and bubblegum tongue were cruel. My heart ached all over again.

Before I realized it, she was done with our conciliatory drink and she was on her way to join her waiting companion outside. I knew the guy she was with; he was an older man I recognized as a professional contact of hers. "Call me." Two whispery words in my ear and I was all hers again—her toy to break and discard. I probably should have picked up my fork and started stabbing, but instead we made a date.

Joan left the restaurant, and Phillip walked into Spoleto about ten minutes later and found me at the bar, already slightly blurred with Dewar's and soda. I was yacking away with Larry, the bartender, who had commented on my tan, my weight loss, and my outfit. A few of my former coworkers had stopped by for hugs, kisses, or chatty banter. Phillip was patient for a minute. Then he sat down and ordered a Dewar's on the rocks, shooing the bartender off. He wanted to know about my trip, why I hadn't called, did I know how freaked out he had been? The little bit he did know guaranteed he would not settle for anything less than everything, not the bullshit lie he knew I had been telling the bartender.

I didn't lose forty pounds from being a bundle of chickenshit nerves, starved and sick with *Giardia* for six solid weeks. No, that was intentional, a strict diet. The way I told Phillip the story, the lackluster training by example Henry had afforded me became ninja warrior preparation. I had been to Paris, to Brussels, to the Ivory Coast of Africa, and to Soule. I hadn't been to Soule; I just threw it in for color. I told him about my cover story. How I was pretending to work for an art expert at a publishing company in Paris. The story was I assisted a woman who was assembling an art anthology made up of graffiti from around the world, which I would find and photograph for her for comparison to current movements in art.

I had adapted my tale from Henry's artful cover story. I had known Henry for a long time. He had been my sister's friend for years, and I had envied his existence for as long. Phillip knew who Henry was too. I guess from his Provincetown days. But almost everything we had thought we knew about him was made-up bullshit. I told Phillip that Henry had been my trainer and that he wasn't actually a successful art dealer; that was his cover story. He was sort of an art dealer, though, but he only represented one artist. That little distinction was what made it so effortless when he lied to Customs about the purpose of his trips.

He would say he had been visiting wherever we'd come from on business. He could tell a Customs agent a whole story about his trip without lying once. His story would be backed up by trinkets and memorabilia from each of the shows or galleries he attended. The point of all of this effort was to get past the first potential obstacle to success. If, for some reason, I was selected by a Customs agent to be hassled, coming back into the United States, a poorly researched or delivered cover story would be my undoing.

The restaurant had emptied out a little and I spoke more quietly with Phillip to match the lowering volume of our surroundings. We had opted to dine at the bar, so I had to be careful not to be overheard. In the mirrors that spanned the restaurant's walls, I saw a waitress I knew was a big gossip come up behind us with our food. I made sure she heard a few positive tidbits as she approached.

She took our salads and served our dinner plates, then asked if we wanted Parmesan on our pasta. We leaned back so the gossipy waitress could reach our plates and grate the cheese. "Life is treating you well in Chicago?" The waitress beamed her famously fake smile as she delivered the compliment and cheese. I nodded a dismissive affirmation, easily made my joy to see her look equally fake, and leaned back into my conversation with Phillip when she was done grating a mountain of Parmesan.

When she left, I continued my story while Phillip gobbled up his dinner: shrimp scampi on a bed of linguini. I told him about having to actually go to art exhibits and galleries in Paris, talk to artists, and learn a bunch of shit. I sarcastically added how my high school French came in handy. Then I told him about Africa, how I went on these amazing expeditions in search of art and graffiti. I was copying Henry's lead and experiencing a life to match my cover story. If I had to tell the lie to Customs, it wasn't going to be a complete lie.

Larry dropped off two glasses of wine. Phillip had a cold glass of pinot grigio and I had a ruby-red glass of Chianti Classico. I took a sip and ate a couple of bites of the angel hair. Phillip touched the sleeve of my jacket, examining the fabric, and said, "Nice." I told him about shopping in Paris, looking for the clothes I would wear on the plane. I described my dress rehearsals for my role, in Brussels and again in Paris. I would get all dressed up and go out to the art shows. I had pretended to be someone I was not, and practicing the role had made it real to me. I had also needed some practice getting used to walking in dress heels. My tomboy gait hadn't fit the image Henry had been hoping for, and it had taken a little work and a lot of blisters to correct. Phillip knew I was unaccustomed to the heel torture most women had overcome by my age. I don't think he had ever seen me dressed up according to society's standards before.

We finished our meal and Larry asked to take our plates away. When he came back to wipe away our crumbs, we ordered cappuccinos.

I told Phillip more about Africa, meeting the Nigerian whom my sister was in love with. I described the scary but impressive train of dinner guests at his huge table every night: an Italian general of some sort, the secretary of something-or-other for the Nigerian government, a council member from Cotonou. I told him about the armed compound I'd stayed at in Benin, the days spent at the round pool and the beach at the Sheraton, the voodoo markets, the marabout priests and Sufis who counseled our host. I tried to describe the flocks of happy kids in Ganvié, a village built atop Lake Nokoué. I recounted one drive up the coast and the fishing tribe we watched pull in the day's catch someplace beyond Porto-Novo. I told of our crossing the border into Togo at a chaotic roadside station and my quandary about the hordes of haggard people trudging by with everything they owned in tow. I had too many vivid memories to recount adequately in one sitting and so many unanswered questions about the things I had seen. I told him about the flight back to Chicago and how scared I had been. I told him about getting up before dawn on the day I was to fly.

I had carried a man's suit jacket stuffed with heroin in my garment bag. Phillip's expression registered surprise when I told him about its contents. This was the first he had heard of heroin being smuggled. When I had been asked and had agreed "to work" in Chicago, we'd thought the whole smuggling business was about diamonds.

Phillip had wanted to go with me then but he hadn't been invited. I'd had to act surprised when the offer was made to me; my sister was not supposed to have told me anything about her friends' and my new roommates' real vocation. Therefore, I couldn't really advocate for Phillip joining us or pass on his interest in doing so at the time. Phillip definitely wasn't supposed to know anything about the smuggling operations going on under his nose. I think he had been disappointed but had accepted the situation for what it was. I had then vowed I would return to Chicago a week later, a few thousand dollars richer.

When we were done with dinner, I told him how Henry and Bradley had prepared and swallowed the big capsules and how the guys had harvested these capsules back in Chicago, counted and cleaned them. I told him about the way we'd had to stay in our Chicago hotel room for days babysitting all the heroin, waiting for it to get picked up and to be paid. Then I ran out of storytelling steam, and besides, Phillip wanted to get to the liquor store before it closed.

The money I had earned was back at the hotel, and I wanted to show him. I thought he needed to see this to believe it all—everything I had just told him sounded insane, made up. I knew it was a lot to take in as quickly as I had spouted it all off, and I had seen a look on his face that suggested he might not believe some of the details. I recalled not believing my sister when she had told me about Henry, who after all these many years admitted to her he smuggled diamonds for a living, and how she had been invited to do the same.

I paid our check, and by the time we left, there was perhaps four inches of snow on the ground and more where the wind had created drifts. It didn't feel as cold as it had when I had gone into Spoleto, but that was probably the scotch or the wine numbing my senses. At the liquor store, I grabbed a bottle of Dewar's and a pack of smokes. Phillip's order was identical. I took him back to the hotel with me. I was happy to have the escort and I was not ready for the night to be over.

He followed me like an excited puppy to the Hotel Northampton, running to pick up speed and slide down the slippery parts of the sidewalk that had not yet been salted in several places. We walked into the hotel and past the empty hotel desk, past the bartender, who had patrons to serve and who looked up and said, "Hello." We passed two other hotel guests on their way out and it delighted me that the hotel no longer seemed abandoned or spooky.

The elevator ride and walk to my room didn't spook me on this trip. In fact, the hotel felt warm and sheltering. I pulled back the drapes and listened to the howling wind coming from the deserted streets outside my windows. My view was partially obscured by the sideways snow precipitating on the glass, but I could see the traffic light at Main Street swaying back and forth, casting its flashing red light into the snowfall. Phillip would have to go soon to make an arctic trek home with his girlfriend Meg. I think I recalled that Meg was getting off work at closing time and he was going to walk home with her from town. This was one of those nights when families and couples stick together—a survival instinct thing, I imagine. I wondered if Joan was alone.

I sent Phillip to the ice machine with a little plastic bucket the hotel had provided and turned on the television to see if I could catch any news about how much snow we were expecting and whether the earlier predictions were holding. This storm seemed to have picked up a little more punch than I had seen in New England in a long time. When Phillip returned with the ice, I dropped a couple of cubes into each of the two water glasses and poured a couple of fingers of scotch. Phillip grabbed his drink and sat down, swirling the ice in his drink before he emptied it in one gulp. He wouldn't be staying long.

I retrieved my money from the safe and showed him the contents of my manila envelope: thirteen thousand dollars in cash, minus the costs of a shopping spree, a plane ticket to Boston from Chicago, bus fare from Boston to Northampton, and the room charges for three nights at the Hotel Northampton. I knew the money made my stories all real for him. Unless I had robbed a bank, an even more preposterous story to believe than the one I had told, neither of us could have that kind of money. He excitedly stared into the envelope of cash, then looked up and handed the envelope back with a strange expression, like he had an idea or realized something shocking. He pulled the envelope back jokingly when I went to take it from him. "Mine!" He held the envelope tightly against his chest with his arms wrapped snuggly around it.

I laughed, prying the envelope from his clutch, and told him he would have to get his own. He could too, of course, if he wanted. "The easiest part of the whole trip was getting through Customs," I said as he released the envelope and let me have it.

He said, "Really?"

I said, "Yes," with emphasis, thinking to myself, *A monkey could do that part*. It was a mistake to have said so, but it was no fun if Phillip was going to be jealous.

He questioned me a little more intently about the actual trip home, now that he knew it was not fiction, while looking outside and then at his watch every few moments. One slowly emptied drink later, he had to go. We said good night and made plans to meet at the Haymarket Café in the morning. He would bring Meg along too, if she didn't have to go to school.

I closed the door behind him and unmuted the television's volume. The newscaster kept me company with updates on conditions around the area while I undressed and slipped into my sweatpants and a T-shirt. Boston was getting walloped. The snowstorm had even caused power outages as far east as Hyannis and Wellfleet. If that was the case, Provincetown was getting buried. I wished for a moment I was there already. All the year-rounders, which included a bunch of my friends, would have gathered at the Grand Central Café. There are so few places open in Provincetown when the summer season ends, it's easy to locate your tribe on a night such as this.

I didn't know what was next for me, but I didn't want to go back to Chicago. I loved the East Coast too much, and besides that, I had way too many reasons not to go back to Chicago. I still had to retrieve my cats though. I wished that I could have brought them home with me on this trip. But until I made a decision about where that would be and got a place to live, I would have had nowhere to put Edith and Dum Dum.

I took one last peek outside. The snow was still coming down heavily and it looked like a foot had already fallen. I turned off the lights and lowered the television volume, then jumped into bed and under the thick covers. I stared at the ceiling for a few minutes. The red traffic light outside cast a soft orangey-yellow hue on the room each time it flashed. I started counting flashes and recalled a French television station's late-night sign-off, which had been playing in the room I'd shared with Joan in Paris. It had been a series of ballet dancers dressed as sheep, leaping in slow motion to the count of *un, deux, trois, quatre* . . .

I woke to the phone ringing just after the crack of dawn. The sky was clear blue—I could see that from my bed—and the wind had died, so the storm had passed. The snow on the glass had turned into crystal, reflecting prisms of sparkling light from the sun. Joan was on the phone, excited as a child on a snow day. She wanted me to meet her at the Haymarket Café. She had to make the scones, but we could have some coffee and be the first ones out in the winter wonderland before everyone else spoiled the virgin snowfall.

3 U-Haul, We Haul, We All Fall Down

Northampton, Massachusetts
April 1993

MY SNOW DATE WITH JOAN ended two days, one drunken declaration of love, and an apartment hunt later. We weren't moving in together, but now I was moving back to Northampton, the town I had sworn three months prior that I hated and couldn't wait to get out of. I was leaving Chicago, the city I had also claimed was a better fit for a thirty-year-old who actually wanted to do something with her life. My flight back to Chicago, where I had left my cats and belongings, left that Monday.

Doing this meant I had less time before I had to go back to work and start earning money the old way to pay bills. I wouldn't have the rent-free arrangement I'd had in the Chicago apartment with my sister, Bradley, and one other drug courier. Hester was leaving Chicago for the same reason I was anyway, except she was not running back to an ex-lover. She was running from one. She was planning on returning to Provincetown for the summer, where she could make plenty of money during the season and have the whole summer on the beach to ponder what was next for her. I, on the other hand, already knew what was next for me.

I figured I could get a job somewhere in Northampton, maybe at Spoleto restaurant. I had also decided to forgo poetry and take on a bigger challenge. With a little money stashed away in my magical manila envelope, I could take what time I did have, before reality set in, to start writing a book. The more I repeated my bullshit story to friends, about working for the woman in Paris, the better it got. I decided it would make a great novel—this double life I had briefly led. It would be fiction though, not a confession.

In April, I moved into a cute apartment on Crescent Street and quickly turned it into my home. I would have no major expenses there, only my phone bill and rent to worry about, since the utilities were included. I splurged a little and furnished my cha-cha palace with reasonably priced IKEA-like finds. The furniture fit well with the hardwood floors and creamy white walls and woodwork. The kitchen and bathroom were nothing special, but the apartment was comfortable and stylish compared to the dumps my kitties and I had lived in previously. We had the place all to ourselves, and my rent was reasonable, so I didn't need a roommate to contribute. My cats, Edith and Dum Dum, loved it there too. We had never had a place all to ourselves before.

I made one impulse purchase, and it was a big but practical one. I bought an Apple Macintosh PowerBook for over three thousand dollars. I had wanted my own Mac ever since the *1984*-inspired Super Bowl ad had aired a decade earlier. Henry's laptop had nearly swayed me to abandon my loyalty to Macs. But when the Macintosh PowerBook came out that spring, it became clear to me: I simply couldn't bear to go on without one. My PowerBook made it possible for me to go wherever I wanted to work. I could even take it into the Haymarket Café to write; all I needed was an outlet to recharge every couple of hours. I could hang out where Joan worked and write the great American novel my laptop would surely elicit from me. *How cool was that?*

Of course, this made a huge dent in what remained of my rotten nest egg. I knew I had to get back to work somewhere soon, but I procrastinated. I had created a bit of an obstacle for myself. I had told almost everyone I knew the elaborate lie about working for some woman in Paris, traveling the world in this dream job and collecting art for an anthology she was paying me well to assist her with. I would have to tell everyone a new lie now. What would I say happened to my dream job? I certainly couldn't tell my old boss at Spoleto the truth: I had smuggled drugs, I was too afraid to go back, and I was broke. No, before I begged to get my job back at Spoleto, I had to figure out my new lie, a story that would put the old lie to rest. I needed to solve this. It wouldn't be long before I wouldn't have money for rent.

My reconciliation with Joan was short lived—just long enough to fall back in love and move back to Northampton. She dumped me again a few weeks after my cats and I got settled in our new home. She had slept with another woman and was unclear about whether she intended to do it again. That was her noncommittal way of ending things. As long as I didn't mind her having a girlfriend and that we wouldn't really be having sex anymore, nothing needed to change. We could still be together. We went to see *Jurassic Park* with some of her friends the same night she dropped the bomb on me. When I felt an affinity with the goat tied to a post in the movie, waiting to be lunch, I left.

I didn't feel as horrible this time—no debilitating depression or the-world-is-ending feeling. It wasn't the same as the first breakup, where I'd had to move to another state. I liked Northampton. I had bigger problems to deal with, though, before I could focus on the simple business of living. There were still loose ends I needed to tie up. Ignoring them until they went away wouldn't work. My sister was trying to break up with Alajeh, our boss, the Nigerian drug lord she had been sleeping with and was supposed to marry. The problem was that she still lived with friends who worked for him. I couldn't relax until she broke up with them too.

Alajeh and his transcontinental business network totally spooked me. At first, Northampton had felt a million miles away from all of that, but more recently, I felt like he was looking over my shoulder. One night I woke in a sweaty panic. I thought he was standing by my bed while I slept—ready to pounce. But that was Dum Dum. Hester, still in Chicago, planned to make the move to Provincetown in May. I wanted her away from Chicago and her friends, several of whom were still tied up in Alajeh's drug empire. But now I learned that Bradley and Henry were going to P-town too.

My sister had sworn it was over with Alajeh when we left Africa and I didn't doubt her sincerity. He had been a complete jerk to her while we were there, treating her like his whore, not his fiancée, and then he'd made her carry bags of heroin home. You don't do that to your wife-to-be. I had seen enough for myself to know that the ring he had given her was total bullshit. He never meant to marry her.

My little sister might as well have been my own daughter. We were only four years apart, but I had raised her. I'd had a little help from babysitters or our very absent mom and dad. Both our parents were professionals with demanding careers to nurture. We were like most children of the seventies, when villages really did raise children, because Mom and Dad were busy climbing the corporate ladder. I had always been the one Hester came to when she needed something. When Alajeh had treated her like his whore in front of me, I couldn't even imagine how he treated her behind closed doors, nor did I want to. But if he hadn't been who he was—didn't have his little barefoot bunch of rifle-toting vagrants, voodoo spells, or hobo priests guarding his compound and tasting his food like he was royalty—I would have confronted him about it or gotten her out of there, but I was too afraid of him, too lost already myself to save either of us.

I knew my sister had issues, but I had never wanted to look at them or what they stemmed from. But when I went to Africa to meet her husband-to-be and my new boss, her issues just about knocked me out. We were staying at Alajeh's compound in Cotonou, Benin, a small country on the Ivory Coast of Africa, when my sister was sick. Actually, Henry, Bradley, Hester, and I all had *Giardia*, to be precise, and we had been throwing up for days. He came to fetch her from the room we were staying in at his compound, presumably for sex. Then he returned her to the room when he was done.

At that moment, I knew he wasn't going to marry my sister, no matter how many times he said it. He had been using her and I felt like a fool for ever believing it was more. I had wanted it to be true, my baby sister getting married to a rich Nigerian exporter. It had sounded so exotic, so wonderfully exotic, when she had told me about her new love. When I learned that in addition to the rice, diamonds, and oil I knew he exported, he moved drugs, I didn't think he would expect her to continue doing that. He was her lover. Why would he risk losing her?

It made me so sad to watch my sister tiptoe back into our room that night, trying not to wake us. She sat in the dark for hours and didn't want to talk when I asked, but I knew she had figured out the same. When he finally withheld all of his affection because she refused to carry jackets full of heroin back to the United States with the rest of us, I was furious. By then, though, I was also more informed. I knew there wasn't a damn thing I could do. He was "God"—that's what they called him. All I could do was get out of there and get her away from him for good.

I worried though. Her so-called friends liked that she was sleeping with Alajeh. Perhaps they thought she would have his ear if they needed his favor at some point, like the poor girls sent to marry Henry the Eighth. I don't know, but it made no sense to me that they would want to see their friend subjected to degradation such as this. Whatever the cause, they tried to justify his behavior with confusing cultural differences she would have to train out of him and they attempted to nudge her back into the happy bride-to-be she had been when we'd arrived. I knew she was smarter than that. But matters of the heart can be very tricky territory. He was tall, dark, and handsome—I thought he looked a little like Wesley Snipes. I was terrified by the prospect that maybe the spell he'd had her under once before could be renewed if he chose to reignite it, especially if her friends helped him. I kept thinking of how horribly he treated her, and that her friends would encourage her to go back to him made me doubt their loyalty to her.

My sister would be broke again soon too, and Henry had always supported her emotionally and sometimes even financially. As long as I spoke to her regularly, which I had every week for the last month since we'd returned, I was calm. I felt I would be able to sense any change in her intentions, even if she wasn't being honest. So I did that, but without Henry and Bradley out of the picture, it made it hard to see an end to the worry. I couldn't be sure that whatever pull Alajeh'd had on her at one time had no conduit.

This meant that a door would remain open for me too. I was trying to forget how easy it had been to glide through Customs and go home with ten thousand dollars. But I couldn't think about my sister's problem without getting distracted by the fact that just because I didn't want my sister to ever go near Alajeh again didn't mean I couldn't. Besides, could I really be certain she wasn't seeing him with my head stuck in the sand. Oh, I had some fabulous rationalizations for doing it again.

I started playing with crazy ideas, thoughts of not getting my job back at Spoleto but of taking another trip instead. I calculated how long I could live on the money I would make without all the expenses of moving and buying the computer and what not. If I behaved this time and was more frugal, I could make the same amount of money last so much longer than I had this time. Now that I knew how fast even that much money could vanish, surely just one more trip wouldn't hurt.

My crazy thinking started with trying to figure out how Phillip could do it. Phillip had been clear about his desire to be invited on a trip. I thought maybe he could go with Bradley and I could get the three-thousand-dollar finder's fee Alajeh had promised if we knew anyone we trusted enough to bring to him. But I realized Bradley would have to lie for me and say Phillip was his friend, not mine; we couldn't bring someone else's trusted friend. Bradley would have to train Phillip too. That wouldn't work. Bradley wouldn't give up that money if he had to do all the work and take all the risk. Then I started thinking about doing it myself and taking Phillip, and that actually sounded like a fun adventure.

The only hitch in this idea was that for Phillip to work for Alajeh, he had to meet him. I would have to return to Africa again myself. I had to be there with my new recruit and personally vouch for Phillip, and I also had to be the one to train him. Alajeh also had to do his weird voodoo mumbo jumbo, have his marabout priests pray for his blessings, and Alajeh had to "look into his face." I don't know what that meant; it just had to be done before he would allow someone to smuggle his drugs. One of my sister's roommates had recruited me, and Henry had trained me. My being Hester's sister made me an exception to the rule. My sister was still pissed at them for that one—not because she didn't get the finder's fee for her own sister but that they had recruited me at all.

I remembered the night in January when Henry walked me into a restaurant in Paris and Hester didn't know I was coming. She thought I was in Chicago with my cats and Phillip, hopefully getting my shit together and selling ads in the magazine Phillip and I had gone there to start, with her financial help. She had paid for printing these beautiful posters we were hanging all over Chicago. But nobody wanted to buy ads in a magazine that didn't yet exist. I was broke, so when her roommate gave me the chance to work, I jumped on it. Hester nearly kicked my ass all the way back to Chicago, but I'm stubborn, and if she could do it, so could I. Of course, I hadn't learned what exactly that meant yet. My poor sister had been trying to save my stupid butt, not deprive me of some great adventure.

At first, the idea of returning to Africa was unthinkable, though I had obviously thought it through. Then Alajeh started calling me. These were the days before cell phones. Connecting with someone who didn't have a landline or voice mail was all but impossible, even for "God."

I had recently had a phone installed, never dreaming that Alajeh was trying to reach me and had gotten my number from either Bradley or Henry. I could hear his frustration in the message he left on my new recorder. My respite was over. The reality was, all this vacillating over whether or not I would do it again had been wasted energy. Alajeh's assumption had always been that I knew he would not waste all that time on someone for only one trip. He was trying to get me to confirm when I would be able to go again, not if.

Bradley answered the phone in Chicago one night when I was trying to reach my sister. Hester wasn't home, but he was eager to tell me all about his second trip. He had made eighteen grand on this latest trip because he had carried an additional jacket home. He was pretty pleased with himself for taking the extra jacket. He had figured out that taking the additional jacket wouldn't make any difference, except in the amount he was paid. He would have been either 100 percent busted or not.

"Where are you now?" Bradley asked and I realized I hadn't talked to him since we'd both come back to Chicago after our first trip. A lot had happened in a month, least of all April and spring had finally arrived. The world had turned from cold, snowy, and gray to warm and pastel so fast, which made it feel like it had been much longer since my wintry return to Northampton and my trip to Africa. But it had been less than a month since I had talked to Bradley.

"Still here. I mean, here again. I moved back to Northampton."

"Why?" He sounded horrified and incredulous all in one. He could've been asking me why I had poked my eye out. Of course, he had a reason to sound this way. He had helped my sister convince me to move to Chicago and start my new life there.

"Things are different." I didn't want to say that I had gotten back together with Joan. Because that would make it clear why I had moved back to Northampton. Bradley would know I was an absolute idiot, especially since I would have to tell him that she had dumped me again already.

"How long were you gone on your trip?" I changed the subject back to him, expecting to hear tales of fright, hardships, and boredom. His trip had been quick and easy, just as Henry had said they would be from that point on.

"Wow, you make it sound so tempting." I referred to his expeditious trip. I hoped he heard my sarcasm and understood. He did. He was alarmed that I would not be interested in working again now that it would be easy and fast. I pondered whether it was a good time to get the word out that I was done and had no interest in returning for another go.

"It scares me." I'd said "it" instead of "he" and I left out any more preaching about not liking how the Nigerian treated Hester. Bradley joked about my being a chickenshit hiding out in lesbian land.

He said, "He asked about you." He meant it was my turn to take a trip. I thought, at first, that it was just sweet banter and the drug lord missed me.

"How nice."

"I'll tell him you're all good?" He was asking a very specific question, which wasn't getting through.

"Okay. You do that," I added to our little coded conversation, which I now realized we were having. A few phone calls later, I accepted the invite to work when I found out Alajeh would be in Europe and that he could meet Phillip there. We could forgo the trip to Africa. For some reason, it scared me so much less to encounter Alajeh in Europe than in Africa. I still hadn't recovered from the culture shock of my first trip into the third world to stay at a drug lord's compound.

Phillip and I flew to Chicago to pick up travel money and left for Paris within a week. My trip with him was more like a quick shopping expedition than a smuggling drama. I discovered Phillip was a closeted fashion whore. We lived in a college town, remember; we were surrounded by students and we identified ourselves as slackers. We had both done everything we could to hold growing up at bay. However, if we had followed the traditional path most did, we would have been a few years into a career by then, working nine to five and dressing up the way he was about to, every day. There was even a chance we would have been wildly successful by then. That is what Phillip wanted to be, wildly successful, so we went about dressing him for the part.

I took him to the fancy little boutique where I had bought my fine leather gloves and expensive Italian leather boots, and we found a similar store for men nearby. We went to a French tailor and had a suit made. The ritual and the fit were both much better than just buying a suit off the rack. Phillip fell in love with his suit, his tailor, and the tiny little shop full of materials and accessories to select from.

We met Alajeh at the Sheraton Hotel in Brussels, where he was staying under yet another name. Phillip wore his new attire for the big meeting and looked confident and handsome. Alajeh had also dressed for the occasion. I had never seen him in a suit. I had only seen him in Africa, where he wore the African garb that indicates a man's power, wealth, and status. In this Western garb that indicates a man's power, wealth, and status, his presence was just as commanding, maybe even a little more so, since it spoke more directly to my sense of what power and money look like on a man, and really the African garb had looked like comfy pajamas to me. Alajeh wanted a little one-on-one time with Phillip after the initial introductions, so I left the two suits alone.

It was still a long train ride to Brussels from Paris in 1993. This is prior to the current high-speed rails that whisk you from city to city in little over an hour and run more than once a day. Phillip and I had rented a cheap room near our intended meeting place with Alajeh. Instead of spending the entire day on trains and making the round trip, which would require taking an even longer night train back, we'd planned to have a little adventure, spend the rest of the day figuring Brussels out, and return to Paris the next day. Once introductions were made and Alajeh made it clear that he wanted time alone with Phillip, I went back to our hotel to wait and worry about what was happening between them. *What is Phillip being asked, and oh my God, what is Phillip doing and saying?* I hadn't told Phillip everything about Alajeh. I'd forgotten to mention that because of his dabbling with a form of voodoo he called zuzu, and the rules instituted by the marabout priests in his backyard, he didn't drink or smoke. I'd also forgotten to tell Phillip that Alajeh liked to test people to see how they act in certain situations—for example, observing if they drink too much. I had learned quite a bit about the man while in his home for a month in Africa.

Phillip returned late and he was drunk. He claimed I was crazy. He thought Alajeh was fun, personable, and interesting, not scary, as I had described him. He imitated Alajeh's accent. "He is my brother!" Alajeh had been so happy when he learned Phillip was not gay. He had invited Phillip to come to Africa, where he said Phillip could experience the most beautiful women in the world. By the end of their short meeting, Phillip believed he had found an exotic friend. Of course, his new friend had apparently also asked for the address and a picture of someone in his family, and Phillip had willingly provided this.

Our trip proceeded in much the same fashion that my first had, except it was just Phillip and I. We flew back to Chicago, pretending not to know each other from the time we got out of the cab at the Charles de Gaulle airport in Paris until we were seated in a taxi together at Chicago's O'Hare Airport. It was an important control to travel separately, because if one of us got caught and we were known to be traveling together, we would both go down.

Phillip slid into the taxi next to me and wore a grin I had never seen on him before. His cheeks were even flushed. He grabbed my hand with his shaking hand. I waited for him to say something, but he didn't. I was pretty sure he was holding his breath. The cab driver, meanwhile, wondered where these two mute idiots in his backseat might want to go. "The Blackstone Hotel on Michigan Avenue," I finally said.

When the cab jerked into motion, Phillip let out his breath and started laughing. "Oh my God! That was ridiculous." I think he was referring to his trip through Customs. "I don't think that guy even looked at me."

I realized Phillip might be about to launch into a story about his trip through Customs, right there in the cab. People sometimes forget that cab drivers have ears, and who knows who they know or who they are. I quickly cautioned him by shaking his hand; he was still holding on to mine like he might float away. I held my finger up to my lips to shush him.

"Save that stuff till we get to the hotel," I said to be clear he understood that what I meant was to shut the fuck up. I nodded toward the driver to indicate to Phillip why I had cut him off so rudely. I didn't want to spoil his good mood. I just didn't want him to confess to Rajid, our cab driver, that we had just succeeded at smuggling heroin into the United States.

Phillip made the call from our hotel room in Chicago to his new brother and best friend Alajeh. He gave him our hotel's phone number and room number before we began our wait for someone to come and retrieve our successful delivery and to pay us for our efforts. I changed out of my travel clothes and into something comfy. Phillip did the same, changing into his normal T-shirt and jeans from his beautiful suit. We carefully packed our cover-story costumes away in my garment bag.

All we had left to do was wait for our contact to arrive. Neither of us unpacked; we just rearranged our stuff. We had to remove the heroin-stuffed jackets we each had smuggled and place them all into the one garment bag Phillip had flown with. We then repacked our own stuff into my bags. We ordered room service and watched pay-per-view movies. The hotel room began to feel like a gilded cage. At first, neither of us wanted to be left alone when the courier arrived.

By the end of the second day, we were getting on each other's nerves. Phillip kept wanting to call Africa again to see what the hell was going on, but that wasn't protocol and any odd behavior could create a problem. So we waited.

I suggested Phillip get out of the hotel for a little air. I was less concerned about the risk of meeting a courier alone than my killing Phillip or his killing me. Of course, as soon as he left the room, someone knocked at the door. I thought it was Phillip and answered the door to our couriers totally unprepared. They busted right into the room like they lived there. It was two women who looked like they had just stepped off the set of *Married to the Mob*. One impatiently told me in her overdone Jersey accent, "We-a ah he-a to pick sumptin' up. We gotta caw waitin'." I handed them the bag full of jackets and they, in return, handed me their shopping bag and left.

The door closed and I laughed, thinking, *What the fuck was that?* I quickly leapt into action though. I looked into the shopping bag, stuffed with cash. An assortment of rubber-banded stacks: fives, tens, twenties, and a few fifties of varying thicknesses, depending on the denomination and the newness of the bills. The fifties were the thinnest stacks; they were the newest bills. I couldn't stop to count it. I just wanted to confirm that it at least appeared to be enough money. It looked like a lot of money, so that was good enough for me.

According to the rules, I had only fifteen minutes to get out of the room and out of the hotel. There were two reasons for this. The first was I was in a room with a ton of money and no protection from being robbed. At the very same time, an unknowable number of bad guys—or girls, as the case may be—knew that I was sitting on a pile of cash, and exactly where to find me, seeing as they had just delivered it.

I quickly grabbed my stuff and crammed any loose tidbits into the cash bag. I piled all of our belongings together on the bed. Then I started cleaning up the room for the second reason I had to be out of there fast: police. Cleaning up is a speedy ritual where we wiped fingerprints off of as many surfaces as possible with a damp face-cloth: the phone, the TV remote, the sink top and faucet, the toilet handles, shower control, etc. I was hasty and did a less-than-Henry job, but I did it.

Henry had explained to me on my first trip that since we couldn't know what was happening once the heroin left us, and the possibility existed that something might go wrong, we didn't want to make it easy for the police to figure out who had just handed the heroin off to the couriers. We had to get out fast and leave no trace behind us. What if the people who came to make the exchange got busted and decided to tell on us?

When I had gotten back to Chicago on my first trip, Henry had been much more anal about this. He had limited the number of things we touched in the hotel room, making a big to-do about it if we touched something not included on the list, like the windows or the bathroom mirror. He made me very self-conscious about remembering what I had touched. Then every night of each day we had waited for our contacts to arrive, we made a thorough sweep of our room, cleaning every surface we had touched. On the day the bags were retrieved and the cash delivered, we only had to make a fast pass at the cleaning because we had stayed on top of our bread crumbs, so to speak.

I had not been so careful on this second trip with Phillip and had been caught unprepared for the arrival of the Jersey girls. This cleaning had to be done fast because the only thing more stupid than leaving our prints all over the scene of a crime was to still be sitting there myself when the police arrived. Fifteen minutes later, I was ready to go and Phillip had not come back. *Shit! Shit! Shit!* I paced rapidly, trying to figure out what to do. His wallet wasn't there, but did he have any money with him? Chicago was a rough place to be stranded with no money. I made the decision to go. I could deal with Phillip's anger at leaving him behind later. At that moment, I was worried about the police showing up or the Jersey girls' boyfriends coming back to the room to rob me.

I walked out of the hotel onto Michigan Avenue. It was raining and barely warm, but I was sweating bullets. I was just about to get into a cab when I heard Phillip yelling my real name, rather than the false names we had used to register at the hotel. I was too happy to hear Phillip calling me to be irritated at the faux pas of yelling out my real name. I'd had no idea how I was going to find him otherwise. Besides, we had to call Alajeh to say our business had concluded successfully. There were probably negative outcomes to making that call too late.

Phillip slid into the cab seat next to me, but this time there was no big shit-eating grin when I made the international symbol for money—rubbing your thumb and first two fingers together. In fact, Phillip looked mad. We rode in silence to the Drake Hotel and checked into a room as Mr. and Mrs. Jeffrey Bloss, without actually addressing each other the whole time. Whatever it was, it passed. I wondered if he had thought I was trying to run off with his money when he caught me jumping into a cab. If that was the reason, I would ask him why he thought I wanted to steal his clothes and shaving kit, since I had also packed his belongings left behind.

After we made our journey back to Northampton, Phillip ran home to Meg and disappeared. They had never before been apart for more than a couple of days, and he hadn't communicated with her during the whole two weeks we had been away. He had sent post-cards, but they wouldn't have arrived yet. Although it had been only two weeks, it was probably a long time for them to be separated. I had been looking forward to a celebratory dinner, one that would include Meg. But she didn't know what we had really done because she had been told our cover story. Phillip had simply adopted mine; he worked for the art expert at the publisher in Paris too. That was all that he wanted her to know. He wasn't sure how she would react to the fact that he had lied to her and become a criminal.

Phillip and I got together for a little celebration not too long after our return. He didn't bring Meg. I let go of the fantasy that he would tell her the truth, that she would magically be fine with it, and we would all celebrate our little triumph together. If he hadn't told her the truth yet, I doubted now that he ever would.

We went to the Northampton Brewery. I think it was because a blues band he'd heard would be playing there. We knew a bunch of people who were going, and it was one of our favorite haunts. I knew our waitress too; we had traveled in the same small circles the summer before. She had been good friends with one of my room-mates and had worked with another one. Her name was Piper. She had long strawberry-blond hair, always pulled back into a ponytail. She had blue or maybe greenish blue eyes and freckles. She was very pretty, but she seemed aloof, like when she spoke to me it was because she had to.

She had my attention though, and I think I had hers. I knew she was a Smith College graduate, which impressed me. I was curious as to why she was still in Northampton. I had always thought she was straight, and the only Smith grads I knew who had stayed in Northampton stayed because of a girlfriend or the endless possibilities of finding one. I had also worked at the Northampton Brewery, when I'd first come to Northampton, so I knew it wasn't the great job she had keeping her in town. She was at the bar, talking to an old friend and a crush of mine, Sheila.

Sheila was in her midthirties. I hadn't known she was gay until we'd gotten to know each other better while working at the Brewery together. Sheila was what I describe as butch-femme and had become more of a lipstick lesbian lately. Both were rare in Northampton. They were more common in Boston or New York City. Sheila was initially a butch-femme, since she did not wear lipstick or sport heels ever. Either of these types were women my age and older who you couldn't quite be certain were gay, but their heterosexuality was debatable. Picture the television character Murphy Brown in leather on a motorcycle—that's a butch-femme. Picture the same in heels and lipstick on a Vespa—that's a lipstick lesbian.

Sheila had lived in Boston prior to Northampton and she had frequented all the same clubs and restaurants I had when I'd lived in Boston in the eighties. I had been surprised to hear her mention Spit, a club that I had thought was the most amazing place on planet Earth when I first came from Ohio. We had nothing comparable to Spit in Cincinnati. We'd once had a lot in common and a lot to talk about when the restaurant was slow and we were trying to look busy.

When I first moved to Northampton, it seemed like everyone was twenty. It was nice to know another gay eighties survivor from Boston. Sheila had lived in Northampton for a while by the time I got there and already had a circle of lesbian friends closer to our age than most of the younger people in my circle at the time. After I had broken up with my twenty-two-year-old lover, I'd started hanging out with the thirtysomething crowd and Phillip. Sheila and I didn't talk much anymore.

Piper appeared to be flirting with Sheila. When Sheila walked away from the bar and left Piper on her own, I watched Piper. She was thinking about something, her chin raised ever so slightly, and she looked down her nose. I kept seeing her profile like this when she stood at the bar, giving drink orders to the bartender, and she looked like an utter snob. I figured there was no way the attitude was real—kind of the same thing where someone always looks mad or grumpy, but they are not. Still, Piper looked like a snob.

I found myself comparing every pretty woman I encountered with Joan, and not with any of Joan's faults. Their eyes were not as faraway dreamy or blue, no wisps of silky blond to tame, their shape not as long and sinewy, or they weren't as witty or smart, they didn't speak French fluently, or as in this case, they were a snob. I would have found something wrong with even Kate Moss at that particular time. If I tried to picture myself with anyone else, the picture always twisted into a memory of Joan—making out on a bridge over the Seine in Paris, kissing in a quiet snowstorm or in the pouring rain after one of those unbearably hot summer days in Northampton, or the two of us playing in the crystal-clear surf of a P-town beach.

It kind of made me sad to think about dating anyone new. Piper was attractive—in fact, compared to me, she was a goddess—but that's not the way my mind works. I don't compare myself to the woman I have a crush on; I compare that woman to my former lovers. I had been very blessed in that regard, as far as physical beauty anyway. But it was probably at least half the reason why I kept repeating the same mistakes. Being an insecure mess doesn't mix well with beautiful companions.

Meanwhile, back on Earth, every time I was midsentence and about to blurt out the details of our crime in my conversation with Phillip, Piper appeared at the table to check on our drink status. She would stay and chat for a moment. Then she would scurry away with her overloaded tray of empties and her brain full of drink orders. The place was packed and she had a bunch of tables to serve. Phillip noted her overattention to our table and my having been staring at her like a stalker. He decided to play Cupid.

Our table got bigger. A couple of Phillip's straight friends showed up and joined us, pulling another small table over to ours. Then this gay guy—who knew Phillip's friends and was Piper's old roommate—joined us, and so it went for the rest of the night, people joining our table until we were an island of randomly merged tables, a patchwork of social-circle intersections.

By closing time, we had our own little party going on. Piper had given up serving our island or her shift had ended and she joined us. I found she wasn't quite the snobby bitch she had struck me as, and I found out she was gay. She was also smart as a whip and had a great dry wit. She kept making me laugh. I was drunk but not clumsy and stupid yet. So when she joked about tables that wouldn't leave and let her go home, I realized she was talking about our table. We were the last group left in the restaurant and she was the last waitress.

Phillip invited a few people to come over to my house for an after-party. I didn't object and offered him a ride. It was within walking distance, but we could get there before anyone else and I could make sure I hadn't left anything out that I wouldn't want in plain view of people I barely knew. I had ridden my motorcycle to the Brewery to meet him, not because I was lazy but because it was my shiny new toy and Phillip hadn't seen it yet. This was a small purchase I had made upon our return to Northampton so I could get around. It was a used but shiny black Honda Rebel 450, a big step up from the little red 250 I'd had the previous summer. Summer was coming and that meant bike trips to all my favorite spots, like to the waterfalls in Florence, to the glacier-dug, granite swimming holes in Shelburne Falls, to Provincetown, or to Boston.

Phillip put on my extra helmet, a small skullcap I kept on the bike for unexpected passengers. He settled in behind me, still holding a snifter full of Courvoisier he had secreted out of the restaurant. I barely had a six-pack of Sam Adams in my fridge. We took off and headed for my house. Phillip held the drink under his jacket when we passed by a police car, before we pulled into the little private road that led to my apartment.

A couple of minutes later, the gay guy who had first joined us at the Brewery showed up with one of Phillip's straight friends and Piper. I was pleasantly surprised she had come and joked about her having gotten lost on her way to the home she had been so impatient to get to. But I had to run off and leave her with the boys and their snifter of Courvoisier for a minute. My cats had both retreated under my bed when the three strangers had come into the house. They needed to know the sky was not falling.

My relationship with the kitties was already on the rocks. I had dragged them to Chicago, abandoned them there with crazy people for six weeks, dragged them back to Northampton, and promptly abandoned them again for a week. Edith and Dum Dum had put up with a lot from me in our time together, and I had work to do to restore their trust in me. In any case, they had been my babies for a long time, and whenever they went under the bed, it worried me and meant real trouble. This late-night intrusion might have been the last straw, and there was a whole arsenal of tricks they might have in store for me, including their favorite punishment: pooping on my pillow.

I was trying to lure Edith out from under the bed, but I was having no luck. Edith even hissed at me when I reached for her, which nearly broke my heart. Meanwhile, right outside my window I could hear something interesting brewing. Phillip and the two other guys had gone outside and I could hear their conversation. What I could gather from my eavesdropping, while prone on the floor with my head under the bed, was that somebody had slept with somebody at some point in the recent past; the somebody else, who was not with them, was pissed. Basically some kind of personal drama was unfolding and I was being a busybody.

In the meantime, Piper had been left in the kitchen all by herself while this evidently secret issue was being sorted out. I could hear her roaming around my house, probably looking at things. I didn't have much, but it was all new, and that's a strange sight in our little college town. Most apartments were decorated in Salvation Army and thrift store finds. She put on a Smashing Pumpkins

CD from my little music collection and came to my room. I was still lying on the floor where I had been begging Edith to come out from under the bed but ended up eavesdropping. I motioned for Piper to sit down and be quiet.

She sat on the edge of my bed, probably trying to figure out what I was doing lying on the floor with my head under the bed. Edith came out the other side and hopped onto the bed, unafraid of Piper. Dum Dum followed and lay down by my pile of pillows. Edith, however, made herself comfortable on Piper's lap. Edith was getting all lovey with Piper. I think she was trying to make me jealous, and it worked. I was happy they had come out from under the bed but a little surprised at how very manipulative Edith had become. She wasn't one of those cats, the kind that loves any Tom, Dick, or Harriet willing to pet her. No, Edith generally shied away from other people. But now Edith wouldn't stop cuddling with Piper. When I retreated and turned my attention to sweet little Dum Dum, she too got up and sauntered over to Piper's side, snubbing me.

Phillip and the other two came to my bedroom door to let me know they were taking off. Edith remained on Piper's lap, digging her claws into her leg as she kneaded. Piper didn't seem to mind having her leg ripped to shreds. I guessed she must be a cat person. I think Phillip thought something much more interesting was brewing in my bedroom; he didn't linger and left.

Piper decided it was time for her to go too. I asked her for her number. I wanted to see her again. I knew if I weren't still so lovesick over Joan, I would have behaved very differently. I wanted to preserve the possibilities if I could. I might come to my senses or she might not come to hers. In any case, my cats liked her . . .

4 Dial *M* for Mule

NOT EVEN A WEEK HAD PASSED since Phillip and I had returned from his first trip as a drug smuggler before "God" started calling. Alajeh wanted us to pack up, turn around, and go right back to Europe to repeat the journey we had only just completed. But neither Phillip nor I wanted to do that. Phillip's desire for intrigue had been satisfied and we'd both had barely a moment to begin spending what we had just earned, much less get desperate enough to consider another round of European roulette. While the fact that the trip had been so easy might make it seem more appealing in due time (we had each cleared ten thousand dollars), we hadn't lost our ever-loving minds. It was way too soon to even contemplate another trip, let alone pack our bags and go.

Phillip had told Alajeh he could only be reached at my phone number, to avoid the risk of Meg accidentally intercepting information that contradicted his many cover-story lies. That meant it was all up to me to deflect Alajeh's repeated attempts to get us en route. I screened my calls and made him work hard to reach me. But he was more persistent than a telemarketer. He called all hours of the day and night. I suppose I had hoped he would simply tire of me and give up. I finally answered a call and told him that we would call him when we were ready to travel again and then hung up before he could object.

Alajeh stopped calling after that. But about a week later it started up again. After a few more failed attempts to reach me, he started having Bradley and Henry call to ask when we could make another trip. They had just returned from a trip themselves and "God" already wanted them to go back. If we didn't go, Bradley and Henry were suggesting that we weren't carrying our load and it would affect them.

Finally, my sister called to tell me that Alajeh was getting angry with me. She was furious that I had taken a second trip. She wasn't supposed to know about that. But some secrets have a very short life span. Thinking Bradley would not disclose my quick adventure was foolish. If I had been under any delusions before this, I now knew I was playing with fire. I just wasn't sure how torched I might already be or how bad it might get. My sister had completely broken it off with Alajeh, and in spite of my worries to the contrary, she'd had no contact with him, not until he reached out to her to pass on the message to me that he was angry with me.

I was very protective of my baby sister and I had made it clear how much I loved her while on my visit to meet Alajeh, my future brother-in-law and soon-to-be boss, in Africa. He had never asked me for anyone's address or anyone's picture like he had asked of Phillip. I would have wondered about the picture request, as I was now doing. What if the reason he collected this information had nothing to do with having someone to connect with in the event of an emergency, like if we were ever caught, as he had explained to Phillip.

Like Phillip had said, Alajeh was a totally affable guy. That was true at first, second, and third glance. He had been a generous host when I was his guest in Africa. He treated me very respectfully. But I wasn't his lover. I would have had no reason to be afraid of him after our first meeting were it not for his horrible treatment of my sister. This was not completely foreign to me. I had known men and women in my past who had married and had kids with worse companions than Alajeh. But I had never seen my sister in a similarly horrendous relationship.

Seeing Hester in the role she had allowed herself to fall into had made me crazy. How could she do that if she loved herself even a fraction as much as I loved her? It was their relationship that had made me want to get us out of there, not the fact that he was a drug lord. Ironically, I think in witnessing her in her so-called Prince Charming and Cinderella fairy tale I had broken the love spell my sister had been under and the illusion had collapsed. At the same time, in focusing my already challenged skills of observation and character judgment on their love affair, instead of the moronic predicament we were both in, I might have missed some big red flags. For example, he had made a joke once about killing Hester if I ever disappointed him, but that was when I still believed they were both in love and he was still the nice, rich fiancé, who also happened to be a drug lord.

Aside from the shame I felt for becoming the one thing that caused him to reconnect with my sister, I had an awful and sudden epiphany. I realized that he might not have been joking at all back then. Maybe the real message being sent was a threat, reminding me he could reach out to me through her, if I made him. My goofy little sister didn't realize it, but she was unwittingly delivering the most potent intimidation anyone could ever direct at me. It didn't matter exactly what she was saying to me; all that mattered was that he had called Hester to have her call me. I got the message.

When he answered the phone and thundered happily in his very deep voice "My friend!" I had this brand-new feeling. It was like ice had filled my chest and I shook like a cartoon character. I wasn't the confident international citizen of the world I pretended to be. I was a dumb-ass from Cincinnati, Ohio, who until very recently had still called Daddy to fix things when they got out of my control. Until that moment, I truly had no grasp of what I had gotten myself into, but I wanted out and I needed help thinking it through. I needed someone to talk to, someone levelheaded and smart, but not Dad, not with this. I couldn't do that to him. It would break his heart to know what we had done. I decided to tell Phillip about my new-found clarity via Hester's "message." Maybe he would tell me I was being crazy paranoid.

Alajeh also had the contact information of someone Phillip loved. I had to get to him to see if he had also received a message from "God" through his contact. If Alajeh had reached out to Phillip through the contact, I could be pretty certain Phillip wouldn't so easily dismiss my concern as paranoid silliness. Phillip told me he had made it clear to Alajeh, he was never to contact that person unless he had been arrested or worse.

Edith jumped up onto my desk and sat on my notebook's keyboard in front of me, causing the laptop to ding repeatedly. She couldn't have cared less about the irritating dings; nor could I. She knew I was upset. She stayed seated on the keyboard, letting the dings from my laptop continue without so much as a look at the noisy beast she sat on. Edith had a sixth sense about these things. I could tell by her worried mews: she was upset that I was upset. But I was frozen in my seat, unable to do anything but have a worried staring contest with my cat. Then a calm clarity finally fell over me.

This had to stop. All of it. I wanted to make damn certain nothing happened to Hester. Phillip wasn't going to like it, but I had to warn him about Alajeh. It seemed to me now that Phillip had also naively put someone he loved in harm's way. I understood that now. I stood up and stretched with purpose, like I was about to run a race. Then I sat right back down wondering where I thought I was heading and how exactly I thought I could just stop this.

I called Phillip first. He was going to come over later. He didn't care how big I thought my emergency was. It wasn't big enough to have to explain it to Meg and blow her off. They had plans and that was that. He would be over afterward. I wasn't about to utter the details of my drama regarding our criminal enterprise over the phone. I knew that would be sloppy and stupid.

I sat staring back at Edith and petting her head. I pushed her off the laptop's keyboard and realized she had been entering text into the word processing program I had opened before all this. I took a look at what her butt had typed. Perhaps I would find my answers there. All that she had typed was a string of the letters L and A, repeated for pages and pages. She had now officially done more writing than I had in the last couple of months. I closed Edith's composition and turned off the computer before she crawled back onto the keys and curled up. I couldn't sit there all night waiting to talk to Phillip. I would go batty.

I started thinking about the worst-case scenario. If I had no choice but to go on another trip, I would need another cat sitter. This time I wanted someone to actually stay in the apartment with Edith and Dum Dum, someone who might be in a position to keep my babies if I never returned. It was time to start thinking about the long term. Mom and Dad's house was definitely out of the question. I would have to explain why I needed them to babysit my girls. Besides that, my mom had conveniently developed cat allergies. I had recently asked her to babysit my kitties while I got settled in Chicago and she couldn't help then. Edith flicked her tail hard once, as if she were responding to my thought.

Edith and Dum Dum needed a good godparent. The cats had liked Piper and she was a cat person. Piper still lived in an apartment with a bunch of people and she might appreciate the "alone" time at my apartment. Piper would never let anything bad happen to my girls if I didn't make it home. It was a long shot and I would have to tell her everything, but I could give it a try. I found her number still tucked in the pocket of the pants I had stuffed into my dirty clothes hamper a few nights before. I had been hesitant to call her without having something concrete to talk about. I no longer had simple stuff in common with anyone and I sucked at small talk. I had no reason to hesitate now though; Edith and Dum Dum needed a godmother and a house sitter.

I called Piper and invited her to have a drink with me. If she agreed to be the kitties' godmother, there were a lot of unusual details better explained in person. She wasn't working that night, so when she agreed to meet me and asked where I wanted to go, I wasn't prepared for such a simple detail to be so complicated. I didn't want anyone listening to our conversation. She worked at the Brewery, so that place was out—too many busybodies interested in Piper there. I would have similar fans at Spoleto, so that was out too. Haymarket didn't serve alcohol, so that was out. Besides, I certainly wasn't ready to see Joan if she was at work. I picked the Hotel Northampton. I wondered if it was a mistake to meet her at a hotel for drinks. Especially since I think she thought I was making a date with her.

Edith woke from a short nap on my laptop when I set the phone down in its cradle. Cats are professionals when it comes to power napping. She stood up and did a minute's worth of yoga, downwardfacing dog, then Halloween kitty. I expected her to hop off the desk and go about her very important business. Instead, she stepped off the desk into my arms and dug in. I was wearing one of my nice new knit sweaters from Paris but sacrificed it gladly when she started kneading. Edith was finally making up with me. She had not done this since my return from Chicago, and it signaled the truce I had been so hoping for. I loved her unconditionally. Though it was conditional, Edith loved me too and she trusted me. I could never abandon her, but leaving her in someone else's care felt like that. She hopped down and headed for her bed.

I had enough time to lie down for a little nap, take a shower, and get to the hotel. I wasn't normally a nap person, but the call with Hester and subsequent call with Alajeh had sent my adrenaline through the roof. It had worn off quickly though, and I was exhausted, emotionally drained. I opened the windows in my room and crawled into bed with Edith and Dum Dum, closed my eyes, and dozed off. The next second my room was dark, Edith was gone, and I had no idea where I was or what I was supposed to be doing, but instantly I knew that it was something important.

I jumped out of bed, checked quickly to see if the cats were in or out, shut the window, locked it, threw my clothes on and my boots, grabbed my helmet, and bolted out the door, then back in the door to get my cigarettes and lighter, then out and onto my bike, then off my bike, back in the door to get my keys, then I stopped, stood still for a moment, and did nothing. I was already late, and when I try to go fast, I end up going backward.

Miraculously, though, I did make it in time to meet Piper. She had been late too, or said she had. I sat down at the bar next to her and ordered a drink. She ordered some big fruity frozen thing. I scanned the bar menu and instantly regretted having chosen the Hotel Northampton. Their food wasn't very fun, just boring crap visiting parents would want. I was in the mood for pizza and suggested we go to a trendy pizza place up the street after our drinks. She agreed . . .

But first, I had to get the reason we were meeting onto the table. I ordered a scotch, took a big gulp, and got right to the point. I didn't beat around the bush at all either. I just came right out and told her what our little date was about.

"If I begged, would you stay at my house for a while and watch my cats? I'll pay you." I wondered if that was overkill.

"Maybe." Piper looked puzzled. "When?"

"I'm thinking soon, but not sure."

"For how long?"

"Hmm. Maybe a week, but it could be longer." It was a little premature to ask her about being their godmother. But my claim that it would be only a week assumed that if I did go, it would be a repeat of the last trip. "Why?"

"Oh, I don't know. So I know when to show up and what to pack." She laughed at me like my not knowing this was crazy.

"So you'll do it!" I jumped off my stool and hugged her.

"Whoa! Slow it down." The expression she chose and her playful smile reminded me of someone I liked. I couldn't remember who, but the smile was genuine and warm. "When you figure out when and for how long, you let me know." Her expression turned serious again, if not a little condescending.

"I will. But you'll do it, right?" I didn't even know this was going to be necessary yet. I just wanted her to say she would do it if she could. If I had someone who would do it, I could work out all the details so they could.

"Where are you going?" she asked, probably not expecting what I said.

"Paris. Maybe Africa."

She looked at me without saying anything for a moment. "You haven't decided?"

"No. I haven't got an itinerary yet. I'm not even certain yet I am going anywhere." I told her I was simply trying to make sure I had someone I could trust with my cats.

"What are you going for?" I guessed Piper had heard the bullshit story that I worked for someone in Paris.

"I'm a smuggler." This sounded so much nicer than saying I was a drug mule. She didn't laugh, so she clearly didn't think I was joking, and she hadn't turned to stone, which kind of describes what I imagined people might do when I told them. I had shared my secret with a few others by then, not just Phillip. Nobody I'd told had freaked out yet though. Everyone just thought it was cool. But this was the first time I would tell someone about the trap I thought I was in.

Piper was slow to respond, but when she did, she didn't seem to mind my occupation. I explained my predicament a little more, that I really hoped to figure out an alternative to going on another trip, and she was very sweet about it. She assured me that she would take care of the cats. She told me I was crazy when I offered to pay her, I didn't have to pay her to do that, and she would stay at the house with them.

I felt like I had made a new friend and it surprised me that I had misjudged her so completely before getting to know her. She was no snob. She was very sweet, quite possibly even a little shy. I felt like I could trust anyone who loved cats so much. I know, crazy, but that's the way we cat people are. Piper listened to my adventurous tales and the unlikely series of events that resulted in my having the tales to tell. I told her I felt like something bigger than myself was at work in my life. It was all too unreal. She agreed completely, and I think she even bought into the idea; it would mean something bigger than her was also at work in her life. I had just made her my confidant after all.

We went to eat pizza and ended up going our separate ways when Phillip finally found me and was ready to address the big emergency I had called him about. His sudden appearance and demand of my attention probably seemed a little rude to Piper at first. But I apologized for it and sent her on her way, telling her I needed to let Phillip know she was in the loop but that first we had to deal with the situation I had explained earlier.

Phillip and I discussed my newly amplified fears and got extraordinarily drunk. One too many drinks while discussing our possibly unsolvable problem made it impossible for me to ride my motorcycle back to my apartment, but it did wonders to douse the fuse of my explosive emotions. Fueled by Dewar's and sodas, Phillip and I came up with a great idea to save our own butts. We would find people who wanted to do what we had done and pretend we were the ones doing it!

Phillip and I simply opened our big mouths up and spilled the beans to people we thought might be interested. When someone we told our story to responded the way Phillip had when I'd told him about my trip and wanted to do it themselves, we added them to a mental list of possibilities. Very soon, we had a small group of friends who knew our secret and wanted a chance to do what we had done. You know what happens to secrets. The first two people who wanted to give it a go were interested because of the adventure, a couple of people were bored adrenaline junkies, and a couple of others needed money. Everybody wanted expense-free travel. I think one was either a sociopath or suicidal or some combination thereof, so we stayed away from that one. What none of our new recruits were was poor, desperate, or stupid. They all came from good families, and that is what would make it so easy. No one would suspect any of these people to be drug smugglers. They came off as educated, privileged, law-abiding yuppies, because that's what they were.

Beyond the desire to go play outlaws and globe-trotters for a week or two, they also had to meet some basic standards, and of course, Phillip and I believed we were experts on profiling the perfect drug smuggler, given our vast experience of just one trip together. They had to be old enough to hold a job that would take them overseas or old enough to be traveling college graduates. We told them enough of the real story, the many un-fun parts, and the danger that Alajeh might be to scare them off. Though we would do everything we could to keep it from happening, if anyone did have to meet Alajeh, there would be no easy way for them to get out. If Alajeh found out what we were doing, he would have to meet them, and our hope of using them to do our work would be dashed.

We explained that this last fact was why we were doing what we were doing, finding our stand-ins. We had both been like our recruits at one point, wanting to go on an adventure, make a little money, and be done with it. What we could offer them was a way to do that without making the same mistake we had made. If someone we did like was still eager to go, with all the negative information disclosed, we had a recruit.

Most important, there were no threats made. As long as everything worked out, they were also free to leave us at almost any time they chose. Heck, we would even pay the change fee for their return ticket if they chickened out. We never thought too hard about failure; I guess we didn't think it was possible.

Phillip and I put our plan in motion. I was to take two of our volunteers to Chicago, pick the money up, escort them to Europe, pick up the drug-stuffed jackets, and put our friends and their nice new jackets on a plane back to Chicago. Phillip would leave Northampton a week after us and meet them coming into Chicago. He would deliver the drugs and get the payment, then pay our friends and finally send them home. A couple of weeks later we would do it all again, but with me in Chicago and Phillip in Europe.

In this arrangement, Phillip and I would no longer have to smuggle drugs. We were only in danger of being busted for drug possession, and that for only however long it took to retrieve the drugs from our friends and hand them off to Alajeh's folk. It would look to

Alajeh like Phillip and I had taken two trips, back to back. He would at least stop bugging us for a minute. We had put a great deal of thought into this plan and we were fairly certain we had devised a brilliant escape route; on the way out we might make a little money and meet some adventurous people like ourselves, all while making everyone involved very happy. Sooner or later Alajeh would decide we had traveled so much that our odds of getting busted were too high. We couldn't be his winning horses forever. We would be out.

The best part was eliminating our own risk, except for that tiny little window of time when we were actually in possession of the heroin. If we made this work, we would be fine, even if it took a little while to completely exit. We thought we were genius escape artists, the fucking Houdini twins.

This was our *Mission: Impossible.* There were a lot of variables to juggle that determined whether or not our seemingly simple plan could work, but we were motivated. Phillip and I were too scared to do it again ourselves. We thought that Alajeh could make us do it if he wanted to, and though he seemed to know we would not get busted, we were both convinced he was wrong. His repeated assertion that as long as we followed his rules, we would be taken care of, even if we did get nabbed by Customs, was not very reassuring. His rules included only two acceptable exits from his service. The first was going to jail quietly were he ever wrong about our not getting busted. The second was reaching an as of yet unknown magic number of trips taken. After that, we would be considered too high risk. How this sum was determined and by whom, I have no clue. I did know about an international flight watch list—that if you were placed on it, you couldn't do the smuggling anymore—but I had as little insight into how Alajeh would have access to this list as I did the calculation for the number of trips it took to make the list.

There was always the possibility that we were being ridiculous. Maybe Alajeh wouldn't follow through on these perceived threats. Maybe it was all just an act, meant to play with our imaginations and maintain control of us. We had considered this, hoped and wished for it. But what if we were wrong? It wasn't our own lives we thought we were betting with; it was my sister's life and whomever Phillip had offered up as his so-called emergency contact.

The most important factors required in order for this charade to work were that Alajeh never find out what we were doing and, at the very least, we had to break even and not lose money on the trips. Our friends knew better than to expose the operation to anyone if they decided to back out or got caught. First of all, what did the recruits know to tell? The name that we called him and country of origin. The name wouldn't have proven very useful, since it apparently wasn't even his real name. Second, if they were caught by U.S. Customs, they would be waiving their access to good lawyers and their fat bonus for getting busted and staying quiet. Yes, there was a bonus for that. It came from Alajeh and we hoped never to have to make that claim. If that ever happened, we would be in deep shit, having to tell Alajeh not only what we had been doing in secret but also that our stand-ins, whom he didn't know about, had been caught.

We knew there would be enough start-up cash for two airline tickets to Paris or Brussels and a modest stipend for living expenses for two. But three of us would be traveling, not two: Phillip or me with the two recruits. The modest stipend made a dent in costs, but we were not going to ask our friends to stay in the dumps that Alajeh's stipends afforded. Phillip and I had to foot part of the bill for each trip, up front. This was part of the deal with our recruited friends. If all else failed, they would get the trip of a lifetime for free. Our friends would be risking getting caught and going to jail for a long time, maybe even as long as two years. That is what we had been told a first-time offender would face.

I finally placed a second call back to Alajeh for trip dates. We had an excellent plan, two perfect candidates, and we were ready to go. We had four other equally qualified candidates in the batter's box, also prepared, when Alajeh said "Go."

Until that happened, Piper, the kitties, and I hung out almost every day. She stayed overnight at my house sometimes, sleeping in my bed with me. There was no hanky-panky there, unless you count her and Edith or Dum Dum's snuggling as such. Piper and I were becoming friends, but that is all. She had a much closer relationship blossoming with my cats. I had been right about her being their godparent. She was perfect for that job. She was a very intelligent and serious woman, she wasn't interested in becoming a drug mule, and I assumed she knew better than to get involved with me. Nonetheless, she was rapidly becoming my good friend and that was exactly all I needed. I was trying to avoid a recurring theme in my life up to that point. I would break up with a girlfriend, go into a tailspin, and fall directly into a new relationship as bad as or worse than the one before.

Piper's presence in my life made it easier for me to manage the void. I had been a tomboy growing up and my friends had usually been boys. Interestingly, most of them turned out to be gay too. My mother once questioned if there was something wrong with our neighborhood. I don't know, like perhaps it was in the water. But the point is, my friendships with girls were always complicated. It seemed like every friendship was based on one having an attraction to the other. It was rare to find a friendship where I felt there was a sort of equal ambivalence. That made it so much easier just to relax and hang out.

Piper was fine with not being invited to participate in any capacity other than as my cat sitter. She had a very calming effect on me, not just on my cats. In telling anyone what I feared might be in store for me if the plan I had failed, it somehow felt less likely to fail. In fact, I started feeling pretty optimistic about things, like I had it all figured out.

Phillip and I stumbled a little bit on the first obstacle to our seamless plan. We learned that the route was changing a lot and the method a little. We were told we would be starting in Jakarta, Hong Kong, or Manila. The trip was no longer a simple hop over to Europe and back. Now it was two hops. Our original plan, where only one of us traveled abroad with the recruits, was bungled. We would also be carrying two pieces of luggage each now. The method we had previously used, where jackets were secretly packed with heroin, was being retired. A new method was starting where the luggage we carried had the heroin packed inside its lining.

Starting out on the other side of the planet on a route we had never taken made us nervous. We had looked on a globe to find Jakarta. Phillip knew approximately where to look; I had no clue. Jakarta was a city on an island in the middle of a bunch of islands, between the Indian Ocean and the Java Sea. All this was between China and Australia. We were to fly from one of these very distant cities—Jakarta, Hong Kong, or Manila—wait for a week, collect our parcels there, and then make our way back to Chicago by way of a brief visit to Europe. It was double the complexity, risk, and expense. But it was more than double the reward. Definitely enough to pay the recruits, stay at fancy hotels, buy all the tickets, play, and still probably walk away with as much as we had made carrying jackets from Europe to Chicago.

By the time Alajeh announced our departure date, meaning it was time to go to Chicago, collect our travel money, and begin our journey, my fridge was no longer empty. Piper had loaded it up with healthy foods Edith and Dum Dum had never seen in our house, like yogurts, fresh spinach, and fruit juices. My cabinets weren't bare anymore either. She had food stored there too, including the new healthy brand of cat food she had found for my cats. My apartment felt more like a home, and it had been a while since I'd felt like I had more than just a place for me and the cats to sleep.

She stayed over the night before I was due to leave Northampton. In the morning, when my travel companions arrived at the house before dawn, we all loaded into a car Phillip had rented to drive us to the airport in Boston. I remember getting warm fuzzies, watching Piper wave goodbye from my porch while we did our last minute do-we-have-everything checks. I watched her go back inside to the cats in my bedroom and turn off the light as we pulled away. It was nice to have a home with someone in it to return to. I felt so much less alone in the world just knowing I could pick up a phone and call my house to talk to my sane friend Piper. I think Piper probably observed my comings and goings like her very own made-for-TV movie, not as the reality she should have been running from.

5 The Day of Living Dangerously

THE FIRST TWO RECRUITS, Craig and Molly, had no objection to a new travel plan or method of transport. They were thrilled but nervous about going to the other side of the planet. Craig and Molly were a two-for-one deal. Not cheaper; they just wouldn't go separately. Craig had long curly blond hair and shocking blue eyes. He was a soccer player, Hacky Sack marvel, mountain biker, hiker, semi-vegetarian, and retro-hippie child of the eighties. He was also twenty-three years old, a dishwasher, and a waiter, and he had just graduated from college.

Molly was a year behind him but smarter. She was a tiny thing, with a mane of black wavy or curly hair, depending on the weather. It was the same length and cut as Craig's, and they synchronized the up and down do days. Neither seemed to have mastered the whole hairbrush concept, but they were adorable in spite of it. Craig had perfect white teeth, and Molly had a Lauren Bacall smile with the sexy gap. She was also a soccer player, Hacky Sack marvel, mountain biker, hiker, semi-vegetarian, and retro-hippie child of the eighties. I never asked why they were doing this. I just assumed it was like going on a trek to Tibet, just free with a big payday at the end.

There was a slight delay in Chicago, waiting to learn our endpoint was Jakarta and not Hong Kong or wherever else Alajeh had said it might be. Craig and Molly played Frisbee on Michigan Avenue and we wrangled tickets to Paris, the first stop. The helpful travel agent Henry had taken me to on my first trip now told us the airfares for Paris to Jakarta and gave us prices for a couple of nice hotels there. Our finances would survive the major game change as long as Phillip and I were willing to risk everything we had left of what we had made so far. Because this was such uncharted territory, we decided we would both escort Molly and Craig. Therefore, we had to cover all costs for our two recruits, and it was pricey.

We had already told Alajeh that we would do the trip, so the only alternative to investing all we had was to just give up and do it ourselves. Compared to our fear of ending up in jail, being broke wasn't much of a risk, so we went all in. We would make the money back and then some at the end of the journey. We were paying Craig and Molly fifteen thousand dollars each for their parts, but we would be getting more than that for the delivery. Enough to cover the expenses for all of us, pay them, and make a few thousand dollars each.

Our companions got their vaccinations and visas in Paris, but we decided that we wouldn't hang out there, which had been part of the original and simpler plan. Go to Paris, hang out, have a ball, swing up to Brussels by train, replace passports as needed, get heroin-stuffed-jackets, and come home. No, this trip wasn't going to be that simple. We got on the first flight we could to Jakarta from Paris. It was a seventeen-hour flight via Singapore.

While Air France still had a smoking area, the move to a nonsmoking world had begun. Phillip and I hated the surprise of the nonsmoking flight this airline sprang on us. By the time we landed in Singapore for a brief layover, I was like a rabid dog ready to gnaw and tear my way out the door. I made it all the way to the exit, only to discover I couldn't get off the plane to smoke during our non-nonstop flight to Jakarta. I sulked back to my seat and tried to sleep through the last couple of hours of the trip.

I didn't know what to expect from Indonesia. My sum total knowledge of this corner of the world consisted of a vague recollection of *The Year of Living Dangerously*. The movie was set in Jakarta in the seventies and featured lots of political mayhem, misery, and poverty. Jakarta fit my hazy expectations. It was a sprawling metropolis that, for some reason, reminded me of the street scenes in *Blade Runner*'s futuristic version of a city at night, with drizzle or sewage sprinkling all the time, all dark with neon everywhere. It might have been the smell that made me think of that, since there were no flying cars or genetic mutants about. But it was dirty, stinky, and overcrowded beyond my immediate comprehension.

We stayed in the fancy and safe resort the travel agent had recommended, a Western resort—"Western" as in American extravagance, not cowboys and Indians. We were only going to be there for a week and we had promised our companions a five-star trip. There were acres of lush green landscaping, flowers, a huge swimming pool, and an outdoor café all nestled inside the resort walls. But it was planted smack-dab in the middle of awful, overcrowded slums that went on for miles. I expected the overwhelming stench of the city to vanish inside the walls of our oasis, but it didn't. It hung in the hot, moist air around us, contaminating the pristine beauty with the smell of cholera and starvation.

Phillip and I realized how prudent the decision was for both of us to come to Jakarta. It would have been unnerving to try to negotiate this leg of the trip alone. I knew Jakarta was too far outside of my comfort zone. The culture was too foreign, the city was too huge, and—whereas every city has pockets of poverty, the desperation that most Western cultures pack into their projects—in Jakarta, the impoverished masses aren't segregated in their own zip codes. Ten feet from our resort, thousands of human beings lived like refugees, in makeshift housing, alongside the stinking canals overflowing with raw sewage. Someone once compared the beautiful canals of Amsterdam to Dante's concentric circles of Hell. The comparison seems more fittingly applied to Jakarta.

With the exception of a couple of seedy nightclubs, a McDonald's, and a mall, we mostly stayed at the resort. I stopped trying to pretend we were some seasoned veterans of the third world. Besides, it turned out Craig had traveled the third world quite a bit with his globe-trotting parents. We hadn't expected our Hacky Sack hipster to have such a prestigious provenance that our field trips out into Jakarta would be a bore.

Craig didn't look to me like someone who had traveled anywhere but to Dead concerts or soccer championships. But he had. This was information we should have known prior to letting him come with us. I didn't know diddly-squat about Indonesia, but I did know a little something about smuggling heroin. The extensive travel already recorded in his passport meant he would not be able to use his current passport to go through border control carrying drugs anywhere, not even Paris, and that was supposed to be our next stop. Stamps in a passport from certain countries created a red flag for Customs agents or border guards anywhere. Craig's passport had so many of these stamps already, a thorough questioning and search were almost guaranteed.

The Golden Triangle is not a geometric shape or a math calculation used to craftily identify likely smugglers of poppy products. It is a region made up of countries known to be cultivators of the pretty flower. Craig had stamps from Turkey, China, and Myanmar. It didn't matter that the stamps were all dated from over three years earlier, as he had argued.

By then, we had all seen the bags they would be carrying—three of them anyway. The true nature of this black leather luggage was very well concealed visually. From the outside they looked like nice black leather garment bags. But a simple search would be the end of the line for Craig. A close look at the bags' interiors would reveal the bags were hiding more than clothes. There was a big lumpy bulge under the leather lining, clearly concealing something substantial, like a mashed bag of flour might be stuffed in the interior of each bag.

Craig was understandably aggravated by the situation. He had just traveled halfway around the world with us, only to discover it had all been for nothing. Phillip assured him he had a better solution than his not being able to participate. He asked Craig to give him a minute to check out one detail. Without explaining what was going on in his head at the moment, Phillip said he would have his answer by morning and told Craig to relax, not to worry, that everything would be fine. I followed Phillip back to our room, where he finally shared his thoughts.

We hadn't thought to ask any of our recruits about their travel histories. We didn't need to for our original itinerary. It would have been corrected by "losing" the tainted passport and going to the embassy in Paris or Brussels to get a replacement. Problem solved. We had never carried the drugs out of the third world into Europe and then into the United States too. If Craig did this trick of getting a replacement passport in Jakarta, he would be okay going into Europe. But he couldn't go to the consulate in Paris and say he lost his passport again so soon after, not without the possibility of raising a lot of suspicion.

The passport quandary worried me. I kept trying to put myself in Alajeh's shoes and think what he would have expected me or Phillip to do after getting a stamp from Indonesia if we then couldn't use that stamped passport going back into the States. It worried me that Alajeh probably expected us to lose the passport a second time in Paris. Was that safe or was this a suicide mission? These were the details that could become failure points. We had to resolve these first as if we were the ones carrying, then apply that same reasoning to our recruits' predicament.

A consulate in Europe might know he had just done the very same thing in Jakarta. If they did know, they would surely make a note or something in the pages of Craig's new passport, which would alert Customs agents. In 1993, our understanding was that government computers were not all connected to one another. We did know there was a watch list for suspicious travelers, but how and when it was compiled, we did not know. We had to assume a stunt like losing his passport once in Jakarta and again in Paris might raise some red flags and get him added to the list. If we were supposed to be using a clean passport in Paris, then both Molly and Craig were screwed. That would mean we couldn't even make it to Europe. *Game over.*

Both Alajeh and Henry had told me about this database of suspicious travelers. Apparently, once a person was on that list, they were done. They could no longer be a smuggler because they would always be questioned and searched. This was a list Phillip and I wanted to be put on. When Craig's issue came up, we thought we had found a much simpler way to solve our problem, one we hadn't thought of. We could do exactly what we were trying to help Craig avoid doing and end up being put on the watch list ourselves.

At the moment, though, we needed our recruits to stay off that list or they wouldn't be able to smuggle the bags in without getting searched. I realized that Alajeh could not have intended us to use clean passports in Paris. The first question they asked is where you just came from. Surely saying you had come from anyplace other than where the plane you just got off of had come from would raise more suspicion than one ugly visa stamp from Indonesia. That cleared Molly unless this was a suicide mission, but it didn't resolve Craig's populated passport issue.

Phillip explained his idea to me. We could use one of the other recruits that we had been planning to use on our next trip to complete the second leg of Craig's trip. They could meet us in Paris and take Craig's bag back to Chicago from there. Craig and the other recruit would then split the payment in half. The solution complicated our plans and meant more out-of-pocket expenses up front, but it would solve the problem.

Garrett and Edwin were Phillip's friends from Chicago. More accurately, Garrett was Phillip's best friend from their college days and Edwin was his boyfriend. Phillip had recruited Garrett, and Edwin was part of the deal. Phillip was able to get Garrett to agree to meet us in Paris to complete the trip. Craig also agreed, once Phillip explained it to him carefully.

A few days into our Jakarta stay, a new problem arose that might have exposed our whole scheme to Alajeh. Henry and Bradley unex-

pectedly appeared at the resort bar while I was having a wonderful
and relaxing escape from everyone, waiting for a quick tropical rain
to make its way through. I was sitting by myself in one of the big
wicker rocking chairs that lined an elegant veranda on the opposite
side of a series of French glass-paned double doors. The open door-
ways, punctuated by big picture windows of the same style beveled
glass, made everything sparkle. The outdoors felt like it was inside,
and vice versa, but the doors separated the veranda from the interior bar and obscured Henry and Bradley's view of my location in
the rocking chair.

The scrumptious veranda with stone floors, a beautiful hardwood
ceiling, and gigantic slow-moving fans overhead flanked the resort's
main building. A long red oriental carpet stretched the entire length
of the exceedingly long, narrow porch. The plantation-like charm
was an odd juxtaposition to the green jungle-like fauna between
the pool and the building but made a perfect perch for me and my
frozen mudslide. Unfortunately, with all the glass between me and
the guys, there was no place where I could really hide, so that was
the end of my relaxing respite and the beginning of a problem.

Molly and Craig had taken shelter at an outdoor table under a
protective canopy, by the poolside café. They were directly across
the pool and beyond the sundeck. I had been waving wildly, trying to get their attention to come join me a moment earlier. But
after I saw Bradley and Henry come in and walk to the bar inside,
I stopped waving, turned my chair slightly, and sat down low in my
seat. They were ordering drinks. Bradley faced my direction, but he
was as blind as a bat. Henry had his back to me, but he kept scanning the room. My only exit would have been to either walk past
them or past Craig and Molly.

If one pair saw me talking to the other, either way, it wasn't good.
I didn't want Henry or Bradley to know what we were up to, and I
didn't want Craig and Molly to meet them and find out more than
they should know. We had told Bradley about what we were planning once, back when the plan we were now executing had been just
a drunk's idea. Bradley had thought it wouldn't work, but he would

know what we were doing if he saw us with these guys. It worried me that Henry might find out.

Bradley and Craig both spotted me at exactly the same moment and started walking toward me from their opposite directions. I lit a cigarette and rocked back and forth in the chair. I was like a deer in headlights, except for the rocking and smoking. This was really going to happen and there was nothing to do.

Bradley got to me first; he was closer. He was genuinely happy to see me. I learned quickly that they had arrived that morning and been sleeping all day. Wasn't the resort beautiful? Wasn't it amazing that we ran into each other? He was talking one hundred miles an hour. I watched Craig get closer. Henry had almost made them take a room at a cheap hotel in town, but they had changed their minds when they got a look at Jakarta. Bradley noticed the fellow approaching us and made a look-at-this-cutie kind of "Hmm." The cutie, Craig, kept coming toward us and he stuck his hand out in a greeting gesture, which thoroughly surprised Bradley. Then Craig asked me to make introductions, which I'm sure confused Bradley.

I introduced Craig to Bradley as someone I knew from Boston. I didn't want to tell Bradley he was from Northampton, so I tried to pass him off as someone I had miraculously bumped into on the other side of the planet who hailed from Boston. I told Craig to wait for me either back at his room or back at the pool café, as if we had plans to get together. I hoped Craig was smart enough to catch on. Bradley was a very smart fellow. If Craig corrected me and said Northampton, our secret would be no secret soon. I saw Henry was on his way over and he was also surprised to see me, but not pleasantly either. Thankfully, Craig got the message and told me it was nice to have run into me and left.

I watched Craig collect Molly, their pool towels and stuff, then head off toward our rooms. Bradley watched Craig's exit too; still cruising him. But as soon as Craig took Molly's arm, Bradley turned back to me, having lost interest or hope in the unattainable Bostonian.

Phillip appeared from out of nowhere and approached us with

a strange look and an apprehensive gait. But as soon as he was in our midst, his expression changed and he greeted Bradley warmly with a "Hey, dude" and they man-hugged. Phillip had met Bradley in Paris on his first trip and had liked him. We had all briefly been guests in the same hotel, the Saint-André des Arts, and Bradley was a totally likeable guy.

Phillip had never met Henry, though he had heard plenty about him from me. Henry was cool and guarded but polite. We all sat down at a table together. I don't think Bradley and Henry could tell I was freaking out, wishing I could run away or magically go back an hour in time to undo this unfortunate rendezvous. Phillip looked nervous and I wished he would calm down. But I couldn't tell him Craig and Molly were safely squirreled away in the room. I guessed he was worried about them showing up, because he kept looking all around us like he had a severe attention deficit. We ordered drinks from the cocktail waitress, who brought us a little bowl full of what I thought were tiny peanuts, but I think they were roasted beans.

We told them everything that we had discovered about Jakarta so far and generally made small talk. We finally got a moment to slip away and speak privately when Phillip went to the bathroom and I followed him. We decided to say we were meeting the couple from Boston for dinner and returned to the table separately. We were just about to try our escape when I saw Molly over by the elevators. She looked impatient but maintained her distance.

I realized we had been sitting with Bradley and Henry already for over an hour and it was dinnertime. Our secret travel companions were getting hungry, I guessed, and the buffet we had talked about earlier would only be open for another hour.

Bradley saw Molly exchange a look with Phillip and remembered her having been the one with Craig, the cutie. He looked at Phillip, then at me, with the expression of someone about to solve a mystery. "You guys did it!" he said, looking back in Molly's direction. I had hoped Bradley had forgotten the conversation we once had, but obviously he had not.

Phillip smiled a devilish little grin and Bradley guessed we had actually followed through on our harebrained scheme. Henry was slow to understand the direction and contents of our conversation. He wasn't really paying attention. But as soon as he realized that I was uncomfortable with him hearing what was being discussed, he got very curious, sat up, and paid very close attention. He then acted like he couldn't believe his ears, and he almost whined, "I want someone to carry my bags. Shit! I'm the one here who should be the most worried." I hadn't expected that reaction. He was right, though.

Phillip jumped at an opportunity to salvage things he thought Henry's reaction had indicated. He told him we had other people and that he *could* have someone carry his stuff. Phillip's offer was a smart move. It was actually the only possible solution, now that the cat was out of the bag. There was no way to keep it secret from Alajeh without including Henry and Bradley in the scheme.

Phillip left us and went to the room to call Garrett in Chicago. He asked if both he and his boyfriend could be ready to come to Jakarta quickly, instead of Garrett going only to Paris. There had been another change in the plan and they were both needed for a complete trip. When they agreed, he told them to sit tight. He would call back later to discuss tickets, vaccines, and visas. Then Phillip called another recruit in Northampton and told him to get ready to fly to Paris when he got Phillip's next call. This guy would be a replacement for Craig on the Paris-to-Chicago leg of the trip now. The only thing left to figure out was how to pay for all their tickets and expenses.

Phillip came back to the table beaming with excitement, and not a moment too soon. Henry was starting to pick at me again about something. Henry objected to Phillip's idea of charging tickets to his American Express card. He thought Phillip was an idiot to even suggest such a move, believed Alajeh would kill us for leaving a paper trail like that, and said so in a very patronizing tone. That slightly aggravated Phillip. He was offering to cover the guy's costs on his own credit card, give away one of his precious recruits, who also happened to be his best friend, and Henry had insulted him as thanks for his efforts. Phillip suggested Henry wire cash back to Chicago, and that idea was similarly objectionable to Henry. Phillip gave up and told him to figure it out himself, and let him know what to tell his friend when he had.

Henry was right on all counts, but neither Phillip nor I could see that. Henry threw his arms up in a clearly bitchy gesture and said, "Fine." He stood up, wobbling a little, which served as a reminder we were all pretty loaded by then. He looked at Bradley like *Are you coming?* Bradley got up, smiled at Phillip and then me, then suggested we sleep on it and sort out the details in the morning.

"He's an asshole," I swore quietly to myself, once Bradley and Henry were out of earshot.

"You weren't kidding." I think Phillip had heard me, but he was agreeing with the things I had told him about my experiences with Henry before. However, the fact was we both knew we had just avoided a catastrophe. Alajeh would not find out. Even if the solution to keeping him in the dark sucked horribly, it still worked.

Bradley had convinced Henry to stay at our fancy resort and not the cheap hole Henry had located in his research prior to their arrival in Jakarta. This upgrade was a treat they were affording themselves. We didn't know if they would agree to the same when they were paying for two more heads. But that was what we had promised our friends.

There was another obvious problem to consider. We weren't expecting to make a mountain of money off the arrangement, just to avoid carrying anything ourselves, and we had failed to discuss that part.

One more problem I thought of was that we had also already collected three of the bags we were taking back with us and were only waiting for one more. I doubted Henry would be happy with us leaving without making sure the recruits we had promised them were standing in front of him.

The following morning I woke with a hangover to the noise of Phillip stomping around the room, snorting like a bull about to charge, and sweating so profusely he looked like he had taken a shower fully dressed. The room was air-conditioned, but he had obviously come from outside, where it was oppressively hot and humid. Something told me Phillip had engaged Henry again on money matters. "I take it you've talked to Henry," I said and sat up waiting for more, a clue as to why he looked like he had just run a 5K and was about to kill someone.

"No, I haven't talked to him. He's gone. He has Craig with him."

"What?" I tried to understand, imagine it—Craig leaving his girl-friend behind and running off with Henry, Henry kidnapping Craig. Nothing made sense, but I was wide awake and Phillip's anger was infectious. "What do you mean?" I crawled out of bed and threw my shorts on. I would need coffee, stat!

"Henry has taken him to the consulate," Phillip offered and threw me my sandals.

"It's Sunday." I didn't think government offices would be open on a Sunday. "Wait. Why the fuck did he take him to the consulate?"

"To get a new passport." Apparently, Henry and Bradley had gotten up early and been quite industrious. So much for sorting out the details with clearer heads. They'd found our friends at break-fast and introduced themselves. In conversation, the problem we had run into with Craig's passport stamps had apparently come up, along with the solution we had already established. Henry had told Craig and Molly our solution was wrong. The solution that Henry had heard about still involved the same recruit who was supposedly going to be Henry's stand-in. Craig didn't know there had been a slight adjustment to that scenario. Henry probably thought we were full of shit and no one was coming to help him.

But Henry had found out about more than Craig's passport prob-lem and how we proposed to solve it. He had also learned that we already had three bags. This had probably also set him off; the fact that we had not told him about this last night would make Henry wonder if he could trust us. Bradley had told Phillip that Henry had said he should tell Alajeh what we were doing. It was hard to deter-mine whether Bradley was working with Henry or not.

Henry and Craig returned later but had not gone to the consulate. The bickering and nonsense went on for a couple of days, making it almost impossible to figure out what to do. The last bag had not yet arrived, so we were stuck there until it did. Henry shared his worries about delays. Then, as if by magic, Henry became civil again. He apologized with an explanation for his state of being and devised a sensible plan to get us through the rest of the trip safely and peacefully.

Henry proposed we all relax for one week somewhere other than at the expensive resort in Jakarta. Henry claimed to have insight into what was occurring and thought that the rest of the bags would get there by then. The plan was, once they arrived we would get Phillip's friends from Chicago to fly over. But if the bags did not show up by the end of the week, when we all reconvened in Jakarta, we would cross that bridge when we got to it. Phillip and I both accepted the terms of our détente with Henry. Bradley reminded us that Henry did, after all, have a lot more experience than we did and that maybe it was for the best that we had this blowup.

We were all going our separate ways for a week. Henry and Bradley were going exploring. Our friends wanted to take a short hiatus to the other side of Java, the island Jakarta is on. They wanted to go to the beach. We sent them packing with a hired driver and car and with an agreement to meet us back in Jakarta one week later. We were happy that they had taken the initiative to find a fun place to go, and it was actually pretty inexpensive. Phillip and I would be staying at the Marcopolo Hotel, the cheap hotel Henry had suggested, and we would be babysitting the heroin-stuffed bags we already had. We would also be there to retrieve new bags if they arrived while everyone was dispersed.

Henry and Bradley were taking a trip to Yogyakarta, a long train ride away to the other side of the island, so they could see some ancient ruins and temples or ancient ruined temples. Henry claimed it would be as cheap for them to go off on this great journey as to stay at the Marcopolo. He was excited. He loved exploring and would have made a great Christopher Columbus type, back when the world was all new. He told me about the eleven-hour train ride he and Bradley would be taking, the bamboo housing they were headed for, and all the trappings of a true adventure. Henry was correct too; the costs for everything dropped dramatically once they got away from Jakarta.

Phillip and I didn't mind getting stuck at the Marcopolo. Henry joked that it was our penance for lying to them by omission when we hadn't told them everything right up front. Henry and Bradley helped us get to the hotel with all the goodies and left behind some of their own stuff in a couple of suitcases, things they wouldn't need with them on their trip. Our hotel wasn't that bad. There was a swimming pool and we were closer to things like the mall and McDonald's. In reality, anything would be better than more time with Henry. I felt like he was a loaded gun when he was around. I think Phillip felt the same. Both of our moods improved dramatically as soon as they left.

This break gave us some downtime, a chance to get our heads back on straight, without the bickering that had been going on for the preceding few days. We were happy to get our friends far away from Henry too. They went in the opposite direction, to the inexpensive beach resort three hours outside of Jakarta. They were going to stay at either one of two resorts, and they both looked nice and safe enough from the brochures Craig had found at a travel agent in the mall. They would call us at the Marcopolo and let us know which they had chosen.

Phillip and I enjoyed our drama-free day, swimming, drinking scotch, and eating ramen. The Marcopolo didn't have big fancy restaurants and poolside cafés. It had a little market on the first floor that sold the staples of low-budget hotel living: hot coffee, tea, cold sodas, ready-made sandwiches, potato chips, cigarettes, liquor, and ramen. The hotel was right in the center of the city, a tall, L-shaped building. The market, pool, and sundeck were its only amenities, and it had lousy air-conditioning. The rooms all had balconies facing the pool and sliding glass doors that remained open in most of the occupied rooms.

Throughout the day at various intervals I could hear the Muslim call to prayer coming from several directions around the city. Some were so close I could hear the crackle of the audio projecting them, others were a faint wailing from the distance, echoing across the city so I couldn't really tell where the sound came from. It was interesting how different Jakarta felt from this new perspective, definitely farther from home.

That evening Craig called to let us know they had arrived at their destination and to make a confession. We discovered that Henry had shared secret plans with our friends to return to the United States without us and with the heroin-stuffed luggage Phillip and I were babysitting. Henry hadn't counted on Craig's apprehension or that he would tell us what Henry and Bradley had been plotting behind our backs. Craig's confession was incomplete; he tried to say this information was all presented in a phone call he had received from Henry when they'd gotten to their current destination. That was impossible, since Henry wouldn't know how to reach them without prior arrangements to do so, and Henry and Bradley were still on the eleven-hour train ride to Yogyakarta.

I realized this had probably been under way before Craig's current change of heart, but I didn't see any point in calling him on it. I asked Craig to think about what he thought Henry had at stake in their safe return home and to compare it to what he imagined Phillip and I had to lose. I wasn't talking about the money alone. I reminded him that we all came from the same place and had some of the same friends. Their fate would follow us all the way home. I asked him if he even knew how to contact Henry when they got back. If they thought Henry would be more likely to get them back safely and pay them, then they should go with him, by all means. But I asked him not to answer. I wanted him to really think about it. We would call them back in one hour.

Phillip only heard my side of the conversation, but he knew essentially what was happening. He and I faced the fact that our grand plans had failed miserably and they would never work. It had been naïve to think we could get away with this with the million things that could go wrong. We would have to take the bags ourselves and hope Craig and Molly would be happy to have gotten a two-week all-expenses-paid trip to Indonesia as their consolation prize and go home without trying to reconnect with Henry. If they did that, they would end up in the same exact boat we were in and it would be all our fault.

Henry's problem with me and Phillip had turned him into a loose cannon. His behavior was increasingly unpredictable from the day he'd found out we had people there, up to this latest development. If he thought he was better suited than us to get these guys home safely, it no longer mattered. We would never believe his efforts were anything but self-serving and deceitful. He had planned this last trick, I guessed, when he pretended to have reached a détente with us to end the dissension created by our mistake with Craig's passport. That brief peace had been a charade. What I couldn't figure out was how he expected to get the heroin-loaded luggage from us. We still had it.

I realized then that they had not escorted us to the Marcopolo to help us find it, to see what the place looked like, or to store the crap they didn't want to have to drag along on their trek to the other side of Java. Henry had wanted to get a key to our room and he had gotten one. I opened the closet and looked at their two pieces of personal luggage, the ones they had left with us. The two cheap suitcases we had assumed held clothes and personal belongings they would pick up when they returned were still there.

I started laughing hysterically. Phillip looked at me with worry but then understood what was so funny when I popped one of their bags open to reveal it was almost empty. Phillip understood what I was thinking. He ran to the bed we had stowed the heroin-filled luggage under and dropped to the floor, announcing that they were still there. I was relieved but pissed off. The call from Craig had been one thing. It had ruined any hope of making the stand-in thing work. But something about this made it feel like such a personal slap in the face. I could imagine how pleased Henry must have been with himself, as he left these props for their subterfuge in our closet and walked away.

I guessed he planned to come back to the Marcopolo, retrieve the three pieces of drug-packed luggage we had already collected, and leave us with the empty suitcases, the suitcases that supposedly contained his and Bradley's personal belongings—the suitcases that made his coming with us to the Marcopolo and getting a key to the room seem perfectly logical and harmless.

Phillip and I packed our stuff, gathered the three other bags, and immediately left the Marcopolo Hotel. We needed to buy ourselves a little time to think. We left Henry and Bradley's empty suitcases behind, exactly where they had been, and took the heroin-filled luggage with us to the Grand Hyatt. Once there, we asked for adjoining rooms, as if we were coworkers on a business trip, and checked in with cash and aliases. The best they could do were two rooms across from each other, but that would still work. Phillip and I could at least find out how badly Henry had really screwed us, while we were not so easy to locate and discard.

We could keep our eyes on the heroin without sitting in the same room with it. Without a credit card, they asked for a cash deposit to cover incidentals. This was the last cash we had. Stupid or not, we would have to use Phillip's American Express from that point on.

We couldn't simply pack it in and go home, not yet. If Henry took our luggage, Alajeh would have expected someone to stay and collect what would have been intended for Henry and Bradley to carry. Henry knew that I recognized that much, even if he did think I was as stupid as a box of hair. It wasn't enough to assume Henry thought we would just wait for his luggage to arrive and do nothing about his trickery. We had to know for certain if he had covered his own ass and told Alajeh what was happening. He could have easily made us out to be a problem he had solved for Alajeh, rather than risk being caught lying to him.

But if Henry believed Alajeh was really dangerous, that meant Henry was willing to potentially sign our death warrants, as well as spoil his own opportunity to use a stand-in. That would make the whole thing pointless, unless Henry really believed we were too stupid to do what we were doing, and he really was trying to save

Craig and Molly from us. It didn't matter why he did what he did anymore, though. We just had to know if he told Alajeh about it. We thought the answer to that would determine if we were in real danger, not just saddled with the bags we had hoped to not carry because we thought we would get busted. We had an advantage as long as we had the three bags packed with heroin and nobody knew where to find us. But we couldn't count on that to last long. I also had a funny feeling Henry and Bradley were much closer than we had thought. All bets were off as soon as Henry found out his diabolical plot or his intended rescue had failed, whichever it was. I had no idea what to expect from him when that happened.

If Alajeh already knew what was going on, the bags weren't just our advantage; they were our hostages for our own safety and our ransom for control over Molly and Craig's fate for as long as Alajeh and Henry did not know where in Jakarta to find us. I didn't know what the bags were worth to him, but if he had already been told what we had attempted to do, we had to assume that Henry and Bradley weren't going to be the only ones who would have surprised us. Absconding with the bags might make Alajeh want to put a stop to it all. That is what the second room was for, a place to scoot after we made a phone call. From there we might have an opportunity to untangle the mess we had made before it got worse than it already had.

We checked out one last detail, a sound check of sorts. Then Phillip sat down in the chair opposite me at the desk in our new hotel room. We were on the twentieth floor and had a view of the blue sky—no telltale signs of the huge, dirty, and stinky city we were in. Jakarta didn't exist, unless we walked right over to the window and looked right down into it. I had done that and realized we were too far up from the street to clearly identify the people down there. Our other room would have nearly the same view but of the entrance side of the Hyatt. But I figured we would recognize Bradley's shock of blond hair even from up here if he walked anywhere below where our view was not obscured. If anyone else was coming for us, we wouldn't know who to look for anyway.

I dialed the Benin number for Alajeh, and he didn't answer. His assistant picked up and asked me to identify myself. I told him who I was, but I knew that he already knew exactly who I was. This was Alajeh's special phone, by the way, the number we used to conduct our quick business calls. He always answered this phone. His assistant took a quick breath and for some reason that breath is what made my spider senses tingle. He asked for my telephone number and room number, and told me he would have Alajeh call me back. Why he did that only made sense if Alajeh thought they didn't already have that information. But Alajeh already had our phone number and room number at the Marcopolo.

These two pieces of information, if combined, were more precise than GPS coordinates: one defined the exact address we were at on planet Earth, the other the exact room in that address. Without the room number, the closest they could get to finding us was the building we were in, and the Hyatt was huge.

I provided the information Alajeh's assistant had asked for—my room number and the telephone number—shook my head, letting Phillip know that Alajeh had not come to the phone, and hung up. I turned the ringer's volume up and left the phone I had just hung up as close to our room door as its cord permitted. We quickly went into our other room. We had already confirmed that we could hear the phone ring from our other room, even with both doors closed. The new room bought us very little time, but that was all we needed. I hoped.

This had the potential of being a very big mistake, but we didn't know what else to do. It was the fastest way we could think of to find out what we needed to know. If the phone rang within a few minutes, I would run like hell to answer it. In that case, it would be safer to assume that Alajeh hadn't been told anything, otherwise we figured we would get an unexpected visit, not a call. We had to accept the possibility that both might happen, in that case we would only have a few minutes to talk to him and alter our fate, but at least we would have that. If it took long for him to call back, then I would have to remain at the window watching the hotel entrance and Phillip would have to stay with his eye stuck to the peephole until either a call or a visitor did come. The plan wasn't perfect and it did not guarantee our safety, but it was the best we could do.

Unfortunately, the phone didn't ring back. It took only fifteen minutes, but it felt like an eternity waiting there in silence with our eyes glued on the entrance and peephole. Then Phillip backed away from the door and waved at me to come over. The expression on his face told me more than I wanted to know. He motioned for me to be quiet and pointed to the peephole. I looked out, just in time to see two young Asians or Indonesians turn and walk away from our other room door, down the hall, and back to the elevators. One of them had been with the guys who had delivered the first three bags. I had never seen the other guy, but he was not a hotel employee. Phillip and I sat in the quiet for a while, checking the peephole every few seconds to see if they came back. They did not.

I hoped to God the desk wouldn't give any information out to people who couldn't even tell them the name of the person supposedly residing in room number 2022. Alajeh would know we had tricked him now, and he would have to assume we knew he had sent two of his people to the room we were supposed to be in.

It was time to call Craig back. I didn't want to talk to him now. I was so afraid that he might have talked to Henry again, and who knew what else might be happening on his end of the line? My hands weren't shaking anymore and I had a weird kind of serenity flooding over me while Phillip and I sat in the silence. I had been praying to myself. "A bad Catholic" is what my mom would have called me years before when I would go to church only on Christmas and Easter, but I didn't even do that anymore. That didn't mean I couldn't pray my heart out now.

"Craig." I listened carefully for anything other than Craig's voice.

"Hi." He sounded tired but not false.

"So what are your thoughts?" I asked instead of launching into hysterics and telling them to get the hell out of there as fast as their feet could run.

"Well, we want to apologize first." I thought he was about to tell me that they were going with Henry. "I was just freaked out about the whole passport thing. He told me you guys had lied to us about important shit and that you had no idea what you were—" I cut him off.

"It's okay. I know this shit got crazy. If I had known he was coming to Jakarta, I would have warned you. But listen. I need you guys to get out of that hotel. Go check into the other place you were thinking about." I said this and instantly realized there may have been no other place; it may have been part of the ruse. Then I remembered the brochures they had shown me.

"We are already packed up and got a driver." They had planned on returning to meet us at the Marcopolo. They didn't know we were no longer there.

"Okay. Hang on a second." I covered the phone and updated Phillip, asking him what I should tell them. They couldn't go to the Marcopolo and they couldn't come to the Hyatt, where we were now. We didn't know what was going to happen yet. I didn't want to freak them out or get them caught up in the middle of the shit we were in. Phillip looked at his watch and he took the phone from me.

"Go back to the Hilton resort. Do not go to the Marcopolo. We are not going to be there when you get back. Check in under the name Adam Douglas and stay in your room. We will be there by midnight, but don't leave your room till then. Seriously, dude. Henry has some shit going down and you do not want to get involved. If we don't get back there tonight, go home." He handed the phone back to me. I told Craig I would talk to him later and hung up.

"Okay, here goes nothing."

Phillip sat down in the desk chair and crossed himself quickly, like he didn't want me to see what he was doing. I dialed Benin and Alajeh answered on the first ring.

"What is going on?" Alajeh sounded frustrated, maybe angry.

"We have a little snag in our travel plans I need you to help me sort out." I had to resist the urge to flip out and instead stay calm and sane while I spoke.

"Where are you? Let me come to you." He didn't mean that he

would come to me himself. He was saying that he would have some-one else come.

"No. It would be better if we solved this problem first."

"You won't tell me where you are?" He sounded like I'd hurt his feelings.

"Don't worry. We're not trying to run away with your bags. I just have to solve something before it turns into a big problem." I tried to sound like a rational businessperson and kept reminding myself *That's all this is . . . It's business . . . It's business.*

"Yes. I know. Henry told me." He quit playing the fake emotions.

"Really? When was that?" His candor had surprised me.

"It's not important." He cleared his throat after he'd said this.

"It is to me." I heard myself and wished I hadn't sounded so miffed.

"A few days ago." I thought maybe he had really talked to him in the last hour. "I can help you. I can deal with Henry, and your friends will be fine. But you have to listen to me. He is hysterical. Is Phillip with you?" I looked up at Phillip and put the phone on speaker.

"He's here. You're on speaker now."

Phillip sat up and focused on the phone.

"Phillip! My friend!" He sounded jovial, not like a cold-blooded kingpin.

"Alajeh," Phillip answered, sounding tired and uneasy.

"You have to give Bradley and Henry two of the bags. They will leave tomorrow." Alajeh said this to Phillip, not to me, but I didn't give a shit who he said it to. It made no sense. Phillip looked at me and tilted his head like dogs do.

"Why two?" he asked.

"Give them two bags. I will send another one to you, and your friends can go back to Chicago then. I will make sure Henry goes now." We wanted this to be as simple to solve and as small a wrinkle in our safe return to Northampton as Alajeh was making it out to be. We wanted it to be true so badly that we believed it was.

We took the bags back to the Marcopolo, where Bradley came

down to the lobby to retrieve them. Henry did not come with him and I did not go in with Phillip to give the bags to Bradley. Phillip got back into the taxi and we headed back to the Hilton resort to wait for Molly and Craig to get there. We would have to wait now for the replacement Alajeh had promised. He wasn't going to make us carry the drugs ourselves anymore, as long as we had someone we could trust to do it for us. In fact, he actually liked our idea. We had saved ourselves and our friends from a potential disaster, but we had pretty much ruined the one out we had. We could be added to the watch list, get searched, questioned, and probed. We wouldn't be the ones carrying Alajeh's precious cargo, but we would be there.

6 The Day After Tomorrow

Planet Earth
Midsummer 1993

HENRY AND BRADLEY left us all behind in Jakarta. I was relieved by the time we knew they were on another continent on the other side of the world. They had made it as far as London and were due back in the United States before the end of the week. Prior to their safe entrance into Europe with the two bags they had taken from us, I had a little nagging fear in the back of my mind that if Henry got caught there—he was so bitter about losing his game—he might just take us all down with him and I wasn't ready for that yet. Aside from that internal sporadic nag, things felt good again, manageable, like we might all get home in one piece.

I knew it was twisted to feel triumphant, since all that Phillip and I had really accomplished was deepening our own hole. We had taken such an incredibly huge risk to confront the situation with Henry and Alajeh head-on the way we had, hiding Alajeh's drugs and ourselves from him and telling him the truth about what we had been up to with our friends. Either of those actions could possibly have gotten us killed. Alajeh was smarter than that though.

He let us off the hook for devising a scheme to have others carry the drugs, but he wasn't at all forgiving when it came to not getting them where they needed to go.

I thought about that second call to Alajeh, after seeing the two men show up at the first hotel room we had been in. Alajeh had told Phillip and me that he had been looking for us at the Hyatt to offer us his help in our complicated situation. I wondered, though, if we had been there in the first room when the two fellows arrived, instead of across the hall, peeping through an eyehole, how differently this might have ended. Would we be alive? Would Craig and Molly leave Henry and Bradley in Chicago, return to Northampton, and then wonder what had happened to us? Would Piper try to find me when I never came home or try to find out where we were? Would Edith and Dum Dum be like Lassie and try to tell her we fell in a well?

We had to wait in Indonesia for two more weeks before the bags intended for Henry and Bradley arrived. Alajeh got more money to Phillip and me, but not enough for us to stay in two double rooms at the Hilton resort the whole time that we would have to wait for Molly and Craig's bags to arrive. Phillip flew back to the United States, and I went with Craig and Molly to Bali to kill time.

Bali was the most beautiful place I had ever been. The beaches were gorgeous and it didn't feel like a third world country at all. It felt more like Provincetown, but instead of being filled with gays from New York and Boston, its tourists were Dutch and Australian. It had the same bohemian atmosphere, shopping, clubs, and cafés, just with sarongs and sandals instead of short shorts and Doc Martens.

We left Indonesia with the new luggage two weeks later. We encountered no problems in Paris. It was as though having an American passport made us either special or not worth their energy—I couldn't guess—but they barely gave us nods as they stamped our documents and let us into the country.

We checked into what was becoming my home away from home, the Hôtel Saint-André des Arts in the Latin Quarter of Paris. Phillip couldn't come to Paris with Garrett, but he assured me his friend was more than ready and able to travel on his own. I stayed at the hotel with our luggage while my friends took the Étoile du Nord—the European equivalent to Amtrak—to Brussels. Once there, they went directly to the U.S. consulate to report that Molly had lost her passport and needed to have it replaced with a new one. That solved the poppy-country-stamp issue. They returned to me at the Saint-André des Arts the following day.

Phillip had arrived in Chicago and would be waiting for Garrett and Molly at the airport the next day. Garrett flew into Paris the same day Craig and Molly returned from Brussels with her newly acquired passport. We had a nice dinner at an Italian restaurant on the Île Saint-Louis that night and we all got to know Garrett over Chianti and pasta. Craig and Molly reminded me of myself during my first trip.

After a month in Africa of choking down goat meat and parasites, we had all come to this restaurant—Hester, Henry and Bradley, and me. We had sat at a table by the window. I stared at the table, occupied by two French couples dining together. The food had tasted like pure bliss in my mouth, even though I couldn't eat my whole serving. My stomach had shrunk quite a bit from all the abuse in Africa. I could almost see us there at the table, laughing, smoking cigarettes, and drinking cognac because Henry had warned me I would need it to sleep before my first trip carrying drugs home. I had been so nervous and happy all at once, having gotten my sister away from the jerk in Africa but scared shitless about the next day. I had been anxious too, anxious for it to be all over, and it had been so close, I'd thought, to that being so.

The waiter dropped the check off at our table and I asked everyone to pony up all their francs, since we would no longer be needing them. Craig and Molly contributed some random coins worth about two hundred francs and I paid the rest from my dwindling stash of French currency. We had more than enough left over for a cab to the airport in the morning, and breakfast was free at our hotel.

It was such a lovely summer night, warm and dry, a welcome departure from the stinky humidity we had left behind in Jakarta.

Just as Henry had done with me only a few months earlier, I suggested we all walk off some of the wine and pasta before trying to go to sleep instead of being lazy and taking a taxi back to the hotel. We stopped on the bridge we were crossing, one of many bridges that anchor the Île Saint-Louis to the city. Notre-Dame's buttresses and façade were illuminated so that even from our angle and at night it dwarfed everything around it. A dinner barge passed under the bridge where we stood, followed by a sightseeing barge, shining spotlights on the buildings it passed as it too slid under the bridge and out of sight, on its way down the Seine.

When the tour guide's amplified description of the Latin Quarter, coming from the barge, died away in the distance, it was replaced by an accordion's version of "La Vie en Rose," coming from the vicinity of the cathedral. It mixed eerily with a violinist playing Ravel nearby. Garrett was staring at his manicured fingers as he tapped a rhythm on the stone rail of the bridge. I could see a hint of nervousness forming in his pensive expression. Molly and Craig stood, in a spooning embrace, and swayed slightly as they stared down at the passing boats.

"Time to make the donuts!" I started walking the rest of the way across the bridge and back to our hotel. It was time to get these guys back so they could relax, pack again for the zillionth time, and do all the weird, stupid things we humans do to calm ourselves the night before something decisive: battles, play-offs, recitals, and the walk through Charles de Gaulle airport and Customs in Chicago.

Phillip and I got a break from the relentless globe-trotting after the trip to Indonesia. We had been in motion since April, I felt like I had been in motion since January, and it was summer already. Phillip had moved back to Provincetown with Meg in May 1993. He had abandoned me again to go take care of his real life with Meg, while in a hotel in Chicago I waited out the week it took to get our pay. Meg still had no clue what he was really up to, so he couldn't stay away for six-week stretches like I had done now twice.

When I walked into the house at seven o'clock in the morning and woke my good friend Piper up, I was probably a little more cheerful than anyone likes another human to be when they are woken by surprise. When she threatened to kill me, I backed off to give her a little space. I took the Tumi bag I had with over fifty thousand in cash to the living room and dumped it out onto the floor. I had to separate out my pay from Phillip's, and a third pile had to go to pay off the American Express bill Phillip was going to shit himself when he saw. Not really. He knew how much we had spent. He had wired us money in Bali several times. In any case, all the cash sitting together looked like I had robbed a bank.

Dum Dum had no idea who I was, at least that's the way she acted. But I knew otherwise. Cats aren't like dogs. If they were, both of my kitties would have been attached to my face doing the I'm-so-glad-you're-home dance the minute I'd walked in the door. Instead, Dum Dum was sitting up, alert, staring at me with her huge green lantern eyes like I might be a burglar. Piper was knocked out, and Edith was curled up right next to Piper's face, almost certainly fake sleeping and trying to be like *Oh, you. Whatever* . . . I grabbed a wad of the cash, went back to my room, and threw the money into the air above the bed. Edith watched with a bored yawn from the pillow next to Piper, but Dum Dum thought it was playtime. It was.

Piper jumped out of bed like I had thrown a snake into it with her, so I played with Dummy and ignored Edith back. Meanwhile, Piper walked toward the bathroom and I heard "Holy shit!" as she passed by the living room. I assumed she'd seen the cash still spread out on the floor. Her made-for-TV movie had just gotten slightly more interesting.

"Go look in the driveway!" My fancy car still had its hardcover roof on it and I thought the car looked like it cost me much more than it did. The Miata had only been out for a couple of years; in fact, mine was from the year it was introduced. It was an impulse purchase I regretted the moment I handed over the cash to some guy in Chicago. I was acting just like the archetype idiot who buys his girlfriend a mink coat and a pink Cadillac after he robs a bank, and I knew Phillip would give me endless shit about it, so I claimed it was a gift from Alajeh. Not a particularly well thought out idea either; Phillip was then irritated that he had not been treated to the same.

Piper got out of the shower and was dressed faster than I had anticipated. I had said I would put a pot of coffee on for us and I hadn't even made it up off the bed. The cats had surprised me and come around very quickly this time. Either they were very comfortable with Piper replacing me and didn't feel I needed to be extensively punished or they knew how much kitty food all this cash could buy. Whatever the cause, they were both being irresistibly cuddly with me. I rather doubt the latter, but who knows? It's hard to tell what cats really know. People are a little easier to read, and I could tell Piper's interest had been piqued by my big pile of loot. This was good. I had an idea growing in my brain, one Piper might like.

I could do anything in the world as long as I did not have to do it alone. I needed a cat sitter, but more than that, I needed a sidekick. I was not yet sexually attracted to Piper—maybe a little, but not enough to risk losing my cat sitter and someone to keep me tethered to Earth. I hadn't had great luck with sexual entanglements of late—or ever. Besides that, I couldn't figure out if she was attracted to me, and unless I was certain about that, I was not going to be the initiator. It's too awkward when I'm wrong.

The idea came to me because I thought Phillip was about to run for the hills and I thought maybe Piper would be a good partner in crime. She could help me recruit people and take over Phillip's role if and when he lost it. Phillip was in a tailspin at the time. I didn't know about what the source of it was. I assumed it had something to do with Meg. He had kept her in the dark about what he was up to and I had no grasp whatsoever how that must be eating away at his soul. He loved her, perhaps more than the person he had used as collateral for Alajeh's trust.

A week later, Craig, Molly, Phillip, and I were sitting in the Brewery, the same restaurant and microbrewery in Northampton that Piper worked at. We were drinking, celebrating, and telling stories, just as Phillip and I had done when he'd returned. Piper was serving our drinks, and my motorcycle was parked where I could see it from the outdoor tables we inhabited once again. But it wasn't the same. Something was lost on the trip we had just completed, but our friends were happy, paid, and done. They had no idea how blessed they were. Phillip and I no longer had a way out, but we didn't have to actually smuggle the drugs ourselves anymore. We were now just well-paid escorts.

Our new arrangement had only a small financial impact on Alajeh. He paid a slightly higher fee to us to deliver the bags and continued to cover the travel costs of however many bags there were needing carriers. If there were four bags, he paid for the tickets and room and board for four. We took our pay and our travel costs off the top of the delivery payment, and the recruit was paid fifteen thousand dollars. Phillip and I could have made a lot more money than we did, by penny pinching. I was incapable of such a feat and this fault fueled Phillip's growing nihilism and my worries.

Piper was a logical replacement for Phillip. If he did lose his mind and try to bail, Piper could step in and help me. It could even be fun. She could be Phillip's stand-in and maybe save him from a horrible consequence. We could get a live-in cat-sitter maid if on a regular basis we were both making the kind of money I had just made. Hester would be perfect for that role and I could make sure my little sister used her time constructively, like going back to school or something.

In my plan, Piper would never have to carry any drugs—she would just help me coordinate the recruits, help figure out ticketing, hotels, and budgets, and all the things I sucked at. I spent most of that July in Northampton with Piper and my cats, but I did a little traveling too. Piper had decided to move to San Francisco when the summer ended. Moving to the West Coast sounded like a good idea to me, so I invited myself to be her roommate, and easily sold her on the idea that my inclusion would make it more affordable. Piper and I went to California. We found a real estate agent and got a place to rent in San Francisco together. We were there for less than a week.

Piper added a stable element to my otherwise adrift life and that would be as true in San Francisco as it had been in Northampton. I had already made the decision to leave Northampton before the impulse to go to San Francisco came up. Phillip was moving to New York in September and I hadn't known how long Piper would stay before she moved on with her real life. She wasn't going to work at the Brewery and cat sit forever, not with a degree from Smith. As long as I was traveling so much of the time, it didn't seem all that important what city I called home.

In the meantime, I could take a little more time to figure out if I really thought my idea was rational, would work, or whether she would even be interested in being an escort. I also had to be sure I could really trust her before I went down that road and wanted to have a heart-to-heart talk with Phillip about my concerns in regard to his mental state. It would suck to be stranded in Indonesia with a bunch of people if he just dropped the ball. I didn't have an American Express card or the credit to get one.

To complicate matters, which is my specialty, I had previously accepted an invitation to join a friend of mine in a home-buying venture in Vermont. Larry still worked at Spoleto. He was the one who had served me my scotch the first night I was back in town. He and his wife were buying a house outside of Brattleboro, Vermont, and it had a second building on the property they thought I might be interested in renovating. What they were really interested in was the cash I could provide for a down payment. I had about twenty-five thousand dollars saved up so far. I liked Larry and loved the idea of rehabbing the little dilapidated carriage house when I saw it. I thought it was a wise investment and that, in the very least, I would have my own home.

I figured the house in Vermont would be a project I could work on slowly. I wasn't going to do the work myself, though, or camp out in a tent with my cats until it was done. So when the San Francisco idea came up, it was a good place to plant myself, Edith, and Dum Dum till our house was ready to live in, and I was ready to live in Vermont. Vermont seemed like someplace to retire to with a partner or to become a hermit. In the meantime, I got to spend more time with my friend Piper and keep my cat sitter. Our plan was to move to San Francisco in August. After we got back from our successful apartment hunt in San Francisco, Piper gave her two-week notice at the Brewery.

Making plans with me at this particular time in my life was a crapshoot. But Piper knew that. She had her agenda and her schedule set for getting to San Francisco, job hunting, and all of that business, and she would stick to it no matter what, even if I did get called out right in the middle of our move across the country. It's a good thing she was so organized and able to easily make her own plans to pack up and go to San Francisco without me, because that is exactly what she would have to do. Fortunately, Alajeh called Phillip and me back to the starting gate *before* Piper and I were actually on the road to California, loaded down with both of our belongings and my cats in tow.

Alajeh had a sudden urgent need for me to get to Jakarta. He wanted Phillip and me to have five people ready in Jakarta and five more ready to go when the first five finished. We couldn't do that. The best we came up with was two rounds of three people. Piper's best buddy, Donald, was now one of our couriers. Donald and Garrett both thought they might have two more guys we could bring, but there was too little time to try to get that all together so fast.

Alajeh settled for what we could do. Since this was going to be potentially two or more round-trips in a row, and half the people knew what they were doing already, Phillip and I made an adjustment to how we operated as escorts. He would cover the U.S. to Europe and Europe back to the U.S. portions. I would cover the Europe to Jakarta and Jakarta back to Europe portions. By doing this, we could move the two groups through more quickly. Our groups could overlap in Europe. Phillip and the second group would fly to Europe a couple of weeks after I left with the first group to Jakarta. Assuming everything went as planned, he could send me the second group from Europe, meet up with the first group returning from Jakarta, take them home, and turn around to do it again. When I got rid of the second group in Jakarta, I could then finish my move to San Francisco with Edith and Dum Dum.

I didn't have to leave that minute, but it was too short notice to try moving myself to San Francisco yet. I would do my move when I came back. Piper and I still had a little time before she would leave for San Francisco without me, and I would leave for Jakarta. But it was not going to be a relaxing two weeks. She had to get ready for her move and I had to get ready for another psychotic mission. I was not particularly thrilled with the idea of going all the way back to Indonesia again, and going alone made me even more anxious. After all, the last trip there had been anything but quick and smooth.

The two weeks that would get cut off on either end of the trip Phillip and I planned helped us out. By splitting up, we decreased the amount of time each of us would have to travel by two whole weeks, but it meant I would not have a sidekick and it would still be a monthlong journey for each of us. I got a bright idea. I asked Piper if she would come with me to Jakarta. I was certain her job hunt in San Francisco wasn't so pressing that she would turn down a trip to someplace as exotic as Jakarta. I would have jumped on it if a friend had offered me a chance to go on this trip when I was her age, no strings attached. Of course, I had ulterior motives; I just wasn't quite ready to share them with her. Piper accepted my invitation.

In the meantime, I made arrangements for another woman to stay at my house in Northampton with Edith and Dum Dum, since Piper wouldn't be there and I was keeping my apartment a little longer. It was just until I got back from the trip and it didn't seem like money was going to be an issue by then. Piper would meet me in Jakarta after she finished her move to San Francisco. I would have a sidekick, even if she were just there to keep me company.

Ultimately, we had everything settled and everyone was ready to go. Phillip and I had our frenzied itineraries full of contingencies for what if this happens or that, and our crew was prepared. Piper was packed and ready for her move. She would get that done and then meet me in Jakarta. If she were going to rule the world with me, she should probably get a peek at how this all worked.

Piper's friend Donald was the one who had most recently joined our secret club. I had a feeling they were going to be very good at our expanding profession. Piper and Donald, more than the others, struck me as people who would never get bothered by officials. They were both tall, with the same shade of strawberry-blond hair, pale but freckled skin, and the same blue eyes. They even shared many of the same snobby mannerisms. Mistaking them for siblings was easy to do, even though they weren't related. I wondered if it would make her a better escort if she actually carried drugs once herself or if it mattered. Really, all an escort is, is a glorified travel agent who babysits.

By the time the trip actually launched, Craig, Molly, Donald, and Garrett were the first four to go. They left Northampton with me. Garrett's lover, Edwin, and two friends of theirs would fly with Phillip a couple of weeks later. Piper would come on her own to Jakarta via Paris, after she finished her move to San Francisco. Molly and Craig's trip went according to plan, not a single hitch. After the debacle they'd had during their first trip, I sent them back first when we discovered only two bags were arriving. Garrett and Donald got stuck in Bali. The bags were coming in two at a time and not quickly.

Alajeh's big rush was turning out to be a big bust. So I left Garrett and Donald in Bali, where we had already been for the two weeks we had planned on, while I went to Jakarta to send Craig and Molly on their way. Phillip slammed on the brakes for the next group to come over to Europe. When he was done collecting payment for Craig and Molly in Chicago, he and Edwin flew all the way to Jakarta. Phillip flew to Jakarta to bring me a pile of cash to get me through the rest of the trip, which was now going to take considerably longer to complete, because Alajeh had told him to.

Somewhere in there Piper flew to Paris and got stuck, because in all the ticket changes I was making, I forgot to have hers waiting for her at Singapore Airlines in Paris. Somehow she got in touch with Phillip to resolve the issue and she made it to Jakarta while Phillip was still there. Phillip flew back to the United States. Edwin, Piper, and I joined Garrett and Donald in Bali, and the wait began.

7 A Midsummer Night's Dream

Bali, Indonesia
Midsummer 1993

POURED A CUP OF COFFEE for myself from the full pot and took my seat at the table on our small porch. There was an assortment of whole fruits and a couple of breakfast pastries on the tray. I grabbed a banana and a croissant, leaving the fruit I didn't know how to eat for Piper to figure out. The little breakfast spread was the same every morning. Piper had ordered it from room service the night before, as she had done every day we had been there. I was getting a little bored with the rituals we had established on our first day at the Bali resort.

My face felt dry and tickled, like my skin might be on the verge of peeling, and the sun was already beating down on our side of the building. The sun had jumped out of its sparkling orange slumber in what felt like an instant and had extinguished the dazzling colors in the clouds and the water it had risen from. Soon it would be too bright and hot to sit comfortably on the porch, and we would pack it in and go to the beach. Piper slid the door open and joined me, closing the door behind her to preserve our air-conditioned escape from the sun.

"Ouch!" Piper held her hand up in front of her face to block the sun while she surveyed the tray and picked out the star-shaped fruit and the pale green fruit that was filled with something very much like snot. But then she hesitated and traded them both for a banana nut muffin. Her hair was a mess and her eyes were bloodshot. I suspected she felt as bad as she looked. We had eaten at the resort's version of a sports bar the night before and she had won a contest involving a meter-high beer glass, which had required assistance to drink from. Donald, Garrett, and Edwin had lost. I had defaulted when I accidentally poured my beer all over the floor and myself.

Piper took the seat next to me and gave me an evil eye, like her hangover was my doing. She grabbed the liter of bottled water and nearly drained it in one shot. Then she ate her tiny muffin and poured herself a cup of black coffee. "I think I will skip the gym today." Her voice was a little gravelly. She had also smoked quite a few cigarettes the night before that were not her brand but an expensive alternative they sold at the bar. They were pretty but tasted like they might be made of asbestos instead of tobacco.

She dressed in shorts and a spaghetti-strap shirt made of air that had just been returned to her from the laundry service. The bill for this tiny luxury was probably higher than what she had paid for the shirt. The breakfast tray, I knew, was costing us about forty dollars a day. I had checked on the remaining cash I had in the room safe and started to worry. I was going through cash like the safe could magically replenish itself while it was closed. Phillip had already needed to wire me more, twice, and that was on top of what he had personally delivered to me in Jakarta a month before.

While we were at the beach that day, I had made a quick decision to put an end to the bleeding and save myself from boredom. We would have one last little party that night. But the next day we were flying back to Java. We were all going to go check out Yogyakarta, the place Henry and Bradley had claimed to be heading to a lifetime ago. I would wait until the party later to break the news about leaving paradise. No sense ruining a relaxing day at the beach. Nobody was going to be thrilled about our next stop.

Later that night, I nearly lost my resolve about leaving when my attempt to convey the new travel plans to my friends was drowned in champagne and revelry. Nonetheless, I managed to make our departure announcement without incident. I realized, though, that the reality of leaving was not going to elicit any complaints until we were actually packing up and exiting Eden.

I nabbed one of the unopened bottles of Veuve Clicquot from the ice bucket, slipped out of the lanai, and closed the door behind me. My friends' drunken sing-along wasn't quite as torturous from the other side of the door, and the Walkman's puny speakers sucked. All I could hear from my vantage point were my friends' voices howling their horrible rendition of 4 Non Blondes' latest hit, "What's Up?" Their voices rose as they got to the chorus, which everyone knew the words to, even drunk: *"Twenty-five years and my life is still trying to get up that great big hill of hope . . ."*

Edwin loved this song. I had too until then. I think Edwin thought they'd written the damn song for him. Not really, but he had tortured everyone for the last month, playing it over and over again, trying to make it his own. Donald, Garrett, and I had been there for six weeks already, and the two extra weeks made a big difference in my capacity for irritants. I was homesick and had been out of touch with my family, my cats, my real life, for too long.

The sing-along I had just escaped had started out as an interruption to my important discussion regarding our upcoming departure back to Java. Edwin hadn't been listening. He never did, and he had spontaneously burst into a pathetically overtheatrical serenade to his lover, Garrett. Like Tom Cruise's impromptu serenade to Kelly McGillis in *Top Gun,* except that in this case, it had been Tom getting serenaded and Kelly had been lip-synching, not singing. I think everyone else had started singing just to put an end to Edwin's performance and Garrett's humiliation from the display.

Watching Garrett's attempts to train Edwin to be a good drug smuggler was nerve-racking. Then listening to the fights they would have after Edwin reached the belligerent drunk status, as he did just about every night, was also getting tiring. I had started considering the possibility that Garrett had recruited Edwin with the actual intent of getting rid of him. There was no way this guy could be trained enough to get home. Failure to get through Customs would certainly put an end to their relationship.

Leaving the lanai, I walked out into the quiet night until all I could hear were crickets and a slight breeze slipping through the palms. I strolled alongside the serpentine swimming pool that crawled through Hilton's Bali resort, casting its bluish-green glow on everything it passed, and considered taking a swim. It was an unusually comfortable night and my champagne buzz was perfect. I continued along the walkway, encountering only a couple of other late-nighters on the long trek through the grove heading down toward the ocean.

I got spooked by a woman behind one of the waterfalls. This was near where a rock bridge arched across the pool. She was well hidden and probably thought she was invisible, but the electronically forced waterfall had a rhythm to it. It created a strobe effect in the lit veil of water cascading down in front of her. She stood in the shadows, but I got a couple of glimpses before I fully understood what I was looking at. The woman was naked and not alone. Happy I had not yelped when startled, I hoped they would not see me. I picked up my pace and walked very lightly, keeping my flip-flops from flapping. After that, there were no other resort residents about in the dark. I walked around the bend in the pool, where it elongated, became wider, and looked as though it reached out to merge with the ocean.

Standing at the sidewalk's edge, I could see the ocean glistening beyond the last row of coconut trees. These marked the perimeter of the resort's green landscape. The moon was bright enough to cast shadows in the beach's white sands, and the tide was in. I stepped into the moist grass, careful not to step on one of the hundreds of frogs that came out after dark and littered the grass and walkways. I couldn't see them very well in the grass.

Stepping on a big old frog in the dark, in your flip-flops, was an awful business. This was not the same as the bugs I probably stepped on daily without ever knowing, and while squishing a frog under my foot is not nearly as horrible as accidentally hitting a bunny rabbit or squirrel with my car, it still upset me to carelessly murder another being so gruesomely with my toes. So I navigated to the beach with great care.

I made my way across the sand and out toward the calm sea. The glassy water reflected the night sky with so little distortion that it looked like I could leap into the heavens from my sandy edge of the world—or fall off. It had a dizzying effect too, when mixed with the Valium and all the champagne I had consumed. I had discovered I could buy certain prescription drugs over the counter in Indonesia and they helped soothe my ever-increasing anxieties. I pulled my loosely knotted sweatshirt from my hips and spread it over the soft sand.

I had come out here on a couple of nights during our long stay in paradise and had already discovered that there were no crabs or any other exotic night creatures to fear here. The beach was wide with a gentle slope, almost imperceptible, and the water's edge a long walk from the start of the sand, even when the tide was full. I think this was what accounted for the lack of surf, or at least a gentler surf than I had seen before. The waves here didn't crash onto the beach like elsewhere; they just sort of rolled in without cresting.

I sat down on my sweatshirt and lay back. This was the same spot where I had been sitting with Piper, hours earlier, watching our last Balinese sunset. Two women we'd met at the resort had been there with us. It was also our last night with our new friends and our fake relationship. We had kept up a ruse about being together and held hands just like they did. Piper had discovered the pair earlier that week. Their room was across from ours and their porch faced ours. Piper had been doing a crossword or reading one morning. They had thought Piper was staring at them. One of the women had walked over to introduce herself to the peeping Lulu. The gaydar signals were confirmed when they learned Piper and I were from Northampton and Piper learned they were from San Francisco.

The women were presently living in Jakarta, working for a bank, and were on vacation. They were not openly gay at work; they couldn't be. They were just a little older than we were. One was in her late twenties, the other in her midthirties. They had lived in Jakarta for over a year and missed the company of other lesbians. Piper had admitted to them we were from the same church (gay) but had added that we were lovers.

I can't recall what Piper's rational for this deception was, but I went along with it. She couldn't come out and just tell them we were all drug-smuggling buddies and we were stranded in Bali because the heroin we were supposed to be transporting had not yet arrived. Instead, she made up a cover story that we had been together for a while, she had just graduated from Smith College, and this trip was her reward. I'm not sure why our new friends never questioned how we could afford such a long stay. I'm nosy about stuff like this and forever asking inappropriate questions, like how much money do you make or how much did that present cost, even when it has nothing to do with me.

We had been hanging out with them most of their trip and we had told them we had already been there for two weeks when we first met them. That was when we'd thought we were about ready to leave. They'd had to save their money for a year to afford the resort in Bali for two weeks. We had taken them out to dinner a few times, and then we had spontaneously decided to stay longer. They never asked me about what I did for a living. I assumed everyone was as nosy as I was and guessed Piper had spun some excellent fantasy, one that kept them from asking.

They kept telling me how lucky I was to have Piper. They said she was beautiful, so smart, and how great we were together. I had figured Piper made me out to be her benefactor and they were entreating me to appreciate what I had. Perhaps they sensed the charade but mistook it for a fading interest on my part. I would have made the same sort of assumption if a couple in this paradise displayed no more affection than holding hands. I suppose they worried I was bored and might dump Piper and move on to the next Twinkie my money could buy so they were trying to talk some sense into me. They could not have been more wrong.

When I found out that they thought Piper was our gravy train, not me, and our good fortune was her family's money, not my money, I realized they had just been stating the obvious. I was lucky to have Piper. She was beautiful and smart, and we were great together. But I already knew that. The idea of becoming Piper's lover had already taken residence in my dreams and was affecting my ability to make rational decisions. I thought of little else. It was good we were getting away from this place, before I spent all my money and Phillip's too trying to entertain her and show off.

In the daytime, I would stride a good distance out into the emerald water and it still only reached halfway up my calves. If I wanted to swim or play in the surf, it was better to head left, farther up, where the beach sloped more sharply and the water deepened quickly. But here, the surf rolled softly and traversed such distances into the beach that by the time it reached its destination, it made only the tiniest little trickle. People sunbathed here sitting or lying right in the water.

The sand was so fine that it squeaked as I walked on it. If I sat on it in the water, the sand felt like a warm yielding body. The water remained shallow until a hundred yards out; therefore, creatures large enough to eat me couldn't reach me. It was probably the most delicious tanning in the world, but I had suffered a few burns doing this when we'd first come here in our milky winter skins.

That had been the spring trip, when Craig, Molly, and I had discovered Bali. It was fall now and I wasn't burning anymore. No sunburn chills anymore, just a radiant warmth that would last through the night and not peel off in the morning. I felt like a battery being charged in the sun and the water, then drained every night dancing, drinking, and running amok. Even Piper and Donald, with their fair skin, her blond hair, his reddish hair, and their freckles, had stopped burning and had fallen into this boho's dream. Now they were both sun-kissed blonds and their freckles had merged into a healthy glow.

In the daylight, cabana boys would make the long hike down to the beach to the marinating sunbathers and make sure our frozen mudslides, strawberry-banana daiquiris, and margaritas stayed full and frozen. I often wondered how frequently tourists drowned in this drowsy luxury. Late at night, though, the beach was desolate and quiet, not even a noisy surf to disturb me. With no city lights competing, the stars filled the sky and mirrored in the water all around me so densely that it looked like an infinite black well of diamonds hanging above, as if I could reach up and scoop out a handful of stars in my hand.

We were leaving Bali the next day and flying back to Jakarta, back to Java and the dirty masses. There, we would hop a train to a place north of Yogyakarta, another city on the island of Java, the most densely populated island in Indonesia, or in the world for that matter. Java is more densely peopled than most places on Earth. It has a population of 143 million, but it's only as big as New York State, whose population is under 20 million. Imagine New York City with seven times as many people. That is what had me unsettled and in need of peace, a combination of excitement and nerves, along with feeling a little sadness. Resorts were lovely, safe places to wait out delays while in the third world, but they were an expensive solace.

If this trip went belly-up, I would be broke, but Phillip would be screwed. He was my true partner in crime. He had been sending me Western Union wires on his American Express. That put him in danger of ending up with a bill he could never pay on a bartender's wages. Never mind the fact that drug smugglers should probably avoid doing business on paper. The best way to slow the spending—or bleeding, as he had taken to calling it—was to leave the safety of our Western resort and travel somewhere inland on the big island. Our honeymoon was over and Piper would probably not be very happy with our next stop. Edwin, Garrett's spoiled little queen, would definitely hate it.

I picked myself up and sat facing the water. I opened the bottle of champagne I had toted with me and took a bubbly swig that went up my nose. The water appeared to be glowing and it was not from the reflection of the sky. I watched as little points of bright greenish light moved slowly in the surf, and I stood back up to get a better view. Once standing, I could see that the entire shallow waterfront was aglow wherever there was movement in the water. I looked around in all directions, thinking a sight like this would bring others out to the beach. But I was still alone in my moonlit silence.

I dropped my shorts, took off my sandals, and stepped out into the water. I knew what it was. I had seen it elsewhere, just not this much of it. It was glowing plankton that swirled around my feet as I waded through the water. I laughed like a giddy toddler in the bath and considered returning to this place, in less stressful times, to do this on mushrooms. I looked behind me again to see if anyone had come out. The hotel permitted nudity, and local laws, if any, didn't apply to the Hilton's long stretch of beach. Some of the Europeans wore nothing at all in the day. But in the dark isolation, I still worried. Some drunk fool, roaming around like myself, might get some crazy idea about my naked butt all alone out here.

I would have to walk too far out into the abyss, where sea monsters lurked in the dark, to actually swim or even legitimately wade, so I decided to be less conspicuous and less likely to be eaten by sitting down in the water right where I was. I walked back up onto the beach to the place where I had left my shorts, champagne, and sandals and took my shirt off. I threw it into the little pile of my belongings, lit a cigarette, and waited for just a couple of minutes to make sure no one was coming. I felt exposed and vulnerable but only for a moment. I grabbed the champagne and headed back out into the glowing water, walking slowly backward, each step glowing in the sand for a few seconds before it faded away. As soon as the water reached my calf, I sat down.

I took a long drink of the champagne and finished my cigarette, scanning the beach constantly. The beach remained desolate and quiet; just the light breeze disturbed the palms a little but not the water. I think this is what sailors refer to as a dead calm. I could barely hear anything, but I kept worrying someone would come to the beach. They would catch me all alone and naked as a jaybird, with my clothes on the beach.

I sat in the water, which looked like Coke-bottle, green-lit glass when I swirled the sandy bottom with my fingers and grabbed handfuls and turned around to face the infinite horizon. The glowing plankton lit my naked thighs in its greenish light where sand slipped from my clenched fists. I reached down into the water with both my arms and gathered it, as if the water were a blanket I could lift. I pulled the water up and out of itself, so that it spilled down my arms and into the air. It looked like liquid neon as it fell from me and hit the water again. Plankton is made up of many living things. As the cascades of pregnant water fell back into itself, the plankton would swim crazily in maddening and bright little circles. I played like a child alone in the world of my bathtub and lost myself, which is why I didn't hear the water swooshing behind me until Piper had nearly reached where I was sitting.

"Wow!" she whispered softly as if she might disturb the spectacle. I flinched a little. I wasn't disturbed by being discovered naked. I had gotten over that with Piper. She was far more comfortable with her body than I; stripping for a skinny dip was as natural as hopping in the shower. I was, however, perturbed at having been discovered so out of my character. I had worked extremely hard to maintain a sort of cold distance between us until we were home again, safe. If I was serious about offering her Phillip's role, and I was, I could not be her lover and partner in crime at the same time. Having a lover at all would make me horrible at my job. Having a person I loved involved in this same mess had already taught me a hard lesson. I didn't need another Hester. In general, I thought it a very good idea that I stay single until I got out of this business. This distance thing was easier to do with the others than with Piper but more important to do with her. There was a chemistry brewing that I had not anticipated.

She sat down in the water beside me, resting her warm thigh on mine. I handed her the champagne and she took it, tossed her head back, and drained the bottle. She'd had a buzz on before she'd arrived and she clearly wanted to maintain it. She pulled from behind her back a new cold bottle of champagne she had brought with her. She popped the cork with none of the decorum the waiter had when he delivered the bottles to us in the lanai. The champagne foamed quickly up and over the lip of the bottle and into the water. Where it fell in the water, the plankton went dark. I tested this and poured another few drops into the water. We watched, and sure enough, small spheres of darkness appeared in the water where the champagne had just fallen.

Piper wanted to repeat the test yet one more time and I stopped her. She was about to empty the contents of the bottle into the sea to make it go dark for fun. Although neither of us really needed any more to drink, there was something profane about simply dumping a bottle of champagne out and pointlessly massacring a universe of plankton. I grabbed a fistful of sand. When I did this, it agitated the plankton and made it light up brightly, and I poured the sand out onto her submerged thigh. She was mesmerized and repeated the gesture, laughing each time it worked.

She lay back in the water, not realizing that it was an inch or two too deep to comfortably rest one's head without drowning, and she nearly choked. The salt water filled her mouth and nose in an instant. I watched as she reclined slowly in the warm water. Specks of luminous plankton stuck to her cheeks and glowed for an instant before the light vanished. When Piper shot back out of the water, clumsily choking, flinging her long, wet hair, and spraying watery moonlight over my dry shoulders, I realized that she was completely drunk. This was not her style.

She had started coming undone over the last few days, just a little, but you could see it if you looked very closely and knew her well. I had and I did. She could ignore her own emotional deterioration as long as she maintained a separation between herself and any semblance of reality. Fantasy honeymoons and alcohol served her well to a point. She had a very hard exterior; no one else could have read from her poised and calm carriage over the last few days the panic and homesickness that had swallowed her. I should have seen it sooner. The waiting was eating her alive.

She sat gasping for air and spitting out salt water. I slapped her on the back with my palm cupped slightly to help clear her lungs and her throat; it was a trick my mom had taught me in some other life when I'd had bronchitis. I handed Piper the champagne and she took another gulp, clearing the salty taste from her throat.

"And you were going to dump this?" I asked.

She turned her back to me, then swiveled around behind me to lean against my back. As she moved in the soft sand, it stirred, releasing a new burst of glowing plankton around us. We sat silently in this position, naked, back to back.

She had slept in the same bed as me numerous times, just as naked as she was at the moment, leaning her back against mine, but things had changed. She slid her hands into the crooks of both my arms and forced her own arms through. We locked elbows and pulled closer. Once we established this comfortable arm lock, we settled against each other, like a warm chair back. I could feel her heart pounding through her wet, slippery back. Her suntanned skin radiated heat, and although the water was as warm as the night, the added heat felt good. I wanted to hold her, but I couldn't move. I had that awful feeling you get right before going over a roller coaster's first summit.

8 Stuck in the Middle with You

IT CERTAINLY WASN'T THE PAYDAY that everyone had waited for in Indonesia, but it was better than a big fat zero. We had all returned to the States a few days earlier after having been rushed out of Indonesia empty-handed as quickly as Alajeh could get us out of there. We did not get to make the trek to Yogyakarta I had been so excited and nervous about. We only made it as far as the Hyatt in Jakarta when the trip was officially declared a flop. But twenty-four hours after our plane touched ground in Boston, we were all summoned back to Chicago.

In Chicago, we were introduced to a new facet of Alajeh's operation—new to us anyway. We were to transport a large sum of money from Chicago to Paris and then to Brussels. We needed three more people than we had available to carry the money. Alajeh was very specific about how many people he wanted us to use to facilitate the move. He would pay each person six thousand dollars to carry approximately fifty thousand dollars. Craig and Molly were sticking firmly to their decision to not do another trip in spite of the fact that this operation felt like a gift more than a risk.

We had flown into and out of both Paris and Brussels several times by now and the security in both airports was not particularly daunting. There was no such thing as money-sniffing dogs, or so we were told, and therefore we were allowed to check our luggage instead of having to carry it onto the plane. I had already broached the possibility of Piper taking Phillip's or my place as an escort occasionally and Phillip's primary objection had been she was unqualified to do so. The money trip was a perfect opportunity to begin grooming her.

In spite of being weary and homesick, Piper agreed to cut her visit home short and earn some easy money. I flew out a day before everyone, and Phillip would be the last one out. I could begin delivering the bundles of cash to contacts in Brussels as Phillip continued to collect the bundles of cash in Chicago and send our friends over. I retrieved Garrett from the airport in Belgium; the next day Garrett retrieved Donald, and so on. No one ran into any difficulties along the way, except Piper. Her bag had not made it onto the same hop from Paris to Brussels. She did get her bag back, but she was a wreck by the time Donald returned from the airport with her.

I paid each courier as they arrived out of the money they had just delivered. Piper's anxiety quickly gave way to a celebratory mood as she told us of her harrowing adventure. None of us had ever had to wait patiently under the watchful eye of airport security for so long—impressive for a first rodeo. Piper's making it through Customs for the first time also made her officially one of the family. We took her out on the town.

The next morning, Phillip came into the room, and in one angry and fluid move, he dropped his garment bag onto my bed and flung his Armani-ish suit jacket onto the armchair by the window. He abruptly opened the curtains and the window, letting fresh oxygen and sunlight pour into my sleepy cave.

With one eyelid stuck at half-mast and my mouth too dry to

form consonants, I mumbled an unfathomable greeting. Phillip's wordless arrival had stunned and woken me, but I was not fully conscious of my whereabouts, the day, or my own name quite yet. He hadn't called and he hadn't knocked. He had just let himself in with a key. I concentrated hard, trying to hurry along a reality reassembly process in my still half-asleep, throbbing brain.

He must have retrieved a key at the front desk. We were Mr. and Mrs. Adam Stern to the Hôtel Carrefour de l'Europe. We never checked into hotels under our real names.

Phillip was pissed off. I knew why. I was supposed to have met him with a car at the airport hours earlier. He pulled his sunglasses off and made a disapproving grimace while he surveyed the previous night's wreckage.

I finally sat up, but too quickly, and saw stars floating around like lightning bugs. They vanished quickly and I looked at the scene Phillip was taking in, including a bunch of empty mini liquor bottles on the desk and an overflowing ashtray. I recalled a few choice bits from the night before and got a little rush of panicky adrenaline.

"Where's the minibar?" Phillip smiled in spite of my fuckup. I think he got a tiny little bit of sadistic satisfaction from catching me in such a sorry state. It was more often the reverse: him hung over, me all bright-eyed trying to get him up to go get coffee or go bungee jumping. He was also probably very anxious to get out of his suit, into his boxers, under the influence, and lying flat on his back. His long legs and economy class seat on the red-eye from Chicago to Paris did not equal the same relaxing flight that the first-class passengers woke from just in time to start the new day in Paris and hop on the quick flight to Brussels.

He noticed that the soft, downy comforter on the other bed had already been fluffed and messed up for him by someone. "Who ate my mint?" He was referring to the chocolate treat that should have been perched on his pillow, in a still made-up bed. I assumed Piper had. I remembered we'd had a little quarrel at the restaurant. I remembered I'd left her there. I also remembered why I'd left her there and felt instantly ashamed and embarrassed.

"Piper must have eaten it. Fuck!" I stopped myself. Phillip didn't need to know about this.

"It's a piece of chocolate." He laughed, but he was understandably perplexed by my overreaction to the missing mint. The night before I had flipped my wig in a little jealous fit, when I thought Piper was hooking up with some woman we'd met at a restaurant. I definitely didn't want Phillip to know about that.

"But it's the mint!" I reached over, punched him in his thigh, and laughed in an attempt to make my reaction out to be a joke.

"It's okay. I'll get another one tomorrow." He went along with the silly banter, feigning sad resignation over the loss of his chocolate mint. After sitting, or rather flopping, his butt down beside me on my bed so hard I almost bounced out, he tried to kick his shoe off and one small empty bottle flew from the tip of his Italian black loafer, across the room, and into the stone wall. It didn't hit hard enough to break, but the clatter it made, bouncing around on the ceramic floor, chiseled into and shattered my fragile head.

Phillip was clearly pissed at me for standing him up at the airport, and rightfully so. I couldn't do math quite yet—my brain wasn't awake—but he had to have waited for me for at least a couple of hours before giving up and grabbing a taxi. Nearly bouncing me off the bed was his sweet way of saying that all was sort of forgiven. The bottle kicking had been an accidental emphasis, not deliberate violence. And I thought his remaining irritation with me could be cured with a little alcohol.

I pointed to the armoire, secretly praying there was still actually some liquor left in there. The minibar was tucked inside the one ornate relic adorning our room. But this one very baroque or rococo reminder was enough to assert that in spite of the otherwise Holiday Inn feel to our space, this was no Holiday Inn, and we were not in Kansas anymore.

Once opened, the armoire lost its European antique charm. It cleverly concealed, behind its faux drawer fronts, all the modern accoutrements of hotel life: a television, a radio, a miniature coffeemaker, a couple of Styrofoam coffee cups, sterilized water glasses, a digital safe, and a minibar chock-full of itty-bitty versions of liquor bottles atop a little fridge. The fridge had been stocked with a beer, wine, and soda assortment.

Phillip and I had devised a jet-lag cure our first morning in Paris, back in the spring on our first trip abroad together. We both drank scotch, and what started out as one polite nightcap between friends at the crack of dawn, intended only to help us fall asleep, ended up as the discovery of our fail-safe jet-lag cure. We always arrived in Europe at daybreak, but our bodies still registered this as last call, Eastern Standard Time. We ended up polishing off all the brown liquor in the minibar, not just the scotch, on that first trip. We passed out and woke up the same evening, miraculously cured of jet lag but starved and thirsty. This jet-lag remedy had become our ritual, albeit an outrageously overpriced custom.

Unfortunately, on this trip the stage for the rite was no longer set. We had not arrived together. Phillip was walking into a used space, not a room with a full minibar and chocolate mints still perched on two creased and fluffed pillows, on two perfectly made beds. The room was a chaotic wreck. Piper had gone through every outfit she had packed suitable for a night out in Brussels and left the ones she had opted not to wear all over the place. The whole gang had started our night out in my room and the trash bin was full of what used to be the mini fridge's contents.

Phillip leaned over the opened minibar on top of the little fridge to discover we had cleaned it out. He opened the fridge and all that was left there was one Diet Coke, opened and half-empty. He stood up, arched his back in a stretch, with his hands on the backs of his hips, staring at the pillaged treasure. "You have got to be joking!" He shook his head, slipped his loafers back on, gave me an angry glare, and stormed out of the room, slamming the heavy door behind himself without another word.

One of those tiny bottles of liquor cost about fifty francs, or nearly nine dollars in U.S. currency; a can of beer cost seven dollars, a bag of peanuts, five, and so on. Not only had I failed to make sure there was at least something left for Phillip, I also had just need-

lessly wasted a bunch of our money when I should have been pinching pennies. There was a store right in front of the hotel that sold
almost everything we had consumed.

Phillip had left his bag and his jacket where they lay, so his return
was inevitable. He was likely heading to housekeeping to request
our liquid treasure be restocked, to the front desk to get another
room if he was mad enough, or across the street to the store to buy
a full-grown bottle of Dewar's. In any case, I didn't have long to get
ready to face the music. He'd be back.

I got up, splashed water on my face and crazy hair, brushed my
teeth, and then quickly toweled my face and hair dry. I waged bat-
tle with my defiant bed head and otherwise tried to return to my
human form before Phillip returned for a fight. I didn't think he
would let me slide on all that I had done wrong already with just
three words and an angry eyeball. Even if he did, I still had a lecture
coming for all the money I had blown in Bali.

I licked my dry lips and considered how long it might take to get
down to the café and back to the room. I knew the boys weren't in
their room either or they would have come in when Phillip arrived,
so I couldn't send one of them to the café for me. I wondered if they
were all together—Piper, Donald, Garrett, and Edwin. I hoped they
were not discussing me. Piper might have told them about my jealous outburst at the restaurant the night before, especially if I had
done anything more to make her seek alliances or solace.

That would be just perfect, if while trying to get an accounting
of the amazing trip to Bali that we would never be reimbursed for,
Phillip also learned I had lost my mind and potentially destroyed
the trust of any of our recruits, much less the woman I had posited might relieve him of his obligations. If only I could remember
exactly how far I'd gone with my totally inappropriately jealous
flipping out. Piper and I were not lovers, which put me on par with
bunny-boiling psychos—I was embarrassed and humiliated, even if
that was the sum total of my actions. The problem, though, was that
I could only recall bits and pieces of the night before, just enough
to worry me.

I couldn't leave the room. If Phillip did come back to finish our conversation and I was gone, he'd be angrier than he already was. It would be much better to have this conversation while he drank the scotch he was probably retrieving from the store I should have gone to. I knew he wouldn't come back empty-handed or before asking the front desk to restock our bar, and I knew he wasn't done with me. His swift exit was a dramatic pause, that's all. If we didn't finish this now, it would be meaner and uglier later, with more consequence than if I just waited for him and got it over with. Phillip and I could put on a good fight when our stresses and the stakes were high.

I figured Piper must have slipped out earlier because her bed was messed up. Had she helped me wipe out the liquor in the minibar? I just couldn't remember if we'd done that or if it had just been me. If she had helped me, she was probably nursing her own hangover, rehydrating with cappuccino, probably at the café on the corner. That is what I would be doing now were I not awaiting my punishment.

I stopped staring at the café outside my window, wishing for clarity or a hangover cure, and called room service. I ordered two coffees, an orange juice, a bottle of water, and a baguette. Both the coffees were for me. Room service didn't offer pots of coffee served with low-fat milk and sugar on the side, like an American hotel might. The closest you could get to a regular coffee here was a tall espresso served with hot condensed milk on the side. They were small, so I'd ordered two. I needed my coffee, a cigarette, and some aspirin—best hangover cure in the world and the perfect start to any day.

You didn't have to wait forty-five minutes for such a simple order.

I had barely gotten a clean shirt over my wet head when the goodies I had ordered arrived. I opened the door to let a young woman with her treasure-laden tray into my room, and I followed her to the desk where she set it all down. She gave my room a horrified glance. Instead of instantly signing the check, I held up a wait-one-minute finger, poured the hot milk into the espresso, and guzzled down the first coffee. I removed the other coffee, my juice, the water, and the warm baguette from the tray, signed the check, and handed the tray back with all of its unnecessary additions still onboard. I wanted to minimize the proof that I had just ordered overpriced room service. Phillip didn't need more evidence of my extravagance.

I found my pill bag in the safe and popped a couple of the codeines I had been saving, skipping the aspirin. The first surge of caffeine, sugar, and hot liquid fortified me in an instant. I took a seat by the open window, where I could see the street below and keep my eye on the café and the tobacco store, the two places Phillip might visit before returning if he'd actually left the hotel. I also watched for the rest of my crew to appear. A wisp of fresh air on my damp face and wet hair countered the warm sun and felt refreshing.

I lit a cigarette and took a long, deep drag, exhaled, and then drank down the cold orange juice. I felt the chilled elixir of vitamins and health going down, coursing through my veins, and reanimating every alcohol-poisoned and dying cell it encountered. A clear agenda for the morning was finally forming in my addled brain: deal with Phillip, find Piper, put last night's debacle to rest, find the guys, and defuse the situation as quickly as possible.

I had woken with the nauseating certainty that I had blown up or done something bigger than just oversleeping and leaving Phillip at the airport.

I recalled coming back to the hotel by taxi the previous night, pissed off at myself for losing my control in the restaurant, feeling dejected, embarrassed, and disappointed. The concierge had asked about my friend, and it had irritated me further. I hated the eruption of irrational feelings that kept coming up, and I had wanted to quiet them, knock myself out, and start over. I had lined up all the little bottles containing brown liquor to drink them. I had awoken to find them empty. I recalled crying but not the exact reason for it or whether I'd had company. The last thing I could remember was Piper's angry expression spinning over my head.

My stomach did a what-the-fuck-are-you-doing-to-me flip,

sending up a coffee and orange juice burp that tried to be more and almost destroyed my resolve to refuse a hangover residence in my body. I needed to eat something solid or I would be sick. I started to worry that maybe old codeine hadn't been the best choice, wondering what happens when prescriptions expire.

The baguette was thankfully still warm, its crust thin but crunchy, its center moist, soft, and bakery fresh. Instead of gently cutting a piece off and preparing it, I ripped one from the soft loaf, slapped butter on the end, and added a dollop of strawberry preserves. I inhaled the chunk in one bite, then repeated until the loaf was gone and my stomach felt settled. I took a sip of my second cup of coffee, which was no longer piping hot but still warm and delicious.

I finally spotted Phillip taking a seat at the café below my window. He looked up and saw me. He nodded but had no discernible expression to gauge his mood by, just a blank expression. He was joined by Piper. She looked up to see who Phillip was nodding at, smiled, and waved. I couldn't read anything from her either. If she was angry, disgusted, or uncomfortable with me, I couldn't decipher any of this from her wave or smile, and she looked away when Phillip said something.

I got up from my seat, intending to head straight down to the café and make sure Piper did not share whatever happened the night before with him. But when I stood, the room felt as though it had tilted slightly. I felt like a ball in an arcade game. I rolled left instead of right and ran out of floor, toppling back onto the bed. Once I was down, that was it. The fluffy bed hugged me and felt so good. I knew getting back up wasn't happening; going back to sleep was a much better idea. *Screw everything,* I thought.

I recalled what had triggered my reaction the night before: Some woman hitting on Piper had asked her whether we were a couple. Piper said no, emphatically and with no hesitation. The emphasis of her response pissed me off. We weren't girlfriends, not even pretend ones anymore, and I knew that. But she acted like it was absurd to even consider the idea of our being together, and it stung.

I had thought of little else since we'd left Bali. I remembered wondering if her animated response meant that she was ashamed of being presumed my girlfriend.

The possibility that she was actually into the woman we were talking to and didn't want my presence to get in her way triggered my unexpected jealous response to the situation. It came to the surface as alcohol-infused, bitter, vitriolic nonsense. It sounded exactly like one of my mother's rants when I replayed it in my head. Piper had looked at me as if I'd had four heads and had told me to go fuck myself. So I had. I'd walked out and left her at the restaurant.

The ruse about being a couple that we had played in Bali had ended when we'd left there. But I couldn't help myself. I was unable to turn it off. There had been more than one occasion since we'd left Bali when it seemed possible that I was not alone in this, that she was feeling the same mad attraction. Silly little incidents happened repeatedly where my heart suddenly fell into the pit of my stomach and turned into butterflies.

I had started anxiously anticipating these moments like a kid on Christmas Eve waiting for morning. I had thought we were close to one of those moments where instead of nervously retreating, still not quite convinced my feelings were reciprocal, I would know they were mutual. I would kiss her, she would grab me, clothes would fly, and the angels would sing, or something to that effect. The point is, I thought we were on the verge of falling in love. I thought it had almost happened on the flight to Paris from Bali and again when we reconvened in Chicago. The last few days had been the most exquisite torture. I had assumed that once we sat still for more than a moment, the inevitable was going to occur. But her actions at the restaurant had proved to me that I was wrong.

I pulled myself out of the bed and sat up again. Phillip being pissed at me was icing on my bitter cake. But it was what I needed: a cold slap in the face, reality, reality, reality. I had spent over twenty thousand dollars in Bali. After Craig and Molly, the next two bags we had been waiting on never came. Our delivery had been canceled and I had just spent a month at the resort in Bali supporting Garrett, Edwin, Donald, and Piper. Were it not for the money trip, we would be in serious trouble. Something somewhere was going very wrong in Alajeh's world and he had wanted us out of Bali, out of Jakarta, and out of Indonesia, entirely and immediately.

We were not safe there anymore and he would not tell us more. That was why we were not slumming in Yogyakarta at the moment. That was why the night before could even happen. That was why Phillip was pissed at me for spending too much money on my friends and emptying the minibar. The last thing he needed to hear was that he had been funding my attempts to bed Piper.

Now that I knew nothing was ever going to materialize out of our faux marriage in Bali, I wanted to make sure Phillip never found out about my little jealous scene the night before. In fact, I didn't want anyone to ever know about it. I wished Piper hadn't seen it. What I could remember was embarrassing and humiliating. I stepped over to the window to see if the two were still at the café. They were not.

I knew I had been up until daylight the night before. I had reassembled most of the previous night now from the wreckage in my head. Not much more had occurred after my insolent exit from the restaurant. I had gone back to the hotel and gotten stupid drunk and written in my journal—another brilliant practice for a criminal, keeping a personal journal on the unsecured PowerBook I toted around the world with me. At some point I must have passed out and ended up on the floor. I woke there at one point early that morning. Piper had been there, standing over me, pissed off. I remembered that. She must have helped my sorry ass to the bed Phillip had found me in when he arrived.

I saw my laptop sitting on the desk. I went to see if and what I had written, how much, and at what time I had closed the file, if I had. My laptop was asleep, not turned off, and it was plugged in, thank goodness. I had run into technical problems before, letting the battery die without closing everything and shutting the computer down properly.

I tapped a key to wake the laptop. There were no open files, but there was a new file, which was good. That meant I could see what time it had been saved and no one else would have seen my writing, almost certainly an example of literary genius. That would tell me approximately when I had last been functional enough to properly save the document. Reading my writing might also jog my memory and shake loose the rest of the night's events.

I found the system time stamps on the document. It had been created at 3:14 and last modified at 6:23 A.M. Considering my typing speed, this likely accounted for all of the time. The subject of the document was no surprise: Piper. There were no mentions of any other contact with Piper or the world, thank goodness. If all I had done after what I had said to her was leave her in the restaurant and make her find her own taxi home, I hadn't said or done anything unforgiveable.

I returned to my bed without toppling over this time, crawled in under the soft down comforter, and curled into a ball. I actually felt a little better. I was still dead tired but no longer felt as though I was going to be sick, and my headache had gone. The codeine even made me feel a little bit euphoric. I set the alarm on my watch to four P.M. If Phillip did not come back and wake me, I didn't want to end up sleeping any later than that. But I did want to sleep now.

———— • ————

I woke to Phillip's voice. He was on the phone with Alajeh, talking about money and Zürich, Switzerland. I lay still and didn't open my eyes. I was not at all ready to talk to Alajeh or even Phillip for that matter. I peeked and could see Phillip was in his boxers, his bed was in a different state of disarray than it had been earlier, and the room was dim, not dark. The call lasted longer than usual. Alajeh was generally very brief and to the point in phone calls—no chatty banter, just quick instructions and goodbye.

Phillip laughed, said thank you, hung up the phone, and hooted like he had just won the lottery. He said Alajeh had agreed to reimburse us for all that we spent. Alajeh hadn't even objected to the fact I had spent so much. He had also told Phillip that we were going to be traveling in three days, and not back to some far-flung corner of the world. We were going to Zürich and, from there, home. "Are you hungry?"

"Starved." I stood up, stretched, and did a little *Flashdance* run in place. I was so happy to be going home. Hopefully, I could stay a little longer this time.

"What time is it?" It looked like it could be either A.M. or P.M., and my glasses had fallen off the bedside table and under the bed.

"It's a little after seven." Phillip noticed my blank stare and added, "It's dinnertime. I told those guys we would eat about an hour ago." He had already pulled his pants on and was fumbling with his belt and stepping into one of his shoes at the same time.

"I need a minute." I ran into the bathroom, stripped, and jumped into the shower before he could object. A few minutes later, I heard the door open and could hear Piper's and Garrett's voices. I rinsed the conditioner out of my hair and heard the door close when I turned the water off. I listened, but there was only silence. I grabbed a towel, dried off, and wrapped it around myself in case I had company, but there was no one in the room when I opened the bathroom door. Phillip had left a note on the desk instructing me to go to Le Bistro and how to get there.

After I dressed, I felt much better about the world in general, and more important, I thought I was almost up to facing Piper again. It couldn't be avoided, and I hoped it would be uneventful or at least quick and painless. I popped one of the last two codeines, thinking it would smooth my edges and give me courage.

I made the quick walk to Le Bistro. I stopped and took a deep breath before entering the crowded restaurant, like one might do before jumping off a cliff or out of an airplane. There were two things that were true about the many restaurants in Brussels we frequented: they were small and they were dark. Two other things that were true then about restaurants in Brussels: they were smoky and crowded. I'm certain the same is true now, except for the smoking. I bet in another twenty years there will be a table, just like ours was, full of young drug smugglers, but it will be tobacco-sniffing dogs they fear.

I greeted the waiter walking by me and waved at the sous chef I thought might be about to catch his face on fire in a blazing skillet. The last to arrive gets the lousiest seat, so I took my place at the corner of the table. Piper sat directly across from me and I did not try to avoid her glance. I had screwed up enough already. I needed to just suck it up and take my lickin's, whatever they were. But all she did was smile broadly and genuinely. Then she handed me her glass of wine and said, "I think you might need this worse than I do."

I cannot begin to express how grateful I was at that moment. Nobody watched for my reaction to her offering, not even Donald. She had said nothing to anyone. She was compassionate, discreet, and it appeared she was going to do the nicest thing anyone could do in a situation such as ours. She was going to simply act as though nothing had happened. I smiled back and thanked her. I took a long sip of her red wine as my heart welled up with codeine and gratitude.

Phillip held his glass of scotch up to toast. Instead of a toast, he announced we were all going to Zürich on Friday.

The next day Phillip and I slipped away from the hotel and our friends to talk in private. We finally had the discussion we should have had when he arrived the day before. He explained to me that he had charged so much to his American Express, wiring me money in Bali, that when he tried to purchase his plane ticket to Brussels, he had been told to speak with an American Express account rep at the ticketing office. We had no money left from what we had managed to make from Craig and Molly's trips, and not only that, he had no money left from his own first trip. We had not taken any cut from the money that was moved, because if our friends didn't get a payday soon, we were afraid they would abandon us like Molly and Craig had done.

Before I panicked about our destination, he told me that Alajeh had had someone named "Antony Benet" in Los Angeles wire Phillip five thousand dollars while I was passed out all day, and "John

Smith" would be wiring an additional five thousand dollars to Brussels from Chicago. The names that Alajeh's people used to wire money were sometimes quite funny. With Western Union, as long as your transactions were under ten thousand dollars and conducted with cash and not a credit card, you could send money from any name to any name you wanted with a secret passcode as your only identification. Alajeh still preferred not doing any cash transactions where a paper trail existed, even if the paper trail led to Daffy Duck.

Phillip was still freaking out that he would end up with a fifty-thousand-dollar debt to American Express before we found our way out from under Alajeh's thumb. He was also concerned about the obvious stupidity of using his American Express card at all. I couldn't argue with that, but it had certainly come in handy in Bali. For some reason, it was nearly impossible for Alajeh to get cash to us there. Besides, I said, "If we get out of this and all you have to do is file for bankruptcy, you should be happy."

He talked about having this trip be the end, consequences be damned. We would make the money from this last trip, get his Amex bill paid, and get out while we were ahead. Once again, we considered our options. We dissected every little thing that had ever happened to make us so certain Alajeh was really a threat, and in the end we came back to the same frustrating conclusion. We simply didn't know if the threat was real or not. We could create a more tenable situation than we currently had though. We couldn't get away from Alajeh, but we could eliminate some of the traveling we had to do.

Phillip had the same idea about his friend Garrett as I did about Piper. Garrett lived in Chicago and Piper was living in San Francisco. Not only could they occasionally travel in our place as the escorts, they also could find recruits. Surely, between San Francisco's and Chicago's gay communities we would have a nearly endless supply of single-use couriers. As noted, Molly and Craig had told Phillip they were not going to do any more trips when they'd left him in Chicago. If our numbers dwindled any more, we would be back to carrying the bags ourselves if we were not careful.

We went back to the hotel in time to get our friends to vacate for a bit while we made a call to Alajeh. The crew was heading out for lunch while we took care of that. We headed up to our nice room. Our view was spectacular. It looked out onto the stone-paved roundabout in front of the hotel, encircled with ancient cast-iron hitching posts connected by a heavily oxidized chain turned green. The roundabout was surrounded on all sides by the stone facades of buildings too old and grand for the modern commerce they hosted. It was easy to imagine things like horses, knights, and carriages filling the small square below our window, where bistros and cafés colored the street level and ornate street lamps would light the way later. I sat down at the desk and opened the room service menu. I asked Phillip if he was hungry. It was likely we would be stuck in the room for lunch.

"Cheeseburger?" I asked while scanning the lunch menu.

"How about breakfast?" He was hungry but preoccupied with unpacking the rest of his bag.

"Too late." I double-checked the lunchtime menu for any brunch items that might suit Phillip and there were none.

"Okay. Cheeseburger." He looked around the room like he had lost something. "Is there a pen and paper over there?" There was.

A while later we were finished with our phone call and brainstorming session. The little notepad was filled with notes and drawings that looked more like a road map or a flowchart than simple instructions. Phillip had made these while on the phone with Alajeh and I was glad he had. We had a very strange new twist to negotiate in order to get home this time.

Piper came back and knocked timidly on the door, probably worried we might still be talking to Alajeh. Phillip grabbed my arm and dragged me quickly into the bathroom, closing the door behind us, but not completely. He motioned for me to be very quiet. Sometimes Phillip was more like a child than an adult. But it was all in good fun. I could see in the bathroom mirror that Piper opened the room door. She stuck her head in, craned her neck, and said "Hello?" inquisitively.

Phillip threw the door open and jumped into her path, screech-
ing "Hello!" right back.

Piper didn't even flinch.

"You better lay off the coffee." She was clearly irritated by the
prank, but her response to Phillip jumping out and trying to scare
her was funnier than the prank itself. At least I laughed. Phillip was
already pulling the brown liquor from the minibar.

"Tonight we are going out to play." He hooked Piper's arm by the
elbow and spun her in a dosey doe. She broke into a smile. I was
glad to see her smile. There was a weird tension in the air between
these two and I didn't like or understand it.

We got to dinner around eight o'clock that night and found a nice
restaurant on our first try. I liked the big blocky mahogany tables
with no tablecloths, austere and functional like the menu: meat and
potatoes.

My favorite dish in Brussels is mussels—seriously. At the restaurant we went to that night, they were served in a little cast-iron pot
in a white wine broth of leeks, dill, chives, and butter and with fries.
No flowery garnish or swirls of anything to decorate the plate like
in Paris, just food. Everything was served by an old guy in a long
white apron and black tie.

We ate our dinners and then started at one end of the Grand-
Place, working our way through the small streets, popping into each
nightclub we found, each one smaller and more subterranean than
the last. Clubs on Boulevard Maurice Lemonnier were on the street
level, but on the older side streets near the Grand-Place many were
almost hidden, down stone stairs so old they curved from centuries
of wear. We were hitting all the bars, not just the gay ones. Phillip
was with us so we had to be fair. We lost Donald, Garrett, and Edwin
when we found a lesbian bar, with a packed dance floor and playing
house music. Piper and Phillip danced and everyone watched. They
looked like the perfect couple; both were tall, well dressed, attractive, and both were good dancers.

I watched them while I waited for our drinks at the bar. They
were trying to have a conversation while dancing. I was absolutely

entranced, watching them move so fluidly. I laughed because a bunch of other girls were staring at Piper too. They were goggling over Piper, but Phillip was eating up all the attention, and Piper had no idea what was going on. Phillip had a thing for sleeping with lesbians. She was clearly responding to his attention, probably unaware of the fact that it was for the benefit of their audience.

Phillip waved me over to them. I had to navigate through the dance floor, trying not to get bumped so hard the drinks would spill. I had my training for this kind of plight slinging cocktails in Provincetown, so getting through this little fracas without spilling a bunch of drinks was nothing. Phillip took his drink and slinked away in the direction of the girls who had been watching them dance. Piper grabbed my drink and hers, set both down on a little ledge nearby, grabbed me, and pulled me in for a hug. "I love you, you jerk." She'd said this with her mouth pressed to my ear so I could hear her, and then she let go and continued dancing.

That would be the extent of our conversation regarding my jealous foible. We danced and danced, eventually moving on to another club, somehow ending up in a raï bar, filled almost entirely with men, but not gay men, mostly Arabic men dancing together to music I didn't know. We stayed there for a round of shots Phillip brought to us, along with a few dozen more he handed out to the fellows nearby. Eventually, we ran out of places to go.

We went back to the hotel and stopped at the guys' floor to see if they had returned. They had. Garrett was passed out and Edwin was in the shower. Donald wanted to come to our room with us, but we were drunk and going to bed.

Piper got undressed and into bed first, all alone. I was sleeping with my husband. What fun a shrink would have with me, sleeping with all my fake spouses. That arrangement—to sleep with Phillip—had been made, however, when Piper and my uncomfortable situation had still been uncomfortable. I didn't think she or I still had any concerns about my little blowup or my misinterpretations about our relationship. I guess in her head we were friends and I should be sharing her bed, just as we had done in Bali. She leaned up on one elbow and pouted at me. She liked to snuggle naked, but there was no way in hell I would do that again.

Phillip saw her pout as a call to action. He jumped out of bed and pushed Piper's bed into ours so the two beds were joined. He yelled, "Slumber party!" as the two beds slammed together. He hopped up onto our bed and was about to start jumping up and down, in his boxers. Piper flung her long leg over me and kicked his legs out from underneath him. He flopped onto the bed next to me, elbowing me in the ribs. Piper laughed and rolled over with her naked back to me. Phillip turned the light out and I lay on my back between the two of them, staring at the ceiling. Nobody said a peep, but I knew they weren't asleep. Piper giggled.

"Phillip, your penis is poking me." I burst out laughing. Phillip had an erection. I have no idea why I was so comfortable with him that his erection didn't prompt a different response. I loved him deeply, like a brother. But if my brother was in bed with me and this happened, I wouldn't have laughed. I would have knocked him out.

"Sorry. I'll talk to him." Phillip scooted away from me and rolled onto his back. "Do you mind? We are trying to go to sleep!" He continued the conversation with his penis, and I considered for a moment how difficult it must be to have a penis and keep your desires secret. Piper and I could snuggle butt naked, for example, and if she happened to notice my heart pounding out of my chest, or vice versa, it could remain unspoken. Men didn't have that luxury. There is nothing ambiguous about an erection.

"Let me ask." He leaned over and whispered in my ear, "He wants to talk to you." Phillip's whiskery face and hot breath gave me goose bumps and tickled. I crunched my shoulders up and retracted my neck like a turtle does, so he couldn't get his scratchy face anywhere near my neck, but he kept trying, which made it worse, and I kept laughing.

He then stopped and stared at me all serious like, and it felt like the floor had just dropped out beneath me when he kissed me passionately. I hadn't expected that. Then he stopped and leaned up on his elbow a little and smiled. "How come you and I have never made love?"

"Maybe because I'm a lesbian." I couldn't help but laugh. "Made love" sounded so serious and polite, considering he had just been conversing with his dick.

"Aha! I knew it wasn't me. I'm irresistible." He flung the cover back, presenting his red plaid boxers. His lack of modesty about his current condition amused me.

Piper, in the meantime, hadn't moved a muscle. Her face was turned away from us, but no way was she sleeping, not after the fight I had put up to defend myself from Phillip's scratchy face. I had kicked her, our kiss had been slurpy, and Phillip had sighed. Besides that, the conversation he had been engaged in with his penis was absolutely ludicrous. But Piper hadn't objected, gotten out of bed, or otherwise expressed any opinion. The twist of reality unraveling next to her certainly warranted some kind of reaction. I made a what-the-hell-are-we-doing face at Phillip and nodded toward Piper. We should have been asking the same question of ourselves, not just addressing the fact that we might be intruding on Piper's sleep or personal space.

Phillip reached over and softly stroked her bare back, then smacked her butt. Piper flipped over quickly, raised her head up, and leaned on her elbow, shooting a killing dagger look at Phillip. "You're joking, right?"

I thought we might be in trouble for a split second, but then I finally got my Hollywood kiss. Not exactly the film I had in mind when fantasizing about kissing her for the first time, but passionate. Piper held my face in her hands for a long time, staring at me. She kissed me once gently, then stopped, gazed at me some more, and then kissed me again like she meant to consume me in one bite. I knew this was more than just a drunken accident of circumstance. But this tawdry, drunken affair is how and when my relationship with both of them graduated from platonic to sexual and unquestionably insane.

My feelings for Phillip had blindsided me, being a lesbian and all.

I kept those to myself. But I slept with both Piper and Phillip that night. Piper and I became lovers, and Phillip became a much closer friend. Acting on his odd impulse when he did, he provided the perfect remedy to the senseless impasse Piper and I had reached. But I wondered about that. He had to have known Piper felt the same way I did or he was just lucky. In any case, I could finally see myself with Piper and the cats, happy in San Francisco.

I hadn't really been in control of much in my life lately except this one thing. I had not jumped blindly into bed with a new partner, the moment Joan left me the first time. It felt like I had been fighting a rip tide for months and months, trying to keep my head above water. In the quiet aftermath of the morning, I watched the rising sun turn our curtains orange, then white, and then I fell deeply into a restful sleep somehow certain whatever came next was exactly as it should be. Piper and I had a real future together.

9 Planes, Trains, and Automobiles

O UR MISSION WAS NOT A SIMPLE ONE. We had to pluck the luggage we were to deliver to the United States from passengers who had flown into Zürich and who would fly back out of Zürich the same day without ever exiting the airport. The easy part of this operation was that we wouldn't know who these passengers were we would be retrieving the luggage from, what flight they were coming in on, or what they looked like until we were inside the airport in Zürich.

Piper, still riding high on her first trip as a cash courier, had agreed to transport one of the bags we were picking up when we required one more body to get the job done. Of course, we didn't actually believe the job was about to happen. But that would be it for her. We were lovers but no *Thelma and Louise*. She would not drive off a cliff with me, just go to the edge. Of course, she didn't realize we were grooming her for a wonderful opportunity even for a Smith College graduate. Not that anyone would want to make a lifelong career of this, or be proud of what they were doing, but there had to be something meaningful and otherwise unattainable in the collective experience of traveling the world under these circumstances.

It was ironic, but were it not for the ever-present threat lurking in my mind of Alajeh taking his grievances out on my sister if I quit, and having no sick days or reliable vacation, I might have loved this job. We could offer that to Piper and Garrett. If they accepted, Phillip and I would be almost free, though we would still be the ones who had to deal with Alajeh over the phone. He could never know about them. We would have to be ready to hop a flight in a heartbeat if something went wrong, and step in for them occasionally to give them a break. But that situation was a hell of a lot better than our current one. If there was no way out, we had to find a sane way to make it work until there was, and this might be it. But we had to get home from this trip first.

Phillip and I were instructed to fly out of Brussels on a specific flight to Zürich. Our friends (Piper et al.) would have to fly into Zürich right behind us on another flight. Alajeh did not want our recruits to see the recruits of the escort we were meeting. I'm not sure why, but the handoff from one group to another in the Zürich airport had to be done by Phillip and me. We were told to search our flight for another passenger. A fellow from Benin who would be wearing a New York Yankees baseball cap and white leather dress shoes. Once spotted, I was to walk by said passenger, but not until the flight was in the air. I was to wipe my brow with two fingers when I had eye contact with said Yankees-cap-wearing fellow.

Phillip and I barely made it through the phone call with Alajeh without bursting out laughing. Phillip repeated bits of Alajeh's hilarious detail back to him, especially the two-fingered brow wiping. He said he needed to distinguish this from clicking his heels together three times and repeating "There's no place like home." Alajeh missed the reference. Fortunately, Phillip could get away with shit like that and Alajeh wouldn't pick up on the fact that Phillip was mocking him. But come on. It sounded like a plot from *Mission: Impossible* he was sending us on, not a simple smuggling operation.

We had already planned to head back home from Zürich. We

were so sure this operation would turn out to be a big bunch of bullshit. Alajeh overcomplicated things when he was lying. We had figured out that much about him, and this definitely qualified as overcomplicated bullshit. He was probably just creating busywork to keep us in limbo and poised to leap until he sorted out whatever the hell was going wrong in his empire. The last call erased all doubt about whether he was lying. The instructions were crazy.

Imagine our surprise when the white-leather-shoe-wearing, New-York-Yankees-ball-capped fellow walked onto our plane in Brussels. I panicked and scrambled to get a few of my personal belongings out of the garment bag that was not supposed to have any personal effects in it. I quickly transferred those objects to my purse and impatiently waited for the Fasten Seat Belts sign to go out after the plane took off. I stumbled out of my seat in a hurry the moment I heard the signifying ding. Of course, I got stuck waiting in the aisle while a fragile old lady made her trip to the toilet at a slug's pace.

When I made my first pass by our contact, we moved so slowly I had time to confirm he wore the white leather shoes and not red slippers. My guy in the cap had his head resting against the lip of his window when I passed and he did not look over at me. In fact, he appeared to be sleeping. Surely, this was my guy. What were the odds of the wrong black fellow in a New York Yankees ball cap and white leather shoes being on the flight?

I helped granny into the bathroom and closed the folding door behind her. I wondered if she would be able to get the stiff doors open when I saw the Occupied sign light up. A flight attendant came up behind me and beamed a what-have-you-done smile. He was there to help the poor thing get back out if she needed assistance. I ducked into the other bathroom and fiddled around for a few minutes.

By the time I walked out, I was hoping to be trapped behind granny again. On the way back to my seat, I would be facing the guy I was supposed to signal. With granny in front of me, I would have more time to think of something to do if he really had nodded off. The flight was barely an hour long, so I had to get his attention quickly before the sit-your-ass-down moment arrived and I fucked everything up.

I could see his eyes were closed as I approached, but I thought I saw him squint just a little, like he was peeking. I wiped my brow once, waited for some sign of acknowledgment, and got none. I did it again but a little more dramatically. Still no sign. I was about to pass him and lose my chance, so I started to reach over and his eyes shot wide open as he deflected my paw reaching to tap his cap. He didn't say anything, but his look said plenty—something along the lines of *I saw you the first time, you moron.* I made my way back to Phillip, sat down, and buckled up.

"Did he see you?" Phillip whispered but didn't turn his head to me to ask the question.

"Yeah! He saw me. It's him."

"No shit?" We sat quietly for the rest of the flight. Phillip did anyway. I was trying to remember enough of my recently relearned French to string a sentence together when I had to speak to the guy. I could ask him how he was, ask for my bill, where the toilet was, or if he wanted mushrooms in his omelet, but aside from that, I had forgotten everything. I sang children's songs under my breath. A Valium would have been helpful; my nerves were a bundle of crossed wires.

Phillip looked at me like I was nuts when I got to the "*ding, dang, dong*" part of one song. The guy sitting across the aisle from me smiled. I think he thought I was challenged, because when the plane did land, he jumped up and grabbed my elbow to help me out of the seat. I didn't care though; I was desperate, and "Alouette" and "Frère Jacques" cured my temporary amnesia.

The guy we were following was about ten rows in front of us and closer to the exit. By the time Phillip and I exited the plane, we caught a glimpse of him turning right down a hallway where passengers could go either left or right. We picked up our pace to match his about-to-miss-a-connecting-flight pace. But I couldn't keep up without actually breaking into a run. I cursed quietly to myself, "Fuckin' long-legged ass-wipe."

"I'll catch him. Just don't lose me." Phillip took the long strides his legs were capable of and I hurried along at my midget's pace. I remember in first or second grade being absolutely outraged that the fifth-graders had as much time to get from one class to another as a first-grader. They had much longer legs. The distance between each of us was growing a little wider the farther we went. I took a last turn from one of the few arteries that spilled out into a big hub lined with duty-free shops and fast food and thought I had lost them.

I searched the crowd for either Phillip or the New York Yankees cap and found the second one first. The guy was leaning against the rail of a café right in the middle of the big hub. There were arteries similar to the one we had just traversed feeding into the hub from all angles and a bazillion people moving in every direction. There were the motorized carts one expects to see bussing passengers with crutches around in an airport, with little spinning yellow lights on poles, beeping at the pedestrians they were about to run over. The cops wore Bermuda shorts and rode bicycles, buzzing around in pairs and armed with big guns strapped to their backs. The guns were a little off-putting, but aside from that, it was just what one would expect in a big international hub.

I waited for two of these policemen to get back onto their bicycles and ride away before I approached my guy. I saw Phillip sit down at a bank of seats that randomly lined the edges of the area we were in. When I reached the fellow we had been following, I sat my bag down next to him and said nothing but "Please walk slower" in my best French.

"*Pas possible.*" He snatched up his bag and took off in his maddeningly fast pace again. Phillip leapt up and tailed him, I tailed Phillip, and we navigated to another terminal, which felt like it was fifty miles away. My shins were burning and my legs were rubber by the time we finally came to a stop. This was the end of another makeshift artery and a smaller hub with a large circle of seats in the middle.

The escort sat down next to an Asian woman and I saw the familiar black leather garment bag next to her. My escort expertly wiped his brow with two fingers. This was his signal to the lady; it indicated that whoever sat down after he got up would be trading bags with her. I nodded to Phillip and he readied himself with his bag to grab the newly vacated seat when our guy got up.

I hoped Phillip would sit still for a bit and give me a moment's rest. He sat down the instant our escort got up. Phillip took his wallet out, looked at something very briefly, put his wallet away, and hopped right back up, grabbing hold of the new bag as he stood. He threw the new garment bag over his shoulder and walked back in the direction we had come from, leaving the bag he had come in with at the lady's feet and me with the sprint walker from Africa.

My guy took off and I followed, praying we were not going far again, or if we were that I would not lose him. We did, but I did not. He wiped his brow again and sat down again, this time in a row of seats facing out of the airport windows and next to a fellow I assumed was also African. My guy got up and I took the seat in his place. I didn't like having my back to the busy walkway. I couldn't get a good look at my surroundings. So I just counted to ten and went for it.

I stood up with my new bag and nearly tripped over the bag I was leaving behind. Then I nearly collided with two of the cops on their mountain bikes buzzing by me. I froze in my tracks. They swerved a little, missed me, and kept on going. I walked away, leaving my guy behind. We were finished with him for a little while.

I ambled all the way back to the café in the middle of the first hub we had come to when we got off our flight from Brussels and landed in Zürich. I saw Phillip sitting in the café in the middle. He had scored a booth and was already sipping coffee when I sat down across from him, sliding my heroin-packed bag next to his at our feet.

"Wasn't that a surprising turn of events?" I said, breathlessly, and reached for his pack of cigarettes on the tabletop.

"Un-fucking-believable." He looked at his watch. "We have some time to kill. You want to stay here or go somewhere else and come back?"

"Not a good idea." I couldn't wait to get rid of the luggage we were now babysitting. We were in a good spot with the bags concealed under the table, and we were exactly where we should be. Edwin, Garrett, Donald, and Piper were due to arrive soon, and this is where they were supposed to find us. Not the café specifically, but every airport has a big central hub or an area where all the duty-free shops and restaurants are concentrated. Fortunately, we had told them to page us from the help desk. We could find each other that way if necessary. There were several areas like this in the Zürich Airport.

"I hope they find this place." Phillip fidgeted with his spoon and moved around in his seat, trying to pull the garment bag as far out of sight as possible. "I could go see what gate they are coming into and meet them there." He appeared to reconsider what he'd offered, possibly because of the look I shot at him when he posited leaving me alone with all the heroin. "No. I should stay here."

"What can I get you?" our waitress, in her late forties, asked with a thick French accent.

Phillip dropped his spoon and held his shaking hand over his cup to keep her from pouring.

"No more?" She retracted her coffeepot-wielding appendage, already aimed at Phillip's empty cup, and paused over mine. "Coffee?"

I flipped my upside-down coffee cup over on its saucer and let her fill it. I hadn't looked at the menu, but if we were going to take up her prime real estate for long, I figured I'd better order something. Phillip ordered breakfast: eggs, bacon, and toast. It dawned on me that we were drinking coffee, American style. A little metal cream pitcher and an old style glass jar of sugar sat on the table. This must be what it feels like for an Asian to go out for Chinese in Cincinnati. The café served the same fare one would expect to find at a diner in Ohio, not in the Zürich Airport.

"I'll have what he's having, but the eggs over medium." She didn't write anything down and whisked away to the next table to take another order, and then another table. I watched her enter everything into a computer terminal at once, then she started loading up a tray with all the various drinks people from three tables had ordered. "Hmm, do you have some cash handy?"

"Yeah! What do you need?" Phillip pulled his wallet out of his breast pocket and I remembered his having done the same when he'd picked up the first bag.

"Rent." I was glad Phillip had worked in restaurants too. He knew exactly what I was talking about. Our waitress was a pro. She could flip our table five times in an hour, as efficiently as she ran her section of the American café. If we were going to linger, we needed her permission to do so, or she would have us fed, paying our bill, and homeless in ten minutes. Phillip handed her a big bill when she came back with my orange juice and he asked her if she would accept his most sincere thanks for letting us camp for a little while. He told her that his sister—that would be me, I guessed—was having an anxiety attack and we needed to sit still for a while.

Just as he said this, I saw Piper and Donald heading our way, looking like a couple of movie stars, and I really did feel an anxiety attack looming. Piper dressed up so well. She wore a blue pantsuit; the jacket was tailored and hugged her waist, and the pants fit loosely, flaring slightly at her ankles as she walked. She wore pumps and pearls, and had I not been feeling so anxious, I might have thrown her on the table and had her for breakfast. Phillip caught me gawking, and he grabbed my leg under our table and firmly squeezed my thigh. His infectious grin spread across his face. "You like that?" He was referring to her look, Piper's confident, worldly businesswoman's costume.

"Um-hmmm." I had a carbon copy of Phillip's perverse grin plastered on my face when she slid into the booth next to me.

"What a coincidence!" Piper was joking of course. I thought she was about to make reference to running into each other in an airport in Zürich. "Weren't you two in my bed this morning?"

Donald plugged his ears with his fingers, turned bright red, and sang "La, la, la, la!" as he scooted into the booth next to Phillip. I'm sure he thought it an unspeakably cruel universe that had the two lesbians at the table, and not him, sleeping with Phillip. Garrett and Edwin hadn't known what was going on for the last couple of days with their friends, but Donald knew. "I'm leaving you!" Donald pretended to break up with Phillip. It was no secret that Donald harbored a huge crush on him.

"Yes, you are!" Phillip agreed with him, but in a very different context. "Want to feel something big?" he said flirtatiously, and Donald blushed again immediately. It was so much fun making him blush; his color changed so instantly and dramatically to red. Even so it registered on his face that he understood what Phillip had meant after he reached under the table and let Phillip guide his hand. As soon as he felt the soft leather of the garment bag, he sat straight up in his seat, looking excited and delighted and doing a weird chicken-wing flap against his side. He looked like a schoolboy when he did this.

"I'm going home?" It was both a statement and a question.

"We can stay in Zürich for a few days if you want," Phillip offered, knowing full well how badly Donald wanted and needed to get home.

"Not!" Donald had barely let Phillip finish his offer of lingering in Switzerland before offering his own curt reply.

Donald and Garrett were the first ones to fly out. Garrett would take Donald to the Blackstone in Chicago and wait for us there. Very soon after their flight left, Phillip and I reconnected with our New York Yankees fan from Africa and started another chase, Phillip right on his tail and me pulling up the rear at a rapidly increasing distance. I considered hijacking one of the electric carts when I thought that I had lost both of them. But they doubled back. They hadn't come back in search of my pokey butt; the guy had gone to the wrong terminal, I guessed. I turned around when he passed me. This put me ahead of Phillip for a moment, but it didn't last. Phillip passed me while heckling me, as if it were a race I was losing.

I lost them again, and again they must have doubled back. Our African wore a panicked look as he passed me this time. I wondered briefly if I was missing something important. *Is he trying to shake us or someone else?* I stopped and scanned the people behind me and then looked beyond Phillip as he came and went. I stayed still. I wanted to know if there was perhaps someone else following the African whom he was concerned about. But from what I could tell, no one was in hot pursuit of either the African or Phillip.

I was fairly certain no one else was on our tail. *If he wasn't trying to lose us or someone else, what the heck was he doing?* I adjusted the bag on my shoulder and took off to catch up with Phillip. I came to yet another hub, but they had not doubled back this time. He and Phillip were standing by the window when I approached. The African spoke rapidly. *"Nous avons un problème. Je ne peux pas trouver mes amis."* I understood that. He couldn't find his friends.

We were all supposed to follow Donald and Garrett out of Zürich on alternate flights. Phillip would meet everyone at the Blackstone Hotel in Chicago. I would be flying back east, picking up Edith and Dum Dum, and heading out to San Francisco to wait for Piper's return from Chicago. I was going to buy this gorgeous iron bed with a canopy she had shown me in a catalog. I really had to stop my premature chicken-counting nonsense. Edwin was the only one who left Zürich that day. He would get a message back to Garrett and Donald to sit tight. We were stuck.

After spending the entire day searching the airport with the Yankees fan from Africa, we had found one of the lost couriers. Our contact was looking at passengers and we were looking at their bags. Phillip, Piper, and I could not fly home until this was resolved. The African was finally ordered to give up the search by *his people* and Alajeh told us to stay in Zürich. The African would get on a flight back to wherever *his people* were. I didn't envy him, having to return there to face the music. The friend of the Yankees fan had either gotten caught in the airport where their flight had originated or stolen the luggage from Alajeh and the Yankees fan's *people*. If that was the case, we would never see this guy again and it was clear the guy knew this. He nearly cried when he told us it was time to give up.

I couldn't help but imagine myself in his predicament, and what remained of my giddy mood from earlier in the day vanished. An apropos sense of impending doom replaced it. I had never considered the possibility that one of our friends might do something as stupid and greedy as steal the heroin. The cozy sense of everything being as it should and some yet unknowable divine plan unfolding crumbled too. Nothing was right—that guy's expression solved all my mysteries at once. *That's how this ends.*

We grabbed a taxi into Zürich, asking the driver to take us to a cheap hotel, and he took us to what he called a "pensione." A pensione is like a cross between a youth hostel and a residential hotel. Each room had two beds, just a little bigger than twin-size, and there were no private baths or toilets. It was quite a step down from Hôtel Carrefour de l'Europe, but we would have to be very careful with the money we had left or we'd find ourselves penniless in Switzerland using Phillip's overused American Express card.

In Zürich, Phillip and I fought—bitter mean battles fueled by our renewed lack of funding and faith and our current dilemma. We argued over who was suffering more. From Phillip's perspective his circumstances were much worse than mine. His mounting lies to Meg were destroying their future, and there was the ever-present American Express bill.

When we weren't fighting, we were on the phone with Alajeh. Apparently, we could not leave Zürich until the fate of the final missing bag was determined. He told us not to worry; he knew we were not responsible for it having been stolen, and he would fight to the bitter end to make sure we were not blamed. Great! Piper made herself scarce while Phillip and I beat each other up over the world we had created for ourselves.

We were found blameless for the bag's disappearance, so we left Zürich. We all went back to deal with our various obligations at home. Piper had already moved herself to San Francisco. She helped me move my stuff, including my cats, up to Vermont, where Larry, my former coworker and bartender in Northampton at Spoleto, promised to babysit them. He and his wife would care for them while I was away. My house was far from livable yet. But I didn't want to pay rent in both San Francisco and Northampton while living in neither place. Piper understood why I was doing this instead of moving the cats out to San Francisco at that moment. There was too much uncertainty about where we were going to be for the next few weeks to try to move Edith and Dum Dum there.

I had to plan for the possibility that I would never make it back to them. Piper knew that already, but I think she put the possibility of getting busted out of her mind, while she was subjecting herself to the same questionable fate. Having the house in Vermont meant we didn't need to rush. It was fall, after all, and Vermont is one of the most beautiful places to be at that time of year. We could take our time, get the cats settled, and enjoy the fall foliage once more, before we all took off for the land of palm trees and fog.

Larry and his wife, Melony, had agreed to let me move up to Vermont while the rehab on the house was being completed. I would use what was intended to be their office, in the main house, as my bedroom and storage facility. Once Piper and I had everything in, I let the cats out of their carriers to inspect their new room. We kept the cats' new world limited to the office-turned-bedroom while we had a drink with Larry. He was dead tired and we were tired too. We'd flown in from Switzerland, driven from Boston to Northampton, packed my house, and landed in Vermont.

We met some of Larry's children. He and Melony had three dogs and four cats, but the main house was a big place, so it never felt like a zoo, more like a circus, and Larry was the great ringmaster. He had a dramatic flair. The first time I'd met him he'd been dressed like Charlie Chaplin, mustache and all. He'd actually looked like him, and it was not Halloween. If the lights had dimmed and he was suddenly standing under a spotlight while he told of how he had worked a double at Spoleto before returning home that night to my unexpected arrival, it wouldn't have added much to his drama. I had always thought since Larry dressed so oddly well, was handsome, and carried himself the way he did, he was gay. But he was more complicated than that. He wasn't quite as gay as I had thought he was either. We had that in common now.

Their chocolate Lab put a quick end to our late-night socializing. He was curious about the new visitors in the office and had gotten into the room with Edith and Dum Dum. Edith was on top of the bed and Dum Dum was under it. Larry grabbed his dog, but not before he tried to give Edith a big wet nose kiss. Edith swatted at his nose and looked like she had seen a monster. Larry showed me how to lock the office door and promised to help introduce the cats to all their new friends in the morning.

My bed looked like it was in the right house now; it matched. I had a great four-post bed made of cherry mahogany and topped with a feather mattress, goose down comforter, and pillows. Piper and I cuddled in our fluffy white cloud with each other and the cats. We slept like babies that night. It was so peaceful there. The next morning, I opened my eyes, in Newfane, Vermont, and it took me a moment to figure out where the hell we were and how my cats had gotten there.

I looked out the big picture window across from our bed, into the endless backyard. There was nothing there but woods. I could smell smoke from a fireplace. Edith and Dum Dum were curled up on opposite sides of the sunny window seat in the window I was looking out of. A big black tomcat, named Blackie, was stretched out in between them. He was twice as big as Dum Dum. He could have easily posed a threat to our serenity and my hope of residing peacefully in the main house until the carriage house was ready. But my girls appeared to be completely unfazed by the proximity of this big stranger.

Blackie clearly had no issue with the girls. He looked like a big happy drunk, lying on his back in a vulnerable position, his back legs stretched out straight and his paws hanging loosely over his chest, like a dog playing dead. I wondered how he'd even gotten into the room. I had locked the door to the office before we went to sleep, but the door was slightly ajar now. I figured Piper had let him in when she went to the bathroom or we had a lock picker among us. *Blackie?* In any case, we had not been woken by a cat fight, and now they all slept like they'd been friends for years, atop the cushions that fit perfectly into the long and wide space under the picture window.

I was also surprised that my cats had already expanded their world from our bed all the way to the window seat. I didn't expect that they would be this calm when they met the two other dogs or three other cats who lived there. Aside from one spitting hiss for the poor chocolate Lab who'd tried to kiss Edith, it turned out to be an uneventful introduction to their new environment. So far.

I got out of bed and walked over to the window to take my place in the cat lineup and to get a peek at the state of my house next door. We had arrived after dark, so I couldn't really see it then. But now the contractor was out there, pulling old roofing up and tossing it aside. The building was lifted up on blocks of wood that had been stacked Jenga-style until the house was level. They were pouring a foundation under it later that week to replace the crumbled rock and mortar mess that had previously failed to support the building correctly. New windows were leaning against an exterior wall, and the sliding barn door had already been removed and the side of the building it used to occupy had been sealed and sided with cedar planks. The new siding would match the rest of the house after it turned darker and grayer with age.

I could hear Larry drop a pile of firewood on the brick hearth out in the living room, and the squeaking fireplace door opened—a thump—then the clank of the heavy iron and glass door closed. There were certainly no helicopters, boom boxes, or car alarms out here. I suddenly got so excited; like on a Christmas morning, I couldn't behave. I had to wake Piper up.

I jumped into my fluffy white down comforter and straddled her, sat up, and started playing bongos on her chest lightly. Piper woke. I can't imagine why. She laughed and bucked her hips up, tossing me off her and onto the floor. I knew she had to love me; otherwise, I'd have been beaten to death.

I didn't move and waited silently, after pretending to fall down the three stairs right next to my bed. Piper jumped from the bed to save me, I suppose, and I laughed hysterically, but not because she was going to save me. She stood butt naked with her hands on her hips, like a mother about to scold me. Behind her, out the big picture window, the contractor had stopped his busy work. She screeched and dove back into the bed. "Oh my God! You ass!" Fortunately for me, she laughed. "Throw me something to wear." I tossed her a terry-cloth robe we had stolen from one of our hotels.

"I want to walk around the house and see how far along they are." I could smell a hint of the aroma from good coffee wafting toward us from Larry and Melony's enchanted end of the house, that and frankincense and burning wood and something baking, plus oil paints and turpentine. "Coffee?"

A sonic-like boom caused all three cats to wake and mine to stare wildly in the direction it had come from, though Blackie didn't seem all that freaked out. Piper and I stared too, until we figured out it had not been an explosion in the main house we had heard, just Larry.

"Check, check," we heard Larry pronounce loudly, deliberately, and slowly. He had turned on his sound system. He composed electronic music when he wasn't painting or bartending.

Melony, the sculptor, was a graphic designer, also going digital. I loved everything about them—their lifestyle, the smell of their home, their happy family of furry friends, the mix of electronics and oil paints. Their whole home was a work in progress, as were they. Melony was in her early forties. Larry, I think, was about thirty-five. They had met in Chicago when Melony was an adjunct professor and taught at the School of Art and Design. I assumed Larry had been her student. I had known Larry for a while, through work at Spoleto, but I had only recently met Melony. I had been stunned when Larry told me he was getting married. Like I said, he carried himself like a gay man—not effeminate but elegant, like English royalty sans an accent.

I imagined living up in Vermont as living with a modern-day Da Vinci and Mona Lisa. The Kurzweil keyboard was Da Vinci's new toy. Larry was reciting something to a tune he had slapped together and was now recording, so Piper and I didn't bother him. We went straight to the kitchen in search of coffee.

"Welcome home!" Melony stuck her head out from the pantry. She was feeding all the animals at once: an old black Lab they called Gramps; a young and spunky chocolate Lab named Hershel, who had tried to lick Edith the night before; and a gigantic blond wolf-hound named Teddy. There was also a tiny nine-hundred-year-old Siamese cat named Tiki, who tapped when she walked, her nails were so long; Blackie, the big black tom that had crashed in my room; Chiggers, a really big tiger-striped gray guy; and Stewart, an orange tabby. "There's a fresh pot of coffee. Help yourself," Melony yelled over Larry's music from back inside the pantry.

"Thank you!" I followed Melony's example and spoke loudly over the music instead of the whispering Piper and I had been doing with each other as we'd made our way through the house and past Larry's so-called recording session.

"You should go grab Edith and Dum Dum." Melony had stepped back out of the free-for-all with a big can of dog food in one hand and a spoon in the other. "They should come out and eat with these guys. They're part of a big family now." She had a great laugh, making a sweep with her spoon over all the hungry beasts at her feet. It sounded like a recipe for disaster, but she was right. It had to happen sooner or later, and I'd feel better if I was here when it did. So far, they'd been pretty good with the new animals. Piper and I ran back to the room. She scooped up Dummy and I grabbed Edith. Edith was the bigger and stronger of the two. She was also the most likely to flip out. I thought it would be better if I handled her.

When we got back to the kitchen, Melony had placed two more bowls of food in the row of dishes now occupied by chomping jaws. Piper put Dum Dum down and she looked at the little Siamese next to her, then started eating. I'd expected that. I put Edith down next to Dum Dum, and Edith hissed and growled at Dum Dum, as if this was all her fault or she'd forgotten Dum Dum was her daughter. She leapt onto the counter, then from the counter to the top of the cabinet, then from the top of the cabinet to one of the large wooden beams that spanned the main room. I could only see her tail flicking madly back and forth.

Melony laughed. "She has to come down sometime."

We sat down with Melony and drank coffee while she asked us questions about where we had just come from. I kept my eye on Edith's tail hanging limply over the side of the rafter. I whistled loudly once and the tail started flicking again. That was not an ideal place for a narcoleptic cat, and all cats are, but it was especially dangerous for one who regularly dozed off and fell from the back of her sofa.

Dum Dum had finished her breakfast and was following Tiki, the oldest cat in the world, sniffing at her tail. Dummy was using her tip-toe walk for invisibility and it appeared to be working; Tiki was oblivious to the curious cat on her tail.

"I wonder if I should call her over to the loft," I said after Edith walked down the rafter and positioned herself more comfortably at the juncture of two beams that was right next to a loft she could easily jump to.

"I would just let her come down when she's ready," Melony suggested.

"It could be a long wait," I warned. Melony must have thought that I felt obliged to stay there until Edith came down or that I was too worried to go away.

"I'll be here. You should ignore her. Let her come down when she's ready. Trust me, if you stop worrying so much, she will too."

"Let's go look at your house." Piper stood up and stretched like a cat herself.

"Definitely get outside. It's so beautiful." Melony was at the sink now, looking at my Miata in the driveway. "It's a great day for a convertible. You should take Piper for a drive, get a look at the neighborhood. Go get some pumpkins," Melony added. She was right too; it was a perfect fall day: sunny, warm, but with just a touch of morning coolness lingering. People drive for miles to come see the leaves change colors here, and we were surrounded by beauty. The "neighborhood" was the woods full of huge bursts of red, orange, and yellow. It was early in the season too, so not many of the trees had turned fully brown or dropped their leaves yet and some were still green.

At some point earlier that summer, I had made a vanity purchase, a car phone for my Miata. I had also bought a huge battery pack and transmitter thing that made it possible to use the phone outside of the car. I guess you could say I had a cell phone, though the bag it had come in was as big as a large shaving kit and had weighed about five pounds. Although Piper and I were way out in the woods in the mountains in Vermont, and I didn't have my own landline yet, Phillip could still call me.

Our peaceful escape to Vermont and from reality didn't last very long. I had enough time to check out the progress on my carriage house's renovation. Piper wasn't interested, though, not to the extent I was. This was my baby, my house. It had been a leaning pile of potential kindling when I'd first seen it; now it was standing up straight, waiting for its new foundation, its solid footing. There were gaping holes where the doors and windows would be, and no stairs inside to get from one level to another, but the chimney had been built and the guts of the hearth installed. If I wanted to, I could build a fire in it. Unfortunately, there was not enough time for that.

Edith came down from the rafter while I was out interrupting the contractor so he could give me a quick tour of everything he had under way. When I came back into the office through a door that led into it directly from the backyard, I found Edith sleeping on the window seat again and Dum Dum was in bed with Blackie.

"She's a little young for you, mister." I had no idea how old Blackie was and Dum Dum was actually middle-aged, but not the way Edith and I saw it. She was always going to be our little girl.

Blackie looked at me and meowed, as if to snub my warning, and I laughed, lay down on the bed next to them, and called Edith over. I dozed off almost instantly, being surrounded by my purring pals. Then the phone rang.

I was instantly irritated. This was a repeat of my last visit home, more like pushing off a wall between laps than an actual visit. It was time to gather the troops and go back to Brussels. I felt much restored after sleeping only one night in my neighbor's house with all my stuff and cats in one place. But I wanted to stay so much longer, watch the leaves turn, watch my house get finished, stack my firewood, drink wine, cook dinners with Piper, and sit with her by my fireplace in the new house. She would never want to leave there if we had time to do all that.

Piper and I threw our bags into the trunk of my Miata, cranked up a Lenny Kravitz CD, and put the top down. Lenny Kravitz, Everything but the Girl, and Terence Trent D'Arby were queued up in the changer; they were our soundtrack, and I expected they would lift my spirits instantly. But I just stared at the house past Piper, then at Piper, then at the house, and I didn't want to put the car into drive.

I had several cords of wood that had been delivered at some point before our coming there. I had arranged this through the contractor doing the work on my house, which was late getting completed. The pile sat in the middle of the circular driveway like a mountain, dwarfing my little car. "Shouldn't you stack that before we go?" Piper asked. I laughed as we pulled away. I hadn't really thought about having to stack all that wood in my little fantasy. Piper was going to be good for me.

When we were driving down the road into Brattleboro, Piper pointed out all these beautiful little sights we had passed on our way to Newfane—a big rock face, a covered bridge, some people in a canoe. The road we were on followed the north bank of a river that leads directly into Brattleboro. The water was crystal-clear where there were not white rapids. Had it not already been October and were we not already on our way to the airport, I would have pulled the car over and we would have gone swimming. Piper must have read my mind. She leaned over, kissed my cheek, and whispered in my ear, "Next summer, honey." Her warm, soft face and her mouth in my ear gave me shivers, and I was sorry we hadn't stayed awake later the night before or gotten up earlier. Stacking wood was not the only thing we should have done before we left Vermont.

10 Hurry Up!

I HAD BEEN HOME for no more than twenty-four hours again and had already learned there were going to be two deliveries, one week apart, starting immediately. There would be four units each, or so we were told. This time instead of getting everyone over to Europe right away, as Alajeh instructed, Phillip and I gave everyone a general idea of when they would be expected, about a week. We decided we would make sure nothing was going to create a delay before the meter started running on expenses this time around. It was time to make some money; Alajeh had said so with great excitement. But we had been here before.

Phillip and I flew to Chicago. I think Piper took the time to visit her family. We were glad we had handled it this way. The urgent call to get everyone ready and move at least four to Europe was a little premature. It took a week of hotel time in Chicago for Phillip and me to even collect the money for their airfare and expenses.

We had Garrett, Edwin, Donald, and Piper ready with us in Brussels for the first group. We had been told the first group would leave on the twelfth and the second group wouldn't go until a few days later. We took that to be longer and held off on bringing the second group over prematurely. Of course, the twelfth came and went, then the thirteenth and fourteenth, and then Alajeh finally called to say he was coming to Brussels. Phillip and I thought we knew what this meant—more delays.

On one of these days in Brussels, Piper, Phillip, and I went out to dinner together. The weather was getting colder, so Phillip wore his long black dress coat, and Piper wore one of her confident, worldly businesswoman's costumes I loved so much. I was feeling very insecure that day. Maybe it was the change of season that did it; autumn closing in has always had a deleterious effect on me. It's the ominous beginning of my new year, the back-to-school-blues season when summertime dies and the pool closes. I was way overdue for this seasonal bout with the universe, probably due to all the travel back and forth through time zones and hemispheres. My seasonal meltdown clock had been jammed, until now. I felt blue, jinxed, ugly, and hopeless, and then it went downhill.

Phillip and Piper were guilty only of being the same height, wearing nice clothes, and being beautiful. Walking alongside them, I felt like a tagalong, like it wasn't Phillip who would leave and go back to Meg. It was me who was supposed to go away. I felt the idea blossom while we were at dinner.

We all ordered drinks when we arrived at DNA, a Belgian version of perhaps a hip San Francisco club or restaurant—maybe a Hamburger Mary's with more neon and less food. The crowd was a mix of thirtysomethings and fortysomethings. It was a Thursday night and the place was hopping with its way-after-work crowd. A fortysomething of the male variety started flirting with me while Piper and Phillip were trying to talk to each other over the loud music. On another night, I would have understood that it was impossible to have a three-way conversation in a nightclub, but on this night, I felt excluded. So I responded to the flirtation of the man who wanted my attention.

He was drunk. He didn't speak English very well and I spoke only the most basic French. He asked me to follow him and I did. I was furious when I walked away from the table and neither Phillip nor Piper even seemed to notice. The guy led me into the bathroom and into a stall, where he kissed me passionately. He was a handsome guy for his age, but I wasn't interested in sex with him, certainly not in a bathroom stall, so I walked out and went back to the table.

Phillip and Piper were standing and putting on their jackets when I returned. I had intended to tell them I wanted to leave. The fact that they seemed to be getting ready to leave me behind, without telling me, infuriated me. The reality of the situation will forever be a mystery, because instead of just asking if they were really going to leave me there and finding out why, possibly apologizing for my ridiculous behavior with the strange guy I had left the table with, I invited the drunk Belgian to come along with us.

We walked back to the hotel, me and my drunk date behind the two of them. There was a chain-link fence along the way that the guy stopped alongside. He turned, and with one arm over his head, he grabbed onto the fence for support and remained there. I took it that he was out of breath or something and stopped to wait for him, but he waved me over and I went to him. He leaned in for another kiss, but he had been peeing. I yelped when I realized he was still peeing—and on me. Phillip turned around and came back to see what was going on when I yelped. He didn't walk right up on us; he was being protective but from a distance.

I didn't want this guy coming to the hotel anymore. He was also much drunker than I had given him credit for, so I told him to go back to the club. When he objected, he did so in a less than gentlemanly way, spewing in his bad English that I was a cock tease.

Phillip did walk up on us then. "Hey, buddy, I think it's time for you to go."

The guy puffed his chest and cursed Phillip. Then he punched Phillip square in the jaw.

Phillip reacted so calmly. He rubbed his face and told me and Piper to go to the room. "Now!" He waved a cab over that had been parked out in front of our hotel. The taxi went around the circle and stopped beside him. Piper and I went into the hotel and to the room as he had asked, or ordered, us to do. She didn't say a word to me and appeared to be very irritated with me.

When we got to the room, she walked over to the window and looked down to see if the taxi had pulled away with my rude date. "Oh shit! They're fighting."

I ran over to the window just in time to see Phillip chasing the taxi from the circle, the drunk apparently inside the fleeing taxi. Phillip looked up to see us at the window and made a dramatic finished gesture, like he was washing his hands, and he smiled crazily.

"Hope you're happy." That was all Piper said.

I tried to apologize, to explain why I had felt as I did, but she wasn't looking for an apology, my rationalizations, or my ancient history. She claimed she wasn't mad. I don't think she wanted to know my deep, dark secrets or hear my excuses. She shut me up by kissing me, and then Phillip bounded into the room, still fired up on adrenaline. He went directly to the little fridge for a beer, then grabbed a whiskey from the minibar—boilermaker, the perfect post-brawl beverage. He flopped down in the comfy armchair and pulled the ottoman over to put his crossed legs up.

He had been carrying a notebook with him recently, an actual paper notebook. The shocking part was he had been dragging it out and writing all the time, like he used to. He had also recently purchased a Discman, the fat offspring of the Walkman, a relatively new arrival to the electronics age. I could hear Nine Inch Nails leaking from his headphones as he scratched away in his notebook, apparently unmoved by the foreplay between Piper and me occurring five feet away.

Though we did have our little audience of one, Phillip might as well have been invisible; he wasn't really with us. He was deep in his thoughts, his music, his pen and paper, writing by the light of one small candle-watt bulb from the desk lamp. He sporadically reminded us of his presence in the room whenever the vitriolic angst of Trent Reznor moved him to sing along and pound his pen like it was his drumstick. *"Black as your soul . . . I'd rather die than give you control . . ."* I wondered, was it really that he was moved by the music or was he trying to use its lyrics to say something specific to me or us?

Without the playful presence Phillip brought to our bed, there were no pauses to the mounting intensity between Piper and me. It felt almost awkward for a little while, like somehow we were more naked, and it wasn't because Phillip wasn't in bed with us or that he was fully dressed. It had nothing to do with him. Very few things in life are as brutally honest as the way someone makes love to you. You can't hide things when you're stripped bare of your decency and lost in the madness of sex's frenzy. This element gets lost in a ménage à trois.

Was Alajeh a sadistic psychic, sensing my horrible state and excited by the prospect of speaking to the dead? I don't know. But I had my third hangover in as many years and his calls had woken me for two of them. Fortunately, this conversation required very little of me, and he was as anxious to get the call over with as I was, since it was bad news. There would be another delay. He projected it would last a couple of weeks and told me we should relax. Something was shifting. I couldn't quite put my finger on it, but the rational fear I had of him was numbing, or he was changing. When he spoke, it wasn't so commanding anymore.

I put the phone down in its cradle and sat up on the edge of the bed. Piper was dead to the world and Phillip had fallen asleep next to her fully dressed with his headphones wrapped around his neck. His notebook was nowhere in sight or I would have looked at the brilliant literature his street fight, boilermakers, and Nine Inch Nails had bred. From the looks of the minibar, he wasn't going to be in any rush to greet the new day. I showered, dressed, and put my shoes on, and neither of my two lovebirds woke. I sat in the chair Phillip had occupied the night before and watched them sleep for a little while, then got up and left the room. I wasn't ready to deliver bad news yet. It could wait.

I wanted coffee, lots of coffee, and some warm fresh bread. Piper and Phillip would need something other than gin, rum, and vodka when they woke and that was all that was left in the minibar.

Later that afternoon Phillip and I called everyone to come down and meet us at the bar in the hotel and we delivered the latest from Alajeh. Piper ordered a grog from the bartender. Grog had become a favorite of ours while in Brussels. It was a mix of hot tea, honey, and cognac. The pub we had discovered the drink in served this along-side a huge roaring fireplace made of the same gigantic stone much of the Grand-Place was built from. It had been a cold, rainy day when we had ducked in there and wanted a warm drink. I was sur-prised to see our bartender recreate the exact same drink for Piper at our hotel. I ordered the same and watched Piper as she stirred the hot brew with the cinnamon stick with which it was served and blew across the steamy top of the hot liquid in her glass cup.

She smiled when she caught me staring blankly. Her smile was warm and her blue eyes sparkled in the low light of the votive can-dle in front of her. An image from the previous night and that same smile warmed me the same way the drink would. In love and intox-icated by its euphoric chemistry, my world's colors were made more brilliant. I was more attuned to the beauty Piper cast on every little thing around me than the mundane task of the accounting Phillip was doing.

Phillip handed each of our friends an envelope filled with the same amount of cash for tickets he had priced earlier. The differ-ence between round-trip Chicago and Boston fares was negligible. He had prepared one for each of them; what they did with it was up to them. Our only string was that they let us know what they were doing. My heart sank with a loud thump in the pit of my stomach when he handed Piper an envelope. The expression on her face when he handed it to her broke the delicious spell I was under. *Is she mad?*

I did not know Phillip had already gone so far as to get the money ready to dole out to our friends. I thought they would decide what they wanted to do for the next two weeks, then we would either get their tickets home or give them money the next day. I certainly had

no idea he had produced one of these for Piper. Did he think she
would go with Donald? Was I wrong to not even think of that? Without a word to me, she finished her drink and left the bar. I didn't
want to follow her to the bathroom. If she had something to say, she
would without my intruding on her in the bathroom.

Garrett and Edwin were going to London. Donald was meeting a
friend in Madrid. Phillip said we were going to Amsterdam. I had
said at one point that I wanted to celebrate my thirty-first birthday there. I assumed that Phillip and Piper had plotted something
involving Amsterdam behind my back. Perhaps at the same time
Phillip had done all this ticket pricing and banking I had missed.
But why then was she mad? She didn't come back from the toilet.

———— o ————

Piper was sitting at the desk and was on the phone when I walked
into the room. Her bag was lying open on our bed and it was already
packed. A T-shirt she had borrowed from me was neatly folded and
sat atop the dresser. I sat down in the chair and quietly waited for
her to finish her call. All she said into the phone was a time and then
looked at her watch. She was apparently repeating this back to whoever had her on hold for a silent century. Piper looked as though she
had the weight of the world on her shoulders when she hung up the
phone and turned her chair to me.

"I can't do this, Cleary." She looked me straight in the eye. *Were
we fighting? Was it the cash Phillip had handed her to go away? Is
that what she thought?* I couldn't read any emotion in her blank
expression. It could have been anger, sadness, hatred. I had no clue.
I could see no hint of our reality staring back at me in her pierc-
ing blue eyes, but my questions did not fit the occasion. This was
no fight. This was an absolute certainty. She was leaving. *Was she
breaking up with me?*

"I thought we were going to Amsterdam for my birthday." I made
no effort to hide my own disappointment or sadness. I didn't cry
or anything as melodramatic as that, and I didn't really care about

Amsterdam. It's just the only thing that came out of my mouth. If I had said what I really felt, it would have been that I wanted to go with her right then, or I would have begged her to please not leave me there, just stay. But I knew she wouldn't stay and she knew I couldn't go.

"I just can't do it, Cleary." Then I understood. She wasn't talking about Amsterdam, or us, she was talking about carrying bags full of heroin home. It didn't matter if it was because she almost lost her luggage in Brussels, or when the bag she was supposed to carry didn't show up in Zurich—she thought it was a bad omen or a stroke of miraculous luck she shouldn't ignore. It didn't matter if it was the lies she didn't want to tell her family anymore, the ones she didn't think they believed. I would not try and change her mind. I wouldn't tell her what Phillip and I had hoped she might do instead. She was doing exactly what I knew she would do, exactly what she had hinted she was going to do, and I had been too caught up in my own plans and schemes for her future to listen to her in the moment. Piper was doing exactly what she should do, and what I wished so desperately I could too: she was walking away.

The phone rang and I stared at it. Piper ran over and picked it up, listened for a minute, and replied, "Okay. Bye." She hung up, then told me where the guys were going. They were waiting, and I should go. We stood staring at each other for a moment, then she told me again that I should go. For a millisecond I saw Piper there, not the stubborn decision she had become, the resolution that wouldn't allow her to so much as smile at me or she might not leave. I didn't go, though. I didn't hear where she had said they were going and I didn't care. I sat while she finished packing. I told her how long I thought it would be before I could be back and get out to San Francisco.

Then she had her coat on, then her bag was on her shoulder, and then she walked to the door. I got up, held it open, and watched her walk down the hallway to the elevators. She turned around in the elevator with a sad smile and said, "Hurry up!" before the elevator doors closed. I couldn't.

11 Going Postal

Brattleboro, Vermont
Up to June 6, 1996

I FLICKED MY VERY LAST CIGARETTE out the car window after smoking it to the butt. The pack was crumpled on the seat next to me, but I checked anyway. Maybe one was hiding in there. I glanced down at my ashtray, full of half-smoked cigarettes from better days. I was flat broke, but if the check I'd written to the gas station and store the day before hadn't already bounced and the bank would let me keep twenty dollars out of my precious deposit, I could buy cigarettes, lunch, and cat food. I could even get the car washed.

The day was gorgeous, making it difficult to maintain my discipline and focus on going to the bank, buying some lunch, getting cat food, and getting back to work. But I had to. Being hungry and out of cigarettes helped to motivate me. I had the windows open, and my wet hair in the wind felt refreshing, though not quite as invigorating as a swim in the mountain spring I was passing would have been. Every time I drove down this road to Brattleboro and saw the big rocks decorated with sunbathers, I recalled Piper promising me "Next summer" with the top down on my Miata as if it were a dream, someone else's life. At the same time, it was hard to believe that two and a half years had already passed.

It had been a long time since I was down to my last cigarette, not a penny to my name, and on the brink of despair. Ironically, it had been just as long since I'd felt this happy and sane. My little paycheck certainly wasn't like the payday I used to have in Chicago, but the three-hundred-dollar check sitting next to me, atop the collection of love letters from bill collectors, meant more than the sum of dollars printed on its face. It meant victory. I was pulling out of my nosedive just in the nick of time.

I was no longer escorting drug smugglers. I had gotten away. It had been almost two years now and nothing happened to me or Hester. I owed my freedom and safety to two guys I didn't even know, two guys who got busted actually carrying the drugs into the country. That had shut Alajeh down, at least for the people I knew. It was over. Bradley got busted trying to collect one of these fellows from the airport in San Francisco. The guy had been caught and decided to identify Bradley, who was waiting for him at Arrivals. They got hurt, but not by Alajeh, and as far as I knew, Bradley was being taken care of. He had kept quiet. He had not gone to jail yet, and I guessed by now that wasn't going to happen. The other fellow got nabbed in Chicago; he was with Phillip. Luckily for Phillip, this guy had not done the same thing as the one in San Francisco.

Vermont's Department of Education had cut the check to pay me for just one half day of computer training for their high school teachers. I was a professional computer geek now. If all I did was that, twice a day, five days a week, I would be sitting pretty. It wasn't the writer I had come to Vermont to become, but I would be able to pay my bills and feed my kitties in a more purposeful way than waiting on tables until I retired. That was what I was so happy about. I was at the end of my rope, flat broke, but my big bet had paid off. I had taken a huge risk on the crazy notion that the Internet was going to be as big as cable, maybe even as big as television, and I had a place in it. Quitting my job as a waitress at the Four Columns Inn and selling my Miata for enough cash to get by while

I turned my hobby into a paying job hadn't been as insane as my friends had warned.

My new friends had good cause for concern too. I had told them all about my crazy past, so the notion that perhaps my grasp on reality was a wee bit shaky seemed more plausible than the idea that I could make a living out of this World Wide Web thing. The Internet was something no one in my new circle of friends had even heard of a year earlier, so they really thought their warning about spending so much time on my computer, quitting my job, and selling the cute car was all prudent advice. The check sitting next to me was my proof; all my work had not been in vain and I was right.

Janice was to blame. Janice was a middle-aged screenplay writer from Los Angeles who had helped me adapt my first horrible novel into an even more awful screenplay. Janice was one of Larry and Melony's friends. She lived on top of Black Mountain outside of Newfane, Vermont, in a little modern cabin. She was an oddball transplant from Los Angeles who had allegedly dated a movie director in Hollywood in her day. I'd met her at one of Larry and Melony's parties. They loved hosting parties. When they introduced me to their friends it was always as a writer and with some people it was clear they had already shared stories about my interesting past.

Janice fit the latter group. She had told me my life should be a movie and had read my first novel, which was a poorly disguised version of my reality, and she had thought it would make a good screenplay. She had wanted to help write it. I knew she was a copyeditor who got to work from home in Vermont for a company in California, which I thought was amazing in and of itself. But Janice was more. She could shop this screenplay to some of her connections out there in La-La Land. I had paid her to work with me to do this. That hadn't worked out, but it had led to a fruitful introduction. She had introduced me as a computer genius to a fellow named Nicholas. He owned the only computer store in Brattleboro. With Nicholas's guidance, I had helped Janice to get online and had fun doing it. Janice's company was asking its contractors (her) to connect to something called CompuServe, get email, and be able to access an FTP server. This was not a simple task in 1994, but Nicholas had walked me through it, then asked if I would do the same for other customers.

Nicholas was an Englishman in his midforties, really tall with short dark straight hair, always well dressed, and oh so proper. He owned the computer store on Main Street in Brattleboro. He was also part of a chess club, of all things, and invited me to join. I liked the idea of playing chess at the Commons Tavern on Sunday nights. It was something new to do, there would be new people to meet, and who knew? I might even find another lesbian living in Vermont. It had been a long time since I had anything bigger than a cat in my bed. They had a big fireplace there, open mic nights, comedy nights, and bands. The Commons Tavern was the heart of Brattleboro's social scene.

Nicholas's chess club included a bunch of computer hobbyists and professionals, and this was when my simple plan to write until I ran out of money was diverted. I had bought a new Power Mac from Nicholas to replace my obsolete notebook and then a modem for myself, after I got Janice online. Nicholas had started paying me to do this for his customers, and so I had some insight into just how many people were buying these doohickeys and getting online. The guys talked about the Internet and how you could broadcast to the entire world for free and communicate with anyone on planet Earth. Nicholas had expressed an interest in offering web design services out of his computer store and I got curious.

I downloaded HTML 1.0, and an obsession ensued. Melony and Larry had gotten photos of most of their sellable art onto Zip drives. In fact, most of the artists who gravitated around them had done the same. Their studio was outfitted with all the new tools of art and design. I already knew my way around Photoshop and Illustrator so I could help, but I wasn't a graphic designer and didn't want to be one. I wanted to build something on the World Wide Web and tried to explain to them that they should be putting their artwork there, not on Zip drives. Everyone but my geek friends thought it was a crazy waste of time and energy. But I knew it wouldn't be long before they would see what the hell I was talking about.

It had been a struggle, but my regular paycheck from Twelve-Twelve, as director, was about to begin. We formed the company on December 12, 1995, the previous year. Nicholas knew business; I knew the technology. The paltry check on the seat next to me from the Department of Education meant that I had been right and all the eighty-hour workweeks hadn't been a waste. The check I was about to deposit, and that would save me and my kitties from starvation in the nick of time, was the first of many much bigger ones to come.

I habitually slowed down to thirty miles per hour at the entrance to Brattleboro, rolled up my window, and turned on the air-conditioning. The cop who usually hid in the roadside lot, right where the speed limit changed to twenty-five miles per hour, was in his usual spot with his radar gun fixed on passing cars. Locals always flashed their lights and honked at him as they passed. I was a local now and the speed trap was for tourists, but police still spooked me. I quietly proceeded by the cop without flashing my lights, checked that my speed was under thirty miles per hour, and avoided Main Street's lunch hour bottleneck.

Instead, I cut over to a tiny side street that ran between the river and the back of the buildings lining Main Street. Main Street was more like a parking lot on most weekdays at noon. Thankfully, the drive-thru entrance for my bank could be accessed via the back alley and I could make my dash into and out of town quick and painless. If I was able to get cash, I would buy a ham and cheese sub from Subway, stop at the gas station and fill up, buy some cigarettes and cat food, and go home.

I made my way down the alley, into the bank lot, and up to the drive-thru window and slowly pulled forward. Once stopped at the teller's window, I signed the back of my little check from the State of Vermont's Department of Education. I would hold out some money, if I could. I wasn't sure if I was overdrawn yet or not. If I was, it would only be by a few dollars, but they still would only let me deposit my check. I wouldn't get any cash back. If that happened, making it back to my house would be dicey with as little gas as I had left in my tank. I wouldn't be able to go to the gas station on the way home, because if I was overdrawn, it would be the check I had written to the same gas station the day before that had caused it.

In any case, I needed a withdrawal slip to try to get cash back, and I had forgotten my checkbook. "Can I get a slip, please?" I asked after handing an already made-out deposit slip and my paycheck to the cashier. The cashier smiled her you-again-with-no-check smile and handed it to me. I quickly filled it out, handed it back, and watched the teller, hopeful she would give me back cash. I was so relieved when the teller started counting out bills.

Until she stopped counting, anyway, and looked up at me. "Excuse me!" the teller stammered strangely. I couldn't tell if she was apologizing or thought I had said something to her. She looked shocked, which made no sense in either scenario. Something flashed in my peripheral vision and caught my attention. It came from in front of my car. I had been too focused on the teller counting out my twenties to notice somebody had pulled a dark SUV into the drive-thru directly in front of me.

The manner in which they had pulled their vehicle into its place was rude and aggressive, but they stayed there instead of maneuvering out of the lot, as I had thought they were doing. The SUV blocked my exit, so that I was trapped in the bank portal. I forgot about the money and the teller for a second and I panicked. Something akin to my cats' instinct whenever they saw their cat carrier brought out into plain view kicked in and I wanted out of there. The only way out of my spot would be to back up. I surveyed the world behind me via my rearview mirror as I twisted in my seat to negotiate reversing out of the trap. But I was blocked in at the rear too. Another SUV was behind me.

Behind that sat a string of state and local police cars with their lights on but no sirens. I looked back at the teller, wondering for a moment if the bank was being robbed. This was not a scene one would expect to find in Brattleboro, Vermont, on a gorgeous summer day, lunch hour or not.

In spite of the traffic, the town was still quiet or I had gone deaf.

There was a smattering of nine-to-fivers, new age hippies, and veg-
etarians milling about in search of food. They meandered down the
sidewalk like they normally did. But in front of the bank, they were
starting to gather. They knew something very odd, something big
was under way at their happy little bank. From their perspective, I
was the spectacle, not just stuck in the middle of it. I saw U.S. MAR-
SHAL imprinted in huge golden type on the sleeve of a man getting
out of one of the SUVs. There were more of these creatures emerg-
ing from everywhere, like they were just dropping from the sky. My
heart stopped. I knew what this was. It was here, the thing I had
begun to believe would never come.

"Catherine Wolters! Please step out of the car with your hands in
front of you!" The guy in marshals' duds had walked up to my passenger door, opened it, and he was leaning in, as though he meant
to join me. Nobody calls me Catherine Wolters but my mother and
bill collectors. "Do you have any weapons in your possession?"

"My name is Cleary." I held up my pen and checkbook in response
to his weapons quandary.

He was not the least bit amused, but he was very polite when he
asked me to step out of the car a second time. I couldn't though. I
was too close to the bank, and in all the excitement, the teller had
left the drawer extended. I wasn't able to open my car door. I put
the car into drive, assuming what I was going to do next would be
obvious to the man in front of me and the guy leaning in my open
passenger door. I needed to pull the car forward a foot, in order to
open my door.

It was not obvious to them. Another cop jumped into the backseat of my car in a flash, and the other moved all the way into the
passenger seat, grabbed my hand from the shift, but not before my
foot left the clutch and engaged first gear. The car leapt forward an
inch and choked. It moved far enough that it scared the crap out
of the guy out who had been standing on the running board of the
SUV blocking me in the front. The guy dove back into his big rude
vehicle and closed his door, like he thought I was about to ram him.

A moment later, he opened his door again and hopped down

from his former perch on the SUV, looking oddly more officious and in charge than the guy in the seat next to me. I say oddly because in spite of his bravado, he had a youthful look, like some people who look the same at forty as they did when they were twelve, just bigger. My guess that he was the leader in this pack was confirmed when he came to my car and told the guy in my passenger seat to get out. Then he very calmly told me, "Catherine, don't resist arrest. This is not going to help you. Step out of the car."

I demonstrated my inability to do as he asked by opening the door and letting it loudly clank against the bank teller's drawer. "I was just trying to pull forward a little so I could get out." He looked like an older Doogie Howser or an adult version of Opie Taylor from *The Andy Griffith Show*. Opie had already turned my ignition off and taken my keys. I hadn't even noticed that happening.

"Come out this side." Opie got out of his seat and stepped back from the door to give me room to crawl my way out from the driver's seat. This was stupid—the gearshift was in my way—but it was easier to agree with him and get out the passenger door. When I stood up, I saw I had an audience forming and wanted to hide. Getting arrested is very embarrassing.

Of all the things to be concerned with at the moment, I regretted that I had not showered and shaved my legs before coming to town. At least I could have put on some nicer clothes than my cutoff sweatpants and sweatshirt, maybe even a bra. But I hadn't planned on getting arrested. I certainly hadn't planned on getting out of my car in downtown Brattleboro dressed as I was. I had cut the legs off my favorite sweatpants because it was hot and they were comfy. But these were for bumming around at home, not for being arrested in front of a bunch of strangers in downtown Brattleboro. It's astonishing the mundane thoughts that surfaced in the middle of this chaos. As if holding on to my composure might make it all go away.

"I have to feed my cats." Opie looked at me but didn't respond when I muttered this on my way out of the car. *I would have to call someone and ask them to go feed my cats if this was going to take long.*

"Can I have a cigarette?" Opie still ignored me. He had hand-cuffed me in one swift movement as I scooted out of the car. He still seemed to be under the impression that I might run off, and he was very focused on ensuring I did not.

Opie loaded me into the backseat of one of their SUVs and he left me there, in the air-conditioned silence. I looked out the window and counted only four men. The other police cars had left the scene at some point while Opie had been talking to me. I couldn't figure out why they had been there in the first place, other than to get front-row seats at the big arrest. *Who were they expecting, Hanni-bal Lecter or something?* The two SUVs and the men with marshals' jackets on were still attracting the attention of every passerby as they argued about something.

The leader of the bunch, Opie, came back to the SUV and opened the door. "You have the right to remain silent. Anything you say . . ." I couldn't seem to focus on what was happening or what he was saying. " . . . a federal information warrant from . . . California." I watched his lips move, though, and nodded as if I really compre-hended what he was saying. "You know what this is about."

As soon as he'd said "California," I knew, and the truly futile hope that this was about an unpaid parking ticket vanished. Then I noticed Opie's badge said U.S. CUSTOMS and DEPARTMENT OF THE TREASURY while all the other guys were marshals. Alan Dressler, my federal lawyer in California, who I had been checking in with every thirty days for two years, had told me to put his business card between my teeth and not to say a word until he was by my side if I was ever arrested.

That had been a great plan when we made it. Not so good now. He was on the other side of the continent and I couldn't be fur-ther away from having the money I needed to pay him. I had paid his retainer, after Bradley was busted in 1994 at the San Francisco International Airport. But paying Alan's fees had been the least of my worries back then and I had never tried to connect with Alajeh to gather lawyer money for myself.

One of the marshals drove my car out of the bank's drive-thru and pulled up alongside the vehicle I was sitting in. The other SUV pulled up behind my car, and the marshal directing traffic hopped into the passenger seat of the vehicle I was in and barked "Go!" into his walkie-talkie. They were so serious, so military, like they had just captured O. J. Simpson. I looked down at my Birkenstocks and hairy knees, then imagined my cattywampus sunglasses and my hair sticking straight up from my head, looking like it was scared. I certainly didn't look my part in this drama, not like the notorious and dangerous criminal they were congratulating themselves for capturing. I felt as though I looked more like a harmless mental patient who had wandered off sleepwalking in her pj's.

I felt obliged to at least right my sunglasses on my nose, but I couldn't, not with my hands cuffed behind my back, so I just shook them off my face instead. They fell quietly to the floor next to a children's book covered in a child's crayon additions. Was this the work of the driver, my captor? I laughed, imagining that Opie was the one who had drawn the barely discernible tiara on the cartoon girl's head and was the one who had placed the magic wand or unicorn's horn atop the little pony's crown. I noticed a few other telltale signs of the car's other identity: dog hairs and crumbs. It struck me as odd that the vehicle I was being carted away in was a family car. "I have to feed my cats," I told Opie again.

"Your neighbors will take care of them." Opie clearly had a pet too and he said this with enough confidence that I believed it. But I wanted to be sure he wasn't just talking out of the side of his head. Larry and Melony were out of town and would not be home until late that night or the next day. I also had neighbors to the east and neighbors to the west of my house. The ones to the west were too far away and strangers who were never home.

"Which neighbors?"

He grabbed the lip of a file and pulled back the cover. Inside was a stack of official-looking paperwork. He read from one of the enclosed forms. "Larry. He'll be back tonight. Does that work?" He closed the folder and his comrade in the passenger seat pulled the file back into a whole stack of these folders in his lap. Opie put the vehicle into drive and we bolted from the parking lot. A policeman was holding traffic so all three vehicles could leave the lot together.

"Hold on!" the comrade warned me too late. I was instantly rolling around like a ball in the backseat. I wasn't playing though. I was sitting forward in my seat when he took off. If you are sitting forward in your seat and handcuffed when the car makes a sudden turn, you can't hold on, so over you go. I stayed down when my face hit the seat. It wasn't the most ideal position to be in, but it worked. I suddenly wanted to close my eyes and wake up from this dream.

The car stopped almost as soon as we had left the parking lot, and it turned. I could feel the bump of another curb. I struggled to get myself up and back into the seated position to see where we were. I knew we hadn't gone far, but I couldn't think of a police station near the bank. I was surprised to see we had pulled into the reserved spaces outside the U.S. Post Office, practically across the street from the bank.

The marshal driving my car parked it next to us, locked it, and handed my keys to Opie. He jumped into the other SUV with marshal number three and they took off. Opie was left with just the one marshal and me. They got out of the car, opened my door, and beckoned me back out of the vehicle. Then they walked me around to the front of the building to the main entrance. I saw the Subway shop across the street with a poster picturing the very sandwich I had intended to be eating at that moment. Had it not been for this little interruption, I would probably be leaving there already, maybe even back in my car, opening a brand-new pack of cigarettes and heading home.

We walked into the post office's main lobby. They walked me right past the front of the small line of people waiting their turn to step up to the counter. Opie had his hand hooked around my right arm and his comrade held my left. I didn't know anybody there, but the odd looks they gave me still hit like stones.

"You're mailing me to California?" Opie and the marshal didn't respond to my feeble attempt at humor. I wasn't being a smart-ass, but when I am about to have a breakdown, I turn into a comedian.

Unfortunately, this defense mechanism doesn't serve me very well, but I can't help it.

We walked around the corner where post office boxes lined the walls on either side, and at the end of the hall was an elevator. I had never noticed it before. It had the look of a freight elevator or some such beast. It had a cage, serving as a portal that we needed to enter before you could reach the elevator door. This is what gave it the look that had prompted me to ignore it all the times I had been here. To my surprise, the cage was locked, and this little detail gave the elevator new meaning.

As we waited for the elevator to arrive, I asked, "How long do you think we'll be?"

As we got onto the elevator, Opie told me, "Play your cards right, and this will be over sooner." "Sooner" didn't sound good. I wished he had said "soon" instead of "sooner."

We took the elevator to the third floor. I thought how odd it was that I had never considered this building in its entirety before. To me, the interior of our post office was made up of the two people behind the counter and the lobby where people waited in line or checked their mailboxes. Nothing beyond that even existed as far as I was concerned.

It was a big old building, perhaps from the turn of the century or earlier. It was made of the same old red brick from which all of the oldest buildings in Brattleboro were made. It was the largest, several stories tall, and yet it had never occurred to me to wonder about the rest of its interior. Who would have guessed, though, that the set from Andy Griffith's jail in Mayberry was hidden in here?

We walked into what looked like a conference room that had been abandoned after the Cold War. I frantically scanned each passing object as if I might find my fate etched into a desk pad. *How much do they know? Had someone given me up? What is an information warrant?* I felt light-headed, hungry, thirsty, and nauseous, but I had to just keep my head on straight until I knew what the hell was happening to me.

The room was big and filled with filing cabinets and a couple of steel desks with big clunky desk lamps and old heavy black telephones with rotary dials. Opie sat down and dialed somebody's number and the sound of the number dial spinning amused me. I went with the other guy down a short dark hall. He opened the door to a room that seemed to be full of sunlight.

Inside the brightly lit room there were two jail cells, side by side. The bars were painted the same creamy white as the walls, and the fixtures inside the cells were made of orange and yellow plastic. There was a toilet and a sink in each of the cells. I felt my stomach turn to the sound of metal scraping metal as the door opened and they released my elbows. I stepped forward hesitantly, knowing the next sound I heard was the fate I had not been able to grasp. The metal clanged as he pushed the cell door shut, and then the grind of the key and lock echoed in my ears. Opie said something, I don't know what, and he and his comrade left the room, closing the other door behind them.

I stepped forward, eyes closed, and turned to sit down on the plastic bench. I opened my eyes and stared blankly forward. For a few moments my mind was absolutely empty, my ears were ringing, and the only thing I could see in front of me were the white bars and the lockwork of the door that held me.

Then as suddenly as a shot fires and horses race, my senses came rushing in. I got up, paced, sat down, got up, repeat. There was nothing to focus on in the room and I couldn't control the barrage of horrid thoughts ripping though my soul: *Edith, Dum Dum, the Subway sandwich, the bank teller counting out twenties, the sunbathers decorating the rocks on the drive into town, a lit cigarette, the back door of my house open, the feds watching me from my woods, Alajeh's face, the goat in his backyard with its throat cut.* My heart was racing and I felt cold and hot all at once. I closed my eyes again and took slow, deliberate breaths, but I kept seeing an image of Hester jump from the fracas in my head.

I couldn't get my mind to slow down, not long enough to have a cohesive thought about my predicament. I was hungry, having a nicotine fit, thirsty, and on top of everything else, I had to use the toilet, and not to pee. There was no clock and I did not have my watch on. *Why hadn't I put my watch on?* An hour might have passed before I finally decided to get someone's attention. It might also have been only five minutes. I couldn't tell. "Hello!" I had to tell them what I needed to do, so no one would walk in on me. "Anyone out there?" I kept calling like this, wondering where they had gone, until I finally heard the sound of footsteps approaching the door.

Opie's comrade, the young, handsome marshal, stuck his head in. "Keep it down! We're on the phone out here." He started to close the door, then popped his head back in. "You okay?" He asked in an impatient way that suggested he had no intention of helping me, even before he heard my problem.

I told him, "I'm fine. But I need to use the ladies' room." He looked at the toilet I was sitting next to, then at me, then back at the toilet.

"It works." He rolled his eyes and pointed at the all too obvious solution to my problem. "Shouldn't be too much longer. We're just waiting to hear back about the rest of your friends. You're all being arrested." He said this as though he was thrilled to be giving me this news. Up to that point, he had not impressed me as being mean, but his snarky comments made him seem less than friendly. I don't know why I would have expected otherwise.

The door shut and I looked at the toilet. I was getting pretty uncomfortable but decided to wait. I didn't want to get caught on the toilet and the marshal had said they would be back soon. The one and only time I had ever pooped in front of another human being was at Alajeh's compound. Hester, Henry, Bradley, and I had shared the same bathroom. When we were all sick at the same time, there had been no room for privacy.

Instead of having a complete meltdown the minute the marshal told me they were busy picking all my friends up, I did nothing. I had no reaction whatsoever. Instead, the gravity of his words slowly sank in and much bigger trouble than I had even considered started to materialize. My pulse quickened. *He said we are all being arrested. Who does he think we all are?*

If they were really arresting everyone, no one would be free to collect money for the lawyers' fees. *Oh my God! Who would assure Alajeh that no one is talking?* Fear washed over me like ice water and I dry-heaved a couple of times, but my stomach was empty, so this just made me dizzy. My thoughts turned to garbage in a blender. You get used to that feeling if it's an everyday thing, you can even function, but it had been too long and I was out of practice. I collapsed onto the plastic bench, doubled over, and started rocking back and forth, rhythmically pushing the balls of my feet into the cement floor.

I could imagine Hester, Phillip, Piper, Molly, Craig, Garrett, Edwin, Donald, and Henry out there somewhere, being watched by the police, or on their way to or already sitting in a cell like mine. I optimistically thought that if Alajeh knew what was happening, maybe he had already dispatched his people to get us the lawyers we would need, post our bail, get us out, and assess the damage. Maybe. But if they really had us all, that would be an awful lot of money and lawyers to come up with. I did the math. They had needed twenty-five thousand for Garrett's friend's bond and twenty-five thousand for his lawyer in Chicago when he was arrested in January of 1994. Bradley had needed the same amount later that year in July, in San Francisco. *Wait! Who had pointed them to me?*

If it was the same guy who had fingered Bradley or if it was Bradley himself who was talking now, they wouldn't know Piper, Garrett, or anyone who came after Molly and Craig. That might make a difference as to who and how many they had arrested. Ten of us would require at least half a million dollars. Alajeh would have to do something with that many potential leaks. Would he just kill us all or get us all lawyers and bail? I thought maybe it would depend on which would be harder to get done fast, and that depended on who and how many of us they really had. It was clear someone was doing an awful lot of talking, even if these officers were wrong and thought they had everyone but didn't really. Alajeh would know our arrests, whoever we were, meant that there were beans spilling.

Whoever they had, there were places we would not be safe, places where Alajeh could get to people quickly. I knew Alajeh had friends in Cook County Jail in Chicago, someplace in New York, and Los Angeles. He used to brag about these things. Would he trust this many people to be quiet? He wouldn't even know who most of them were. He would know Hester, but she was in Austin, Texas. It might take a minute longer to get to her and me—me in Brattleboro and wherever they may have taken her in Texas—but if he thought any of us might spill the beans, he would be expected to make sure we didn't. Everyone else I knew would be taken right to the places where Alajeh had friends and he could easily act quickly. He would know me, Phillip, Hester, Henry, and . . . Had Garrett ever been introduced to him?

The sun that had filled the room was growing weaker. As it sank in the sky, a shadow from the window crawled slowly up the wall. When it reached the ceiling, I couldn't take the waiting or the silence any longer. I had to deal with the situation while I could. Alajeh wasn't going to send lawyers or bail. That was stupid wishful thinking. I didn't know how much time these fools thought they had before my sister and I were dead, but it was more time than we thought we had. I started banging on the bars with my Birkenstocks, buckle side up, yelling and crying out whatever nonsense I could get out from the blender in my head. "You're going to get everyone killed!"

12 Wheels on the Bus Go Round and Round

I STARED AT A SMALL BLACK ASHTRAY sitting on a wooden end table. Both looked completely out of place in the bright sterile room my cell was in. The ashtray was old and chipped, made of plastic, and scarred from its former life probably in a Burger King smoking section. *Is it possible to smoke in the post office?* Every time I stood up again and started pacing, I saw this empty promise, this stupid piece of plastic, and it made me want to scream. I knew nicotine withdrawal was intensifying my panic, but the wave would pass. I sat down and tried not to look in the direction of anything that bothered me: the door, the ashtray, or the clipboard sitting on the end table next to the ashtray. *What is on that clipboard?*

I imagined similar clipboards somewhere in San Francisco, Chicago, and New York, each containing a list of everyone they were arresting today, and I got angry. I recalled the risks I had taken in Jakarta to make sure Alajeh never got to know who my friends were, and just like that, these morons could produce a handy list for him. I had no doubt he would find out we were all in custody and he would find a way to get to that list if it existed, especially if there was a copy available in Chicago. There were plenty of people in law enforcement who were working with Alajeh or for the organization that owned him. I had to find out two things fast: who all had been or were about to be arrested, and were the guys who had me in this cell squeaky clean. The answer to the first question determined what I hoped was the answer to the second.

The two men finally came through the door. The marshal stood against the wall, and Opie, the U.S. Customs agent, pulled a wooden straight-back chair in from the outer room and placed it in front of my cage. I don't know why, but I remembered Eliot Ness, the guy who went after Al Capone during Prohibition. Maybe because he was a government agent too. I wished it were Ness here. Eliot Ness hadn't been corrupt, and he'd been invincible. But the government had sent Opie Taylor to question me, not Ness. *Can I trust him? Even if I can trust him, can he handle this right? And what about his young, handsome comrade, the marshal?* Opie sat down and told me a story about the limited seating on a bus. If I got on his so-called bus, I might still get a seat. He explained it was too late to be first, but I didn't want to be last. What he was really explaining in his condescending analogy was that they already knew I was an accessory to a serious crime and there was a race on between me and everyone else they had arrested to get seats on his bus.

I asked him who else had been arrested. He assured me that everyone had been picked up already or would be soon. But I still didn't know if he really even knew who "everyone" was. Maybe, to him, "everyone" just meant me. Maybe it meant me and Phillip, and maybe Garrett. It didn't seem likely though. He had made it sound like they had a bunch of us.

I looked for clues to Opie's true nature as he spoke, watching for a wink or a nod, some indication as to whether he was a pawn of Alajeh's or not. I could hear his watch ticking when he leaned forward to talk and held on to the bars near my face. My heart was in my throat. These seconds slipping away might determine whether my sister and I, and my friends, lived through the night, not whether I would get a seat on his stupid bus. Alajeh was impetuous. His response to this situation would be quick. I couldn't predict what he would do when he found out all of his escorts and couriers were in custody at the same time.

It became clear the only hope I had, if they really had all of us, was Opie. If he was on the right side of the law and wasn't a pawn of Alajeh's, he was the only way I could make sure nobody got to the others, *especially my sister*. If Opie was somehow connected to Alajeh, then I reasoned we were all dead anyway.

If that was the case, I might as well get my inevitable demise over fast. But my poor sister. I had to push out of my head the idea of her being afraid like I was at the moment, dying alone, being murdered in some cell in Texas, or I could not function. I wished Phillip was with me—not that he was arrested, but that we could sort the dilemma out together one more time, to know for certain what was the right move. If I was about to die or cause the same to happen to Hester, and Opie here was my assassin, surely he'd let me smoke my last fucking cigarette. It's not like I might slip away. *Hmm.* If Opie let me light up in a federal building, that would be pretty telling.

"Can I smoke a cigarette?" I blurted out my first response to his incessant storytelling and stood up from my bench.

"Yeah. Go ahead." He turned and grabbed the ashtray that had been taunting me for hours. I didn't have any fucking cigarettes though. Of course. Time wasn't going to stop while they found me a cigarette and I tried to figure Opie out.

"I don't care about the seats on your fucking bus. If you want my help, there are some people you have to protect." I sat back down and paid very close attention to Opie. Whatever his response, I couldn't miss a word of it or a gesture.

He adjusted his position in the seat, uncrossed his legs, leaned forward, and asked, "From who?" The question infuriated me. He was either a fucking idiot or thought I was, no matter which side he was on. He knew who I needed protection from.

"If you don't know, then we need protection from you!" My filter was gone. My reply made sense to me, sort of. But his question was like a firefighter asking why he'd been called while standing in front of your world burning to the ground. Apparently, though, Opie didn't realize how stupid his question sounded to me.

"Who is 'we'?" He moved closer still.

"*We* are the people who will be dead soon, because *he* knows we are all sitting with someone like you right now being asked dumb questions." Then I fell apart. I was crying so hard I couldn't speak if I had wanted to. My nose was running and I started pacing back and forth like a caged animal. I found the toilet paper and blew my nose. "I want a cigarette."

Opie looked at the marshal still standing by the door, and the marshal shrugged his shoulders and left the room. *Oh shit!* Opie asking the marshal to leave him alone with me got my attention and scared me. Meanwhile, Opie got up and searched around the room we were in. I watched, wondering if he was looking for a weapon. He eyed the small end table sitting against the wall where the old black plastic ashtray had been sitting and pulled the table over to the bars. I couldn't figure out how he would use the table to kill me. He reached into his pocket, pulled out a pack of matches, and placed it in the ashtray, both an inch beyond my reach. "Catherine, we can't help you, your sister, or your friends unless you let us."

He didn't return to his bus analogy and now I knew they had Hester and at least some of my friends. Either Opie was trying to confirm he should kill me or he was for real, just a law-abiding agent trying to get me to confess. If he was for real, I think he knew I didn't care about his bus seats. He stopped talking about them. "Can I call my lawyer?" I asked.

"You have a lawyer?" he asked this as though I had actually admitted to murder. "He's not going to warn your boss, is he?" I wondered how he knew my lawyer was male and it spooked me. I thought for a split second that Alajeh might have gotten to my lawyer too. It had been two years since I'd retained him. *Did I ever tell Alajeh my lawyer's name?*

"No. I need a lawyer and I have a number in San Francisco for one."

The agent explained that if I needed to, I could also have a lawyer appointed by the court. I could do this at my arraignment, but as soon as my arraignment happened, it was a game-changing event. I didn't know what he meant by that. He was very clear, though, about my right to have a lawyer present during any conversation that we had. He looked back toward the door and then put his hand on his own forehead like he was checking himself for a fever. "I want to help you." He sounded tired and frustrated.

It didn't seem like his frustration was directed at me or my refusal to cooperate with him or was about whether he should kill me or not. I didn't think it had anything to do with me. I recalled the children's book in his car. Opie was just doing a job. At the end of the day, he would go home, get drunk, and forget the day. I was probably making him late for the babysitter or something. He looked like he lived in Vermont, not California or Chicago. He was not part of Alajeh's long reach. I couldn't say what it was exactly that made me so certain Opie was on my side. I just was.

"Alajeh is going to know we have all been arrested," I said.

"How will he know that?" Opie asked.

"Somebody who works for you guys will tell the wrong person or is the wrong person. I don't know, but he will find out. As soon as he does, he'll just finish us all." By "you guys," I meant law enforcement in general. I had no idea exactly who Alajeh's connections were, but on my last trip for him a couple of years earlier, when he'd sent me not to smuggle anything but to check out the viability of smuggling drugs into various entry points in the United States, he had said he got his information about the best and worst places straight from the horse's mouth: people in Customs.

"We are not going to let that happen." His young comrade, the marshal, walked back into the room with two packs of generic cigarettes; one pack was menthol. I was happy to see him. The fact that Opie knew what I meant by finishing people had worried me for a second. That was an odd way to describe killing someone. I had never heard it from anyone but Alajeh.

Opie held the two packs up and I picked the red one, not the green menthols. He opened the pack, handed me a cigarette, and lit a match for me. "Smoke your cigarette. I will be right back." He got up and left, ignoring my objection to his leaving me. The young marshal stood by the door, leaning against the wall, and said nothing.

The marshal was my age, I thought, but at thirty-three it's hard to tell. He could have five years on me, plus or minus. He was very tall and really good-looking, and he had a sweet smile. "Everything is going to be okay now. You're making the right choices." It wasn't a choice. I wanted to try to explain to him how that was not the case. I didn't want him to confuse me with a good person. I did not feel like one at all, and there was no choice here. I was doing exactly what I had to do, the only thing I could do.

Opie came back into the room with one of the big clunky black phones from the desks we had passed on our way to my cell, the cord trailing behind him, and a notebook under his other arm. He plugged the phone into a jack on the wall outside my cell. He looked at his watch. It was a little after seven, so it would be after four in California. He handed me the receiver. "It's before five in California still. Do you know the number or do you need information?"

"I know it." I had been calling this number once a month for two years and had it memorized. I think Opie almost rolled his eyes when I said this but tried to pretend he was looking for something in the corner of the ceiling.

I considered what I could say in front of Opie while the phone rang, and I realized I hadn't followed the attorney's advice at all about saying nothing till he was there. I never really thought I would ever get *here*. But now, *here* I was. I realized we hadn't really thought this event out very carefully. Or we would have considered what to do about the distance between here and there. I got his answering machine. I left a message and hung up.

Opie called the assistant U.S. attorney—AUSA—in San Francisco who was in charge of the case and told her I was willing to make a proffer. I had never heard the term before. Opie told me a proffer is a statement that is inadmissible in court. It is what would make it possible for him to help me, my sister, and my friends without losing any precious time, while I tried to reach my lawyer. The AUSA apparently agreed to make sure that if my proffer—the inadmissible statement Opie had just told me about and that I was going to make—showed that protection was needed, she would do everything in her power to make sure that it was provided and quickly.

Once the call was over, the agent took the phone back into the other room and closed the room's door when he came back in. I assumed the marshal was right outside of it and that Opie was trying to make me feel a little safer about communicating my fears with him. Either that or he didn't trust the young marshal. Either way, I did feel a little less anxious.

"Okay, Catherine, so what are we looking at here?"

"I don't know exactly. But if the guy I used to work for finds out that a bunch of his former employees have been arrested at the same time, he will do whatever he has to, to make sure we don't talk." I knew my face was beet red. It made no sense that I would feel this way, but I was suddenly embarrassed.

"This is the African, Alajeh?" Opie sat with his hands on his hips, all ears, the clipboard and a pen just resting on his thigh.

"Yes."

"Do you think you are in danger now?"

"Yes. So is my sister. Please, you have to get to her. He will use her if he thinks he can and I think he might kill her if he can't use her. Did you arrest her?"

"No. We haven't arrested your sister." As he told me this, he seemed to think that this would make me happy. It didn't. I didn't want my sister to be arrested; it's not that. But I didn't want her unprotected. If she was completely unaware of what was happening right now, and . . . I saw an image of her in my head again, except now it was nighttime, and she didn't know someone was watching her. My heart started racing again. I could feel the emotion bubbling up like I was a soda and someone had just shaken me up. Opie asked, "What do you mean he will use her?"

"If he gets to her, I can't talk to you!" I started sobbing again and couldn't stop it. There were hiccups getting mixed in with my sobs too, so I couldn't speak. I had tried so hard to remain calm the whole day, but I was falling apart.

Opie reached through the bars and put his hand on my shoulder. "Come on, Catherine, I want to help you. It's going to be okay now. Tell me who we need to protect. We can get someone to them to keep an eye on things if that will make you feel better."

"Yes." I gave him an abbreviated list of names: Hester, Phillip, Piper, Garrett, Bradley, Henry. Just the ones I knew Alajeh knew for certain, Garrett cause I wasn't sure, and Piper because I didn't want to be responsible for her murder. I said she had been my lover, that's all, but like my sister, Alajeh might try to use her. Opie wrote the names down as I rattled them off. He told me not to worry, he was going to put things in motion, and we would all be okay.

About a half hour later, he came back, opened the cell door, and let me out. I followed him and the marshal out to the larger room. We sat at a big table with a big old cassette tape recorder sitting in the middle of it. Their questioning began by reading names off a list, one at a time, and asking me how the person was involved in our enterprise or with me. They had everyone's names, even people who I hadn't named and who didn't belong under their microscope, like some hooker I had met once in a hotel bar in Lagos. I had given her my address in the United States and told her she should come to America. I hadn't slept with her. She'd worked the bar at the hotel where Phillip and I had stayed. I felt betrayed by this, that Opie had already known so much. But for me to honor the proffer agreement with the AUSA and for them to know who really needed to be considered for protection, I had to answer their questions.

When we were done talking it was late, maybe ten o'clock at night. Opie asked if they could search my house. They were going to send two agents there and I could have them bring me back an outfit to wear. By agreeing to this, they would not have to get a search warrant. I would also be able to pick out the clothes I wore to court. *Going to court?* I would be going to court in California. I was still going to be extradited. I assumed I was on their hook now until they got Alajeh. I was about to agree when the other guy added that otherwise, I would be stuck with whatever the agents brought back for me to wear and I would have to spend the night in jail. That rubbed me the wrong way for so many reasons.

I was wearing what I had slept in, my sweatshirt and cutoff sweatpants. I hadn't planned on visiting with people that day, only two quick hops out of my car. All I had meant to do after the bank was grab a sandwich, get cat food and cigarettes, and pump gas. For these activities, my grungy getup was haute couture for Brattleboro, circa summer 1996. I was fine with what I was wearing, and they had just made it clear I wasn't going home to stay, so insinuating that letting them search my house meant I wouldn't be in jail was disingenuous if not outright deceitful. That is what irked me. I was entrusting these guys with my life.

Opie was quick to pick up on the damage his idiot friend might have just done to the trust he had taken all day to build with me. He recovered quickly, though, by smacking the other agent on the back of the head in a big you-dumb-ass gesture, and said, "Marshals!" as if he already knew all marshals were morons.

I agreed to the search, but only if I could be there when they did it. I feared they would leave my cats outside. I didn't want my Edith and Dum Dum to be eaten by a coyote, a fox, or a bear. They were not country girls and didn't have the sense to run. Edith would pick a fight and Dum Dum might want to play.

I had left the back door of my house open earlier, since I was only dashing into town. But that had been before lunch and it was dark out presently. In Newfane, nobody left their pets out overnight if they expected them to be alive in the morning. Even the feral barn cats stayed in the barn after dark. The girls weren't going to come inside for a guest and they would definitely hide from strangers tearing their house apart. If I could go with them, I could get them in, feed them, and let my neighbors know I would be gone for a couple of weeks. "At least," Opie added.

Opie and I drove out to my house, and the marshal and some new guy who showed up in the post office parking lot drove my car behind us. I hoped they wouldn't run out of gas but also secretly

wished they did. They had said no to stopping at the gas station
and market where I could get some cat food. I didn't have any cat
food. All I had was some sliced turkey in the fridge. I could cut that
up and feed them. But the principal of their not stopping for one
minute to get a can of cat food bugged me. Even Opie didn't budge
on this one thing and he clearly had a dog at home. Edith and Dum
Dum weren't part of this. They would eat the turkey, but they would
know something was wrong, and then when I didn't come home
later . . . *My poor babies.*

I felt horrible when they made me wait outside my own house
and come into the house only after Opie and the marshal had
checked it out. It was such a silly thing to get upset about, but it was
clear to me no one was in the house waiting to jump us. I guessed
they wanted to make sure the cats were not armed or that I wasn't
hiding an arsenal in there or that I would not turn on them and
run. Opie finally waved me and the new guy he had waiting with me
inside. Dum Dum was on the couch just starting her yoga moves,
so they hadn't scared her, but she gave me a funny worried look
and stopped her yoga short. I looked around for a minute and found
Edith crashed on my bed. She didn't budge, which was uncharac-
teristic behavior. She should have already been under the bed.

I flipped on all the lights. My house had art gallery lighting, so I
could make the interior as bright as a sunny day if I wanted. Opie
commented on how surprised he was at how nice my house was.
It looks so much smaller from the street. Dum Dum jumped onto
the island in my kitchen and sat by the water faucet. I turned it on
so that a small trickle of water came out and she started lapping it
up. I stared at her drinking the water while Opie asked me where to
look for certain things like phone bills and pictures and correspondence. I knew they were going to be disappointed by their so-called
search. I had nothing in my house. I had gotten rid of every shred
of my past and hadn't broken the law, not even the speed limit, for
more than two years since I'd walked away from that life.

When he wanted to see my pictures and I told him I had none,
he didn't believe it was possible. I told him about a day shortly after

Phillip's friend was arrested in Chicago when I had lost my mind, burned my phone bills, ditched my laptop, and packed all my postcards and photographs, even those that had nothing to do with the period spanning 1993 and 1994, into my favorite bit of luggage. I took the bag to the Dumpster but decided that was too obvious; someone might look inside a piece of nice luggage in a Dumpster or at the dump—Dumpster divers would spot my luggage for sure. Instead, I drove way up into the Northeast Kingdom of Vermont to get rid of it.

Northeast Kingdom is a largely uninhabited and mountainous area of Vermont that stretches for miles and miles. I didn't intend to take my suitcase of photos that far away; I just kept deciding I wasn't far enough away. I finally stopped when a snowstorm mandated I come to my senses and turn around. I had pulled off to the side of a deep ravine that dropped sharply at the edge of the small road I had been on, and I'd done a twirling curl, hurling the bag as far out, over, and down the ravine and into the woods as I could make it fly. I didn't think they would be interested in searching for the stupid bunch of pictures I had ditched. There wasn't anything useful there to find Alajeh with anyway. I think I had been trying to throw my whole past away.

They tore my place up, emptying drawers onto the floor, pulling my dishes out; even the food in my fridge was subject to their search. One guy asked if I would log on to the computer for him. He didn't need my help; it would just make it easier. I sat down at my desk, took one last look at the world from that seat, and logged in. The reality that I was leaving and might not be back set in when I stood up and gave him my seat. He started making copies of the files on my computer and looking through my email account at Sovernet.

He didn't mess with any of the Twelve-Twelve files and acknowledged knowing what we did and what we had already developed. "I don't understand why someone as smart as you got involved with drug smuggling. Was the money that good?"

He hadn't been present for my flip-out at the post office. I think he was a private consultant Opie had called in for this. He knew his way around my computer and some of the less user-friendly applications too. "It wasn't the money." I had to laugh at the irony. I would have probably been a millionaire a year later, as CTO of Twelve-Twelve. I went to my room to grab a comfortable outfit to wear on a plane and to court, and to pet Edith on the bed. She was not interested in being woken up. She almost acted like she was sick. But I knew that wasn't it. I think she knew I was going away for another trip. I hoped it would be quick.

I was stunned when they were finished searching my house so quickly and ready to go. I was also worried. It was past midnight and I had hoped Larry and Melony would get home in time for me to let them know I would be gone for a while and to ask them to feed the cats. My heart ached when Edith wouldn't get up to eat the turkey I had cut up for her. I grabbed her food bowl and put it on the bed with her. I picked Dum Dum up and gave her a quick hug and kiss on her cute little head, told her not to worry, I wouldn't be gone as long as I used to be gone, then put her down. I wrote a check out to Larry for two hundred dollars to get cat food and jotted a quick note explaining I had an emergency and had to leave but would call with details the next day about when I would be back. Then I followed the guys out the door, leaving the lights on for the cats and making sure Dum Dum didn't slip past anyone. She was a quick one.

Opie took the check and the note over to Larry and Melony's front door and slid it under. I sat in his SUV and stared at my own doorway. Dum Dum always jumped up to cling to the bottom edge of the window in my front door whenever I left the house. She could pull herself up and peek over the edge. She would be there when I came home too, peeking out the door, hanging on to the lip of the glass frame. It was cute as hell: a cat's version of the dance dogs do when their owners come home. I loved seeing her little head pop up every time I started the car to leave or pulled into the driveway. Not this time. I watched her pop up in the window. She held on until I couldn't see her little head silhouetted in the doorframe anymore. *Goodbye, baby. I'll hurry.*

13 Leaving on a Jet Plane, Don't Know When I'll Be Back Again

"THIS CALL IS FROM THE Chittenden County Jail from . . ." There was a slight pause in the computer-generated message, and then the recording I'd made earlier of me saying my name was played, like it had always been part of the sentence and I wasn't a transient interloper in the prison's phone system. "Cleary." I heard my own recorded voice saying my name and it sounded weird, not like myself. "This call will be monitored and recorded. To accept this call, press one. To refuse this call, press two. If you . . ." I could hear my father fumbling with the phone. God, please don't let him hit the wrong number.

Of course, he did not hit the wrong number. Dad was someone you wanted to have at your side during a serious crisis. Movies like *The Russia House* and *The Hunt for Red October* made me homesick. My father acted and looked so much like Sean Connery. My mom was the complete opposite; she was the screaming girl who always broke a heel at the wrong moment or had to be slapped out of hysterics if, for example, she was late for an appointment.

"Hello . . . Cleary . . . What's going on?" I had needed to psych myself up in order to make this phone call. I had never been in trouble with the law before, much less called home from a jail. I didn't think my parents had ever received a call like this from anyone before in their lives. What I hadn't prepared for was the phone system just coming right out and telling my father that I was in jail. He sounded calm, not angry, when he answered. But my father never sounded angry; if he was actually mad, he still sounded calm. But this wasn't that kind of calm. It was the concerned kind. I was ready for his angry calm, the look-what-you-have-done or you-made-your-own-bed-young-lady calm, but not this weary concern.

"Dad." My fucking voice was cracking already. I couldn't even say that much.

"Honey. Tell me what's wrong. Why are you in jail? Start from the beginning." His voice was so soothing. Maybe every father's voice is like medicine to every daughter in the world facing a personal crisis of this magnitude. But my father was the only person on Earth who could say two words and make any problem, even one as big as I had just dropped in his lap, feel survivable.

I heard my mother screech "What?" in the background. My father must have covered the phone with his hand. There was a brief muffled conversation, and then I could clearly make out him saying "Be still." There it was. That was his angry calm voice, stern and commanding. But it was directed at Mom, who was probably acting like our nervous Chihuahua, Lizzy, did right before she peed on the floor. Mom was not the calm type, not even for small things, and her daughter calling from jail was hardly a small event.

"Cleary, your mother is here with me. Tell us what is going on before she has a nervous breakdown." There was Dad's dry wit. I couldn't help it. I tried to control my emotions, but like bats in a cave set to escape, one got out, and I laughed out loud inappropriately. I loved my dad so much. Mom too, but only Dad could do this trick, make me laugh when it hurt to breathe.

"I'm okay, Dad. But I'm in really big trouble." I had to stop for a second and take a deep breath. It turned into a sob, and the rest of my sentence probably sounded like "Mwabla blubber blubber, and then Mwaaaa blubber blubber."

"Honey, did you murder someone?" I could hear Mom's audible gasp when he said this.

"No, Dad. I didn't murder anyone. But blubber, and then Mwaaaa blubber blubber."

He interrupted my unintelligible gibberish. "All right, honey. Whatever it is, it's not the end of the world. We'll get through this. Take a deep breath, Cleary. We're here. We're not going anywhere." Then he was quiet with me. He was a thousand miles away, but we were *being still,* as if he were right there beside me, and then I was breathing again. I was also sniffing and hiccupping and about to throw up, but I could take a deep, soothing breath again. If I were at home, he would sit quietly with me like this, being still, and with something this bad, he would put his arm around me until I stopped sobbing, at least stopped long enough so that I could breathe right and speak coherently. I could hear Mom asking to talk to me, then he covered the phone again for a second. "Okay. Let's start from the beginning. What happened?"

"I'm being extradited to California for smuggling drugs." I got that out. Now all I had to do was ask if he had heard from my sister, his little baby girl, and I had to make sure I didn't run out of time on the phone. There was a fifteen-minute limit on phone calls; after that I would be cut off, and it was a long wait for the phone if I didn't finish my conversation in one shot. "I'm so sorry."

"Dear God." It sounded like I had just knocked the wind out of him when he said this. I had never heard this helplessly wounded calm before. I stood up straight, sucked my sadness, fear, and angst up in one big deep breath, and stuffed it down as far as I could push it, as far as I needed it to be to convince my father I was all right. We would be cut off in moments and I couldn't let this connection die, not until I knew he could handle my being locked up, my being so far beyond his reach and his ability to fix this for me. It would make him crazy. I would rather he be mad at me, furious even, than have to think of him worrying about me.

He could help me, though, by helping my sister. I needed him to write me off as a lost cause, but in good hands, and focus on saving her. "Dad, I love you so much. But this call will get cut off soon. I have a lawyer. I'm going to be all right. I will give you his number and he can tell you everything that is going on. But right now I need you to do something." I got this all out as fast as I could.

"Anything, honey. Tell me." I could tell that he had just put me on speakerphone and it worried me. I didn't know if being on a speakerphone was allowed. There were so many rules for phone calls in the Chittenden County Jail. Not all of them would be obvious, like someone picking up a second phone in the house could be considered a three-way call. I didn't know. But the call would get cut off, and I would have my phone privileges suspended until I could see a counselor. So I hurried through the rest of the information. I had to make sure he got it before something stupid like that happened.

"Call Hester and tell her to come home. Don't take no for an answer. She is in trouble too. She needs to know that the people who arrested me will help her, but she has to trust me and be honest with them, completely honest. Tell her not to be afraid." I listened to the dead air between us, praying he didn't drop dead from a heart attack while he absorbed the impact of everything I had just said to him. Mom was silent, so she had either passed out or Dad was sitting on her.

"We will get her on the next plane home." His voice was calm again, a flat calm. "Your brother is here now." I could hear the subtle change in his voice that told me he was going to be all right. My father was as smart as a whip, and he knew what was going on. I didn't need to fill in too many blanks. After I had written my first novel, and before I burned it in my backyard, I had asked him to read it. Dad was an editor, after all. He had asked me how I had come up with such a great plot. I confessed that I had actually lived parts of the fiction. This, of course, was the reason I later burned the novel in my backyard.

"I'm going to give you my lawyer's phone number. He will update you." I hoped they had a pen nearby. The phone had just beeped three times. That was the three-minute warning we were about to be cut off.

"I'm ready. Go ahead." It was Mom. She sounded so business-like, not hysterical at all. I gave her my lawyer's phone number. She read it back, then asked me, "Is there a number where we can reach you?"

"No, Mom. It's for outgoing calls only." I was referring to the phone I had called them from.

"Do you know your counselor's name yet?" I was stunned by this question. How did she know about stuff like that? I had only just found this out myself, that a counselor was assigned to me and that I would be meeting with him the following morning. "You mean my lawyer?"

"No, honey, your counselor. You will get one even if you are only there long enough for that. When you find out, call us back and tell me." I remembered my mom was teaching adult basic education in the Hamilton County jail in Cincinnati. I told her the man's name and added that I didn't know how long I would be there. "I love you." She said this and I believed it, but it was almost disorienting having my mother be so matter-of-fact about the conversation we were having, when she should be in hysterics.

"I love you too, Mom. I'm so sorry." I made the short, sharp gasp of a fresh surge of sobs about to escape. Mom could tell or she was psychic.

"Don't let the women see you cry like this, honey." When she said this, I could almost hear Rod Serling welcoming me to the Twilight Zone. My mother coolly telling me not to cry was a sure sign we had entered a parallel universe. Mom was the crybaby, not me.

"Okay." I took a deep breath and held it, waiting out the passing wave of tears and snot.

"Cleary!" I heard my father interject this and knew it meant to quit it, that I should breathe. But I would sob if I let myself exhale.

"Gene! Cleary isn't in the right place to have a breakdown. Honey, you listen to me. Pull yourself together until you can find yourself a private little corner. Go there and have a good cry, sweetie. Go to the chapel. That is a safe place. You can cry there." I heard muffled conversation again. We were definitely in the Twilight Zone now, no doubt. This was probably Mom covering the phone to tell Dad to calm down.

"Hello!" I couldn't let the time run out on our phone call while they bickered, although that was more normal behavior.

"You are going to be fine. You know what, honey? Saint Anthony tried to jump today!" Mom came back and was all excited and happy when she told me this, like everything was clear to her now and all was well. I knew exactly what she was talking about. I was so happy she was her Looney Tunes self again.

A whole team of those crazy bats escaped from my chest and I burst out laughing instead of crying. We had a statue of Saint Anthony in our library at home who occasionally wanted to end it all by jumping to his death from the bookshelf he lived on. The statue didn't actually jump, but no matter what we did to correct the vibration causing its slow move to the edge of the shelf, every once in a while we would find him facedown in the carpet.

Mother, due to her slightly superstitious and deeply Southern Catholic genetics, accredited our Saint Anthony statue's suicidal tendencies to messages from God. Of course, his messages were usually a bit more trivial than what she suggested now. Saint Anthony was invoked in our household with prayers for lost keys or earrings; his leaps were to announce it was time to look again. Mom recommended I go to the chapel and find a copy of Saint Anthony's prayer to recite until I could get my head on straight. I supposed a lost mind could be considered worthy of a jump from Saint Anthony.

"Your brother Gene wants to say something before we go. We're going to call your sister Hester when we hang up the phone." She gave the floor to my brother. I could hear her heels on the ceramic tiles in our kitchen as she walked away from the phone. I could picture the three of them huddled around the phone there. Mom always did that, say "your brother Gene" or "your father Gene." This introduction added clarity when having a phone conversation, such as we were, since they had the same name. But she also did this for Hester, which struck me as funny. She was my only sister and the only Hester we knew; the distinction was unnecessary. Mom also signed all her letters to me as Catherine C. Wolters, aka Mom. Maybe she did that in letters to my sister and brother, but again, the distinction in my case was superfluous. I would know I hadn't written myself.

"I love you, Cleary." I could tell my brother was crying by the way he pronounced his words so deliberately. I didn't get to respond.

The phone call was cut off and I turned away from the wall to find a rather large and angry woman staring me down as if I was on her phone, in her house, on her time. I was, but I didn't know that yet. She picked the receiver up before I had even gotten clear of the stool in front of the phone, then slammed it against the plastic box on the wall. "No, you didn't!" She held the receiver out to show me.

There was evidence on the phone handle of the sweat I had broken out in while on the phone revealing the news to my parents that I was in jail. I had thoughtlessly failed to clean it off before this woman had picked it up. It was bad etiquette, and gross, like failing to wipe down a stationary bike in the gym. The angry woman starting going off, very loudly, about how nasty I was. I was a white trash bitch and a number of other not-so-niceties. I tried to wipe the receiver down with my shirt, but before I could make that mistake, a lady jumped from the line and handed me a wad of tissue.

"She's federal." The tissue lady said this to the angry woman, who now had her arms crossed against her chest and was towering over me like a giant. She uncrossed her arms, stepped back, and apologized. It was the weirdest thing. The nice lady who had saved me with the tissues told me she would come by my bunk when she got off the phone and give me the lowdown on "this fucking romp-a-room." She was referring to my temporary new home. "Don't talk to these imbecile bitches." She pointed her chin in the general direction of the TV room, a space shared by the inhabitants of a handful of rooms in our wing of the Chittenden County Jail where everyone sat, glued to an episode of *Jerry Springer*.

There was a desk against the wall near the phone bank, home

to an overly made-up woman in a uniform. She had a long chain attached to her belt that had so many keys on it, it passed for a gaudy accessory, rather than a functional collection of keys. From what I could tell, her job was the sitter at the desk and the keeper of fire. I had literally jumped for joy that morning when I'd arrived there after my brief engagement in the courthouse, feeling suicidal, homicidal, and overdressed and overheated in my multilayered travel outfit. When I first saw her go to a doorway separating the sitting room from a very small grassy triangle outside, where she lit the cigarette of either an astonishingly young girl or a dwarf, I had nearly cried I was so happy to get to smoke. I had learned that smoking cigarettes was permitted when that door was open. Lighters and matches, however, were forbidden. In order to smoke the permitted cigarettes, the guard had to light them for us.

I asked the keeper of the fire where the chapel was located. She told me it was closed. I was not, by any means, a religious individual. But in much the same way chocolate pudding and mashed potatoes are comfort foods, I found that religious icons, churches, and priests could be soothing, just without all the calories. It probably had something to do with being raised by my father, the almost-priest, and my guilty Catholic mother, and then spending all that time in Catholic school with the nuns. Whatever the cause, Mom's suggestion had given me something constructive to do the next day if I was still there.

Two weeks later, when two marshals finally arrived to whisk me away to California, my bunkie inherited most of the commissary I had just received, my sneakers, and a couple of bits of precious comfortable clothing that a friend from Brattleboro had brought to me. Even though a lot of what my bunkie had counseled me about was useless bullshit, she'd also had a lot of commonsense advice for me that was priceless.

She had already completed a five-year federal sentence but had screwed up on the last year of her federal probation. She blamed this on her being reassigned to a new officer for her supervision. She said this new officer turned out to be a nut job. He got her fired from her job by repeatedly harassing the people she worked with. He then followed her from that job to her next job and did much the same, by walking up to a table she was taking an order from at lunch rush and handing her a cup to go pee in. While she was in the bathroom filling the little portable specimen cup, he asked both her manager and the owner of the restaurant for their driver's licenses. He told them he needed to run a background check on them because my bunkie could not associate with other felons. She lost that job too. She gave up and turned herself in to the probation office. She told them she was unable to comply with the employment requirement.

I flipped my wig while listening to her tell the story. I asked why she had not gotten a lawyer involved, reported the guy to his superiors, anything other than what she had done. She had laughed at my inexperience with the system, which was about to swallow me whole. I prayed she was wrong. I prayed that her story was bullshit, that she and her hippie-looking husband, who I had seen with her in the visiting room, were addicts or something. Maybe she had fucked up and gotten high and didn't want to admit to being so stupid. What she'd said couldn't be true. Otherwise, I could not completely discredit the one piece of advice she'd repeated more than any: "Don't cooperate with those motherfuckers. They're evil." I hadn't told her that I was relying on them to protect my sister, my family, and all my friends.

Two marshals—a man and a woman in their midfifties—picked me up that day. They drove a burgundy SUV unmarked by the presence of family life, like Opie's vehicle had been. It seemed like they were an older married couple or they could have been longtime professional partners. The woman shackled me while the man handled the paperwork for their parcel, me. The woman was very apologetic about the shackles but assured me I would be happy that she was the one who put them on and not her partner.

I told her about the bruises I had gotten from my last adventure in shackles. I shuffled into the backseat of their van and realized she hadn't been any more generous with the room she'd left for my ankles in the cuffs than the previous guy had been. We started our drive.

About two hours into the drive, I asked them where we were going. My query triggered a conversation between the two of them, but not an answer. They were trying to decide where to stop and grab something to eat quickly. They chose a McDonald's drive-thru. They placed their order and turned to me as an afterthought. "Do you want something?"

"Yes, please. Thank you."

"Okay. Don't tell on us." She smiled, a weird, crooked, toothy grin, and her hairline jumped backward when she did so.

"Okay," I responded blankly.

"Add a small Coke, cheeseburger, and fries to that!" She yelled into the drive-thru's intercom without asking me what I wanted.

"Do you have to use the little girls' room?" She made the weird smile again, and again her hairline moved as if she were wearing a wig that moved when she smiled.

"How much longer till we get to where we are going?" I didn't really have to go, but I could make it happen if we were going to be driving for much longer.

"Yes or no. Do you have to go?" She was short with me and didn't turn to me to add her big scary smile and wiggle-wig head trick.

"Yes." I wondered why she wouldn't tell me where we were going.

"Okay, that wasn't so hard. Let's eat while it's hot. You're not going to pee yourself, are you?" She laughed, turned, and did the freaky smile again.

"No."

The guy pulled the SUV over into a parking space. She handed me my food and my Coke. I had never had to negotiate something so simple with handcuffs on. I was wearing my layers again, a long thick knit skirt for court over my cutoff sweat-shorts for leisure time. This made it difficult to place the cup of Coke between my legs and apply the right pressure without popping the plastic lid off. One near miss was enough to convince me not to try. I held on to the cup with one hand and ate with the other. I finished my food quickly, not wanting to be the holdup. When the lady was done with her lunch, she hopped out of the front seat and opened the sliding door.

"Lunch is over. Let's go." She took the Coke from me and tossed it on the ground. I slid over on the seat, twisted my feet out in front of me, intending to step down on the running board and then to the ground. The woman made a twirling motion with her finger at about the same moment I realized I could not step down with the shackles on my ankles the way they were. I turned around and backed out of the SUV without doing a face-plant and she took hold of my elbow. It dawned on me that we were going inside McDonald's to use the restroom.

"I can wait." I didn't want to be paraded in front of the people in the restaurant.

"Trust me. Take care of this now or you'll regret it later." She nudged me forward and I followed her lead, focusing only on the ground in front of me and not any of the people we passed.

She followed me into the bathroom but thankfully not into the stall itself. Getting my skirt, shorts, and underwear down was no problem, but getting them back up after I finished my business was almost impossible with the handcuffs and the chain wrapped around my waist.

"Hurry up in there!" the lady barked out, and I heard another customer in the restroom object and say she wasn't in any hurry. My escort laughed and told her we were late for a flight.

"I can't get my skirt up in the back."

"Open up." She knocked on the door when she said this. I opened the door. She reached around my back and roughly pulled my skirt back up and pulled the chain out of the way. I laughed nervously; it was like she was hugging me.

We finally arrived someplace about an hour later. I have no idea where, but it was past the Connecticut state line, an airfield of some sort—not a commercial airport, but there was a runway. It was surrounded by a few enormous airplane hangars. There were also several other SUVs, each with a pair of drivers like I had and passengers of their own. Two drivers to every sad sack like myself. I found it oddly comforting that there were other human beings on my side of this strange situation. Apparently, I was not getting my own private jet to San Francisco, as I had imagined.

Another hour passed while I sat in the back of the SUV. During that hour, a white bus pulled up to join our little line of vehicles. Four armed guards hopped out of the bus and started unloading. There were about fifteen men packed in the little bus, all dressed in khaki scrubs. They were struggling with their shackles, trying to shuffle down the aisle, negotiate down the stairs, and disembark. As if on cue, a huge plane was landing in our deserted airfield, much bigger than the group of people assembling on the tarmac would require.

When it finished taxiing and stairs were secured to its open doorway, a few militaristic marshals came down the stairs. A couple of them quickly positioned themselves around the plane. They were armed with M16s, dressed in dark blue tactical uniforms, and ready for war or a photo shoot. The other marshals had come down the stairs a little slower, dressed similarly but armed with clipboards and paperwork. These marshals waved the group of shackled men forward. The prisoners were led by the bus driver and their guards over to the plane. They were each subjected to a strange ritual they all appeared to know—lifting hair, sticking their tongues out, getting patted down—then they were prodded up the stairs, where they were greeted by a gigantic black woman. She wasn't fat though. She was big, as in football-player, don't-mess-with-me big. She had the meanest mug I had ever seen on a woman, and, well, I'm a lesbian.

When it was my turn in line, the guy who had driven me there walked me over and handed my paperwork to one of the marshals, who scanned his clipboard for my name. He found it, dismissed my escort with a nod, and waved me off to his side. "Wait right there." I waited by his side for everyone else to board the plane. I was soon joined by one of the armed marshals and then three other passengers like myself. According to the computer printout on his clipboard, I was listed as a flight risk. I told him it was a mistake. He laughed and fitted me with a nice little metal black box. It closed down over the intersection of the two handcuffs in such a way that it locked my wrists into a fixed position. He tightened my wrist cuffs and locked the box with a click. *Ouch.*

I stepped onto the plane and took in the jet that the marshal who had arrested me had told me about, the jet he'd said the U.S. marshals were preparing for me. There had to be more than a hundred men, dressed in the same khaki scrubs the guys from the white bus had been wearing, already seated. There were a couple of women in the front seats and I was directed to sit next to an older woman having an exceptionally bad hair day. She was dressed in street clothes like me, black-boxed like me, but she looked far more ragged than I felt. She turned and looked at me curiously. "Where are we?"

"Eyes forward, no talking, stay in your seat!" the big female marshal yelled as if she were trying to address a packed stadium, not the close quarters of our portable pokey.

The lady next to me ignored the big girl and repeated her question a little impatiently this time. "Where are we?"

"I'm not sure. I think we are in Connecticut." I still didn't know exactly where we were.

She accepted my answer and let her head fall against the window, closing her eyes and I think falling asleep the minute her head settled.

The guy in the seat behind me started pushing on the seatback. "Hey, why you got da box?"

"No idea." The big black marshal was walking back up the aisle, talking to one of her associates, so I ignored the persistent attempts of the guy behind me to get my attention and chat. He quit as soon as she passed by us and the plane started taxiing.

The ragged lady next to me popped her head up without opening her eyes and said, "That's right, baby. You don't know nothing," then slipped back into her nap.

The cabin smelled like it was suddenly infused with dirty oil, and the plane shook as it picked up speed for the takeoff, until it vibrated like it might be about to fall apart just before we left the ground. The noisy vibration stopped and I could feel the wheels being mechanically retracted back into the plane's belly with a squeal as something struggled to close. A little square plastic bag of water dropped onto my lap, then another onto the lap of my companion, as one of the marshals passed. I grabbed it before it slid off my lap and held on to it. I had never seen a bag of water before. The man sitting in the aisle seat across from me bit the bag, tearing it slightly with his teeth, and sucked the corner he had torn until the bag was empty. Then he made an awful face and dropped the bag on the floor between his knees. I decided the lady next to me had the right idea. I closed my eyes and tried to fall asleep.

14 Welcome to the Hotel California

San Francisco to Dublin, California
July 1996 to January 2003

LOCKS, WATCHES, AND CALENDARS are funny things. Every second is supposed to measure the exact same increment of time as every other second, right? Wrong. Some hours last days. At the same time, though, years can pass in a heartbeat, even if some of the days contained therein take forever. According to the calendar, almost seven years lapsed from the time I stepped onto that rickety jet full of convicts somewhere in Connecticut and the day I finally surrendered myself to the care of the Bureau of Prisons in Dublin, California. It took this much time for the wheels of justice to do what would normally have taken a few months. Two facts, in particular, best describe this long period: I was not living, nor was I doing my time. Time passed all the same. I turned forty, waiting.

I was thirty-three when the marshals got me out to California after my arrest in Vermont; I was released from jail while the courts made up their mind about me, but not released from California or their clutches. I was ordered to stay in the very same halfway house in San Francisco that Bradley had been in two years earlier. The residents of my new home in the heart of the Tenderloin referred to the place as just "Turk Street." That was not its real name, and its entrance was on Taylor Street. But it sits on the corner of Turk and Taylor Streets. It wasn't obvious to me why the residents opted to call it this, since both streets were equally dismal.

Turk Street was a far cry from my converted carriage house in the quiet, woodsy mountains of Vermont with Edith and Dum Dum. The first and most notable adjustment I had to make was to sound. The soothing noise of chirping birds and crickets at night was replaced with blasting boom boxes, sirens, arguments, cars backfiring, and gunshots. The second adjustment was to smell. The corner of Turk and Taylor Streets reeked of urine-soaked sidewalks and desperate poverty.

The day that I was released on my own recognizance, no bail, I was released directly from the courthouse and rode with Alan to his office, located in the financial district. When I left his office on foot, I had an hour left to get myself to the halfway house. Santa Rita, the county jail I had been deposited at for a few days, had lost my box of clothing, which should have followed me, so I had been sent to court wearing a pale yellow set of scrubs. The layered outfit that had made it with me all the way there was lost. I was released to my lawyer in the same yellow scrubs that I'd had to go to court in. Interestingly enough, nobody looked twice at my outfit as I walked down Battery Street and turned up Market.

I had no money, not one thin dime. I was starving and hadn't smoked in days. It had not occurred to me to ask my lawyer for a few dollars before making my walk to the halfway house. I had been too narrowly focused on getting from point A to point B in time, terrified I would screw up and get popped back into Santa Rita Jail. But the fresh air did a number on me, and I began to slow down and relax my frantic pace. I asked the few smokers I passed in the financial district if they could spare a cigarette, and they pretended as though they didn't see me or flat-out said no. I laughed when one really well-dressed young man shook his hands in front of his face and scurried away. I couldn't quite figure out the meaning of his gesture, but I knew what a beggar feels like for that second.

I recalled one time when I was in New York City. I had refused to reach into my pocket for money because I was afraid I might accidentally pull out a big bill instead of a single and get mugged. I was younger and had never been in the Big Apple. I had been cursed by the old woman who had asked for my change with scripture: "There, but for the grace of God, go you." I stopped in my tracks on Battery Street and laughed hard for a minute, wondering if I too had the power to curse people now, then continued on to Market Street. I looked over at my reflection, trudging past a storefront farther up Market, and almost tripped over someone sleeping on the sidewalk.

My reflection horrified me. I looked like hell. My hair was standing straight up like those little troll dolls, and my outfit made me look like an Easter egg. No one would recognize me, and I was grateful for that. I imagined running into Piper right then, and running to her, then chasing her down the street, all happy and open armed. "Hey, honey! I finally made it to San Francisco!" This amused me. She would poop her fancy pants.

I stopped short before stepping on a sleeping lump and realized there was a whole crew of young, dirty, tattooed, and pierced bodies lining the sidewalk. I asked a girl sitting among the odd youth of San Francisco, and smoking, for a cigarette. She pulled a pack of Rothmans out of her dingy, torn leather jacket, riddled with large silver spikes. She lit the cigarette for me, looked at the black lipstick she had left on the butt-end, handed it over, and announced she was STD-free. I wasn't sure if there was more I should say, other than thank you, in response. It took me a few steps more to figure out that STD-free meant she had no sexually transmitted diseases and I shouldn't worry that she had just had the cigarette in her mouth, not that the cigarettes were free.

Then I entered an astonishingly bad neighborhood and found my new home. Each floor of the building served a different community. One floor was for drug rehab, another for state criminals. The top floor and all of the first floor except the entrance to the building were reserved for federally sponsored residents of one sort or another. This was made up of mostly men who had completed their sentences but were doing the last six months in the halfway house, a handful of pretrial detainees like myself, and one older woman who was serving her whole six-month sentence at the house. She was my roommate.

Turk Street wasn't as bad as being in a county jail the size of Santa Rita. If you thought I was a crybaby in the Chittenden County Jail, it was nothing compared to my crying binges and panic after just a couple of days in Santa Rita Jail. The women there would have drowned me in the toilet in no time. It was more like an overcrowded dog pound where they just tossed the pit bulls and Chihuahuas in together and served them all shitty food and ding biscuits (psych meds).

I could not leave Turk Street for a while, but eventually, I was required to go out and find a job, work, and turn over 20 percent of my gross pay to my hosts. My stay at Turk Street was a condition of my release, but I could always go wait out my pretrial period in Santa Rita Jail if I didn't want to comply with the facility's rules.

I got a job as a software tester at an Internet start-up in San Francisco. Larry and Melony eventually repurposed my home in Vermont. It became their art studio and they adopted my girls. I had to let them go, all of them, and everything I owned except for the clothes on my back I had left there with. I discovered something very interesting about myself. I only cared about losing the cats and the people, not the stuff. I didn't have ten cents to buy a stamp for a while, but my sadness stemmed entirely from missing my cats and my people. Aside from that loss, I was happy, once I got used to my new digs and poverty.

I knew Edith and Dum Dum were in loving hands and I had to accept the bittersweet truth: they would be happy too as soon as they forgot about me. Larry and Melony would also be safer if I simply cut ties with them. They had nothing to do with my sordid past, but I had learned a federal indictment of conspiracy is like a contagious disease. The federal government could pull innocent people into a conspiracy, seize property, and indict them on nothing more than a whisper.

The panicked confession I had made in the post office was not admissible in court, but it certainly helped to build admissible cases against me and everyone I had named. It also confirmed what their lengthy investigation had already uncovered. I cannot take credit for the mountain of information they'd already had in Chicago and I don't want to go so far as to say I was tricked, but the protection Opie had promised for everyone, if my inadmissible proffer had showed it was needed, was never dispatched. I guess they decided it was not necessary.

They had not arrested everyone that day either. To this day, I don't know who else they picked up the day I was in the post office. But it did not include my sister or Piper. They were not indicted until 1998, and my grand jury testimony preceded their indictments but not everyone's. Basically, the confession was the stupidest thing I had ever done in my life, and clearly, that bar was already set very high. Ironically, it was the right thing to do.

Almost seven years after my arrest, I was finally sentenced in the same federal conspiracy that included Henry, Bradley, Hester, Phillip, Garrett, Edwin, Molly, Craig, Donald, Piper, and a few guys I didn't know. Henry was the only one who dared to plead innocent, refuse to cooperate, and risk going to trial. Everyone else arrested accepted guilty pleas and an agreement with the court that mandated cooperation. Interestingly, the guy caught coming into San Francisco with a bag of heroin was not made part of our big conspiracy in Chicago. I think that guy was sentenced in San Francisco before he could be added, but I couldn't find out for how long he was sentenced. The guy that was arrested coming into Chicago with a bag of heroin was included. In fact our conspiracy was named after him. He was the first arrest of all, the first on Opie's metaphorical bus—the bus Opie tried to sell me a seat on. If my co-conspirators' sentences were any indication, there was only one good seat on that bus and it was taken long before Opie got to me.

That guy was sentenced to seven days. The only exception to all of this is Alajeh. He has still not been in an American court.

Alajeh was arrested in London at the request of the U.S. authorities, but they were unsuccessful in actually extraditing him to face charges. Twice. He was released back to Nigeria and claimed it was a case of mistaken identity—that he was not the drug trafficker, that it was his dead brother. Nonetheless, his efforts to have the charges dismissed from abroad have also been unsuccessful and the United States still considers him a fugitive.

Life went on without me in Vermont. My dream of being the CTO of a successful Internet start-up became the only casualty of my exile; Twelve-Twelve died almost immediately after my departure. Once in California, I was not permitted to leave. I learned I would be going to jail no matter what and that my confession had helped to ensure it would be for much longer than if I had followed my lawyer's simple instructions and said nothing. In any case, I would be gone a bit longer than the two weeks I had imagined. This was not going to be a quick drama, not at all like an episode of *Law and Order*.

I wasn't allowed to leave the halfway house for anything but work, so I spent a little more time than usual at the office. It's astonishing the advances you can make in your career when you have no personal life. I actually fit in very well with the whole technology start-up genre in San Francisco. I wasn't the only one who lived at work; I was just the only one who got excited when we had to work into the night to make a release date.

In December of 1997, I was released from the halfway house and moved into a crappy residential hotel near Union Square. The idea of putting down a security deposit and first and last months' rent on a lease in San Francisco seemed crazy while I was checking in with my pretrial officer once a week and waiting to find out when I would be sentenced and go to jail. A year later, I moved into a really nice house at the corner of Mariposa and Arkansas with a friend, a gay stockbroker. He was the greatest roommate, so clean, so responsible, no drama, no drugs. He was a social butterfly too, so I finally made friends with an interesting bunch of people—some through him, some through work, and some through a few feeble attempts to go out and play with the lesbians of San Francisco.

I had to check in weekly with a pretrial officer, report my income and spending, submit to surprise drug tests, and stay out of trouble or go back to Santa Rita. There was no room for lessons. A mistake would not be something to learn from; it would be the end of me, especially since it was very clear a stay in Santa Rita would not be short. In my brief role as a prisoner, and by way of the extended exposure to people on their way out of the system in the halfway house, I learned one very important thing to avoid. The most potentially disastrous element in my predicament would be a bad lover. Since I wouldn't typically discover I had saddled myself with a problem until long after I had fallen in love with someone, it was a bad idea for me to play with that fire.

I behaved but lived vicariously through the exploits of Natalie, my new best friend. I had a mad crush on her the entire time I knew her, but the fact that she had no interest in me made her a perfect remedy for my problem. Unrequited love can be nearly as exciting as actually consummating a love. She was a gorgeous Amazon, way too tall for me though. That is why we were never going to happen; she only liked other tall girls. She was also dating an alcoholic jealous psychopath who liked to circle Natalie's house with a shotgun each time they broke up. Natalie was professionally successful, and she rode a vintage BMW motorcycle and drove a Land Rover. Aside from alcohol, she was drug-free.

Drug-free was important. I was paranoid about the drug tests. I couldn't be around illegal drugs at all, only drugs that were legally prescribed to me. Fortunately, my job paid well and I had health insurance. By my fifth year in San Francisco, I started to think I was never going to go to jail, not after all the time that had passed, and I started dating a woman. I had also turned forty. My caution about getting involved with someone until my legal predicament was behind me was starting to make less sense. What was I thinking—I would wait till I was a senior citizen before dating again? I should have known not to tempt fate that way.

January 2, 2003

"Sit in this spot, one last time, and savor this . . . this fleeting shit!" I bellowed loudly, throwing my voice and an empty pack of cigarettes at the wall. I sounded like the schizophrenic downstairs on Jones Street, condemning everyone to hell, the whole city of San Francisco. It was a bit too much melodrama for my sleepy cat. She opened her eyes a slit, then closed them again, and I laughed.

The computer screen, the keyboard, and the occasion reminded me of a similar death, almost seven years earlier. If I closed my eyes and tried, I could still see my big oak desk as if I were sitting there and the watery green halo of light on the floor. The light had come from the glass edges of my desk lamp, the one that had illuminated my keyboard in Vermont. I could see it as clearly as the glass desk I currently sat at and the code scrolling by on my screen. Tomorrow this too would have to live behind my lids. It was time to die again.

Miss Kitty had no interest in my noisy musings or my dinner. But she still didn't budge. She had been sleeping, curled up, between the monitor and my keyboard, or within petting distance of wherever I was, for the last twenty-four hours. I hadn't been out of the house all day, and it was already over. Miss Kitty and I would be taking our last late-night walk together in a little while, and I think she knew that. I think she was trying to delay the inevitable, as if in sleeping longer, it wouldn't have to happen. I remembered doing the same thing when I was a kid, and it was time for school.

Miss Kitty had been my guardian angel, my little Dum Dum surrogate. I had both lived and worked in her neighborhood, the one I spotted her in when we first met, three years earlier. I chased her up De Haro Street in San Francisco, sure that she was Dum Dum and had made the miraculous journey across the continent to find me. I had a complete nervous breakdown at the top of De Haro, cried my eyeballs out, when she got away. A couple of weeks later, I found her sitting in my backyard. I lived one block over from De Haro. She clearly had a home, but she still came by to hang out with me every day after work. Eventually, she started spending the night with me.

That's when I got a collar for her and put a tiny note inside a little charm: "If you are wondering where your kitty has been, call me," and I listed my number. Her daddy called a couple of days later and we had a good laugh about his kitty cheating on him with me. She didn't get along with his dog, so he was fine with my adopting her when I moved away from Potrero Hill a couple of years later. I told him I would return her if anything happened to me.

She was the coolest cat in the universe. She liked going for walks really late at night, when the city was quiet, and with me on her leash. She would drag me up Jones Street, an easy climb for a tiny black cat but not a hill an overweight smoker enjoys. The last few bits up the hill are so steep the sidewalk turns to stairs. We would go to the top of Jones, where Grace Cathedral looks out over the city. There is a fountain up there; she liked to walk around its edges. Then we would go back to our apartment building on Jones Street and head up to the roof one last time. Jones Street would be my last address in San Francisco.

Miss Kitty had two moms now, as Julie and I had moved in together shortly after starting dating. But it wasn't one of those dates lesbians are famous for, where someone brings a U-Haul. There had been a fiasco involving a faulty sprinkler system where I used to live. Julie had let me and Miss Kitty move in with her. "What the fuck are you talking about?" she now responded to my burst of poetic grumbling. She was irritated, and who could blame her? I was horrible company. She probably couldn't wait for the morning to come, so she could be rid of me.

I pushed my pieces of sushi around on the plate and popped another Vicodin, chasing the pill down with my miso soup. We had ordered sushi and miso soup, a meal we usually shared with *The Sopranos* on Sunday nights, not Thursdays—I don't mean Miss Kitty; I mean Julie. Miss Kitty didn't like television or sushi.

Julie and I couldn't possibly have been more incompatible, but there were strange forces at work in my life. Forces probably managed by Miss Kitty. She loved my roommate.

Living together was supposed to have been a temporary arrangement while I found a new apartment. But that was when I finally got the call from Chicago, the call I had convinced myself would never happen. It had been just over six years since my arrest in Brattleboro, Vermont.

That was back in August. On September 22, 2002, I finally stood in front of a judge in Chicago. So much had passed to bring me standing there, in that spot, in front of the man about to tell me where I would be spending the next few years of my life. I had come to terms with that. I'd had years to come to terms with where I would be spending this time—probably in the federal correctional institution in Dublin, California. I realized, though, that I had neglected to come to terms with what would happen right there, right then, in that courtroom.

My entire family and some friends from the neighborhood where I had grown up were there. The friends had traveled to Chicago from Cincinnati with my sister, my brother, and our parents to support them through this horrible day. Hester would be sentenced immediately following me, and a few other defendants were either before or after us. We knew this because we had seen their names posted on the schedule outside the door of the judge's courtroom.

We hadn't actually laid eyes on any of them, which was a little disappointing. I would like to have seen what everyone looked like after almost seven years of this bullshit. Henry was fighting his charges; he was going to trial. He would get more time when that finally happened. I knew by then that they punished you by asking for much longer sentences if you went to trial. He sure as hell couldn't win. Every one of us had accepted a plea agreement to avoid going away for an eternity. But part of that plea agreement was that we would testify against co-defendants if anyone decided to go to trial, the assumption being Alajeh was the only one who would do that.

Henry was charged with conspiracy, like most of us had been. Conspiracy law can be used to convict people with hearsay evidence alone. It's a crime to conspire to do something illegal if you actually do any part of what you conspired with others to do, even if you don't actually follow through. It was invented to get at the

untouchables, I'm told, but has been used for much juicier goals
than it was intended. Someone explained to me McCarthyism was
made possible by conspiracy law, but its more common abuse was
by questionably ethical prosecutors pressuring people to cooperate with the threat of an inevitable conviction. Normally, it requires
actual hard evidence to convict someone of a crime, and hearsay is
not admissible in court. But with conspiracy, hearsay is allowed in
court, and all it takes is enough people saying something happened
and it is accepted as having occurred.

One other very important thing to know about conspiracy law: If
you are convicted of conspiracy, you are held responsible for everything that everyone in the conspiracy did. We had been shown a
list of the sentencing recommendations. For the time being, Phillip, Bradley, and I—I thought—were getting the longest sentences,
which was to be expected. But at the time, Hester and I were the
only two out of all the co-defendants who were in the courtroom.

Our parents sat behind us, holding hands. They both were trying to look calm and collected, but it wasn't working. They had
more of an our-daughters-are-getting-beheaded look going on. The
law would sweep both their girls out of their lives for a long time,
period. Mom and Dad couldn't come to terms with the length of our
sentences. We had talked about this with them numerous times,
but I don't think they thought it was possible. Like I said, Mom had
worked in the Hamilton County jail for years as an employee of the
Cincinnati Public Schools, and she thought she knew better.

She had ironically taken this assignment on long before my sister
and I had ever become entangled with the justice system. It was
kind of a blessing for her. It had helped her deal with much of what
had already occurred to us. But her experiences had the opposite
effect in regard to our sentencing. Only cold-blooded murderers got
this kind of time; rapists didn't get half of what we had tried to convince her that we were going to be given. She always believed this
was just prosecutors trying to be scary.

It was hard for them to understand, when viewed through parent
goggles, that their two daughters—who were so smart, so beautiful,

so innocent, with such promise—could be facing this court as the outlaws we were admitting to being. I heard a throaty noise from behind me. It had come from my dad. I knew he was upset; this was the throat-clearing noise he made when emotional. I had only heard it a couple of times in my life, but it was unmistakable.

I was first up. I was dressed well, in a tailored tan pantsuit and a black turtleneck, with my long hair pulled back in a bun. Up until this moment, I did not look or feel like a criminal. But when I stepped up to the bar with my lawyer, that is what I became. I wanted to turn around and tell Dad that I was all right, I wasn't afraid. But the judge had come into the courtroom and I was frozen—breathing and alive, but I couldn't turn around. I realized I was shaking. Well, trembling; shaking seems more deliberate. I wanted to have my sister right by my side, where I could see her, maybe hold her hand, or comfort her. But she was behind me with her lawyer, watching what was about to happen to her happen to me.

The judge started speaking to me about letters he had received on my behalf alleging what a great person I was. His words turned into white noise. I thought I could hear Mom and Dad's heartbeats more audibly than what the judge was saying, but I think it was my own heart doing double time. I knew my sister was afraid for me and it bugged me that she had to be there right then. I was more afraid for my sister than I was for myself. I felt sorrier for my parents than I did anyone. My poor brother must have been completely freaked out. I said a prayer in my mind that he wouldn't have a seizure. My brother is epileptic and stress is a trigger. I realized we had to be setting a record for twisted emotions and family drama. I thought it couldn't get worse.

The judge looked over my shoulder and to the people behind me, acknowledging someone who wanted his attention. I heard his words perfectly then and was stunned. "Yes, sir. Would you like to address the court?"

"Your Honor. Yes, I would like to say some things on behalf of my daughters . . ." Dad paused. Dad was comfortable on stage, but not this one. He still looked like a star though, and while I was embarrassed, he was actually responding to the judge's request to the peanut gallery for input. I was proud he stepped up and identified himself as our father. "I am sorry. My wife and I were parents of the seventies—good parenting was to be permissive, let them make their mistakes and learn." He paused again and looked flustered. "I don't understand this."

The judge was patient. Eugene Wolters was not before him for sentencing; he was not a criminal. He was a father. The judge was a father too. I knew the judge would know, without a doubt, this was a good father, this was a good family, and now he had to see me and Hester, not just the data in our presentence reports. Dad turned to my mom and held her hand more tightly. "This sentence extends to all of us here today." Dad made a sweeping gesture toward our cheerleading section from Cincinnati. "Your Honor, as I said, my daughters have never been in trouble with the law." He stood silent for a long moment before he could continue. "I hope that this court shows us mercy."

Hearing this from my father took my breath away. In all of this, I had never been able to quantify or genuinely acknowledge the pain and suffering this predicament had caused him and Mom. But there it was, their pain flooding my ears and my heart like molten lava. I felt like my heart had stopped pumping blood out but kept pumping it in, and it would explode.

The judge spoke about how horrible my crimes were and how, in spite of his compassion for the family, the crimes demanded harsh sentencing. Besides, it wasn't in his hands anyway . . . "mandatory minimums" . . . blah, blah, blah. I heard the judgment: "Ninety-four months to be followed by five years supervised release." He asked me something, but I have no idea what. Alan, my lawyer, responded for me, and it was done. Alan and I were excused from the court and walked out. I felt like I had left my sister to be torn apart by wild dogs. My father gave me a sad smile as I walked by.

The weirdest thing imaginable happened when we left the courtroom. I felt great, fucking fantastic. I felt like a ten-thousand-pound weight had just been lifted off me. It wasn't until that moment that

I understood how heavy it had been, the not knowing, the waiting, the hoping, for over six fucking long years I had been dead. But I felt alive again, like someone had just zapped me with those electric paddles and my happy heart was beating again. I could now see an end to this. It might be years away, but it existed. My whole family would celebrate when that happened. I could see it: Mom and Dad, probably at the Bankers Club, popping corks and cheering.

My sister came out of the courtroom a few minutes later and my elation vanished. She looked pale as a ghost and pissed off. Her lawyer had prepared her for forty-eight months; she got seventy-two. My brother came out next and looked lost. Then Hester's husband of six months—a Tom Cruise look-alike named Matt—Mom, and Dad came out with my sister's lawyer and formed a huddle, probably about the surprise addition of two years to Hester's sentence. Hester walked toward me and Alan while digging in her bag. She pulled out her pack of cigarettes.

"Tell them we're outside smoking. We'll be there waiting for them." She'd said this to my lawyer, Alan, assuming he knew whom he was to deliver the message to and that he would hang around waiting to do so. She grabbed my hand and yanked me in the direction she had told Alan we were heading, gripping my hand and towing me toward the elevator. I passively followed her to the elevator and I saw a smile form on her lips while we were waiting. I think in spite of the nasty turn of events, she was having her strange minute of joy too. We were given three months to turn ourselves in, so I hoped she wasn't planning on making a run for it, not right then anyway. We were stopping for a cigarette outside though, so I knew I would have the length of a cigarette or two to talk her out of jumping if that is what the happy smile on her face meant.

"Are you all right?" I asked her while she pulled a cigarette from her pack and lit it.

"I'm fine. I'm relieved." She leaned against the exterior glass wall of the Dirksen Federal Building in Chicago and took a long draw off her cigarette. I lit my own, and we said nothing for a few moments. "What about Matt?" I could see her chin trembling. "Six years."

"Hester, think about how long we have waited for this, how long he has waited to know the ending. He has a date now. There is an end to this." I started to paint the same picture I had been creating in my head when she came out of the courtroom. The celebration, the end of our long journey. It was in sight and we would all make it there.

We wouldn't know for sure where to turn ourselves in, not until we were given a destination by the Bureau of Prisons. Hester got her letter first. She was going to a place in Lexington, Kentucky. It was the facility closest to our family and her husband. She had been so relieved. He could visit her there. So could Mom, Dad, and Gene. She had made Cincinnati her home again, so all of her friends were there, and they would all support her and Matt while she served her time. I was happy for her but not so much for myself.

I had assumed I would get designated to the same facility. I wanted that, I could see my family, but I was also sorry I wouldn't get to see any of the friends I had made in San Francisco. I started cutting my emotional ties with all but a few of them.

My letter didn't arrive until December. I wasn't designated to Lexington, Kentucky, as I had expected. I was designated to Dublin, California. I was secretly relieved that I did not have to go to the same place my sister was going. I'd had time to consider it and I was very worried about being in the same place as she would be. I knew she would be better off that way; so would I. In my brief encounter with the world we were heading into, seven years earlier, I had seen how dangerous it was to love anyone in there with you. People used that vulnerability like a weapon. I had met so many nice people who didn't belong in the circumstances they were in, but I couldn't easily pick out the monsters among them. But they were there, just waiting to pounce on naïve little fools like me and my sister.

"You sure you should do that?" Julie stopped me from grabbing the pill bottle on the bureau. The poor thing hadn't signed up to babysit a morose drug addict on her way to jail or to adopt Miss Kitty. But that described our brief, tumultuous relationship in a nutshell. She wasn't in love with me anymore, I was long gone, but she loved the little black kitty I had chased up De Haro Street. She was just baby-sitting me, and they both deserved much better. Before that could happen, I had to vanish.

"I'm fine. I just finished the site. There's nothing else I can do." This was an odd reply to her quandary about my taking too many Vicodin.

"Have you called your mom and dad?"

"That's the last item on my list. It's three hours earlier there."

"It's three hours later." I thought for a moment and panicked. She was right. It would be midnight soon. So I sat down, took the pill she thought I shouldn't, and called them.

"Hello, Cleary." I laughed at Dad. He knew I was the only person who would call him at midnight on a work night. "Your mother and I have been waiting for your call. We thought you meant nine o'clock Eastern Standard Time." I could hear him muffle the phone and wake her. They were probably in bed. Mom had probably dozed off and Dad was probably sitting up doing the *New York Times* puzzles. I had told them I would call at nine; that would have been at six o'clock my time.

"Have you talked to Hester?" Miss Kitty jumped from the desk and walked over to me, jumped into my lap, and started kneading my leg with her sharp claws.

"We have. She's ready for her big day. They came over last night for a last supper and she had a good cry. But she will be all right. We will make sure of that."

"Are you taking her?"

"No. Matthew is delivering her. We will be going down Saturday to see how she is doing. Are you ready for your big day?"

"Ready as I'll ever be."

"I'm so proud of you." I laughed when he said this.

"Yes, I bet you are." He laughed back. Laughing is the best medicine in the world, second only to talking to parents who love you and could actually say they were proud of you for going to prison.

"Seriously. We are so proud of you girls for doing what you have done." I knew he didn't mean the drug-smuggling part and I felt like maybe I better not make any more jokes. My dad was not the most emotional kind of fellow, not outwardly. When he said things like this it wasn't easy for him to keep his cool lid battened down. "You are so brave to go through this all alone."

"Dad, I'm never alone." I lit a cigarette, took a drag, and tried to think of a witty punch line for that one but came up blank. "You and Mom are always only ten numbers away." I thought of something funny. "And now I can interrupt *West Wing* and *The Sopranos* without fail. I promise to call you every night at ten o'clock."

"We'll leave a daily update for you then, on our answering machine. But do give us a call sometime when you want to talk." He was kidding. If I called in the middle of him having a heart attack, he would pick up the phone, and he knew that I knew it.

"Drats! Okay. I won't call during prime time."

"I don't know what we can do to help. But if you have problems, anything, please don't keep it to yourself. We will do everything we can." He was quiet for a minute. But quiet on the phone with Dad wasn't an awkward silence or dead air where someone might think the call had dropped. Oddly, it was the part of every phone call where I felt he was closest to me. "Are you scared?" I don't think he really wanted to ask the question.

"Yes, but it's the same scared as when I went to school in Fulton," I lied. "I know what to expect, 'cause I had to do that whole extradition thing, remember. I met some of the women I will be living with now, or women like them, and they told me all about the place I am going now," I lied some more. "You would have thought they were on their way to camp." That was true. "I hear there is even a pool there." I knew this wasn't true. "They call it Club Fed." That was true about a decade earlier. "Best of all, I can go back to school and not have any distractions." The last item I could neither confirm nor debunk in the little bit of digging I had done online about my new home. But the idea had been appealing and in California the governor offered educational grants. If you were in the pokey and wanted to go to school, it was free.

"My goodness, you're making me want to rob a bank." His voice sounded crisp and clear, not perilously close to a meltdown. There was one thing in this world I knew I could not take: hearing my father cry. "I don't want you to be disappointed." I relaxed, content with the fact that we had gone from him being worried and scared about me going off to jail all by myself to him being concerned I might be overoptimistic about my upcoming vacation. I didn't want him to think I was crazy.

"Dad, I know it's going to be hard at first. But I'll be fine. We humans are such adaptable creatures. We can get used to just about anything."

"Truer words have never been spoken. Your mother is going to explode if I don't give her the phone." I laughed and agreed to call the first chance I got, once I had moved into my new place in Dublin.

"Honey. Are you all right?" Mom sounded frantic. "Tell me everything you just told your father." I knew if I didn't, she would drive my dad insane, if he dared to try to paraphrase. So I tried to recall every single thing I had said and did a pretty good job of it. I could hear my dad snoring in the background when I finished. "Don't worry about tuition, just find a school that will let you take correspondence classes. Look for reputable universities too, not some fly-by-night operation, or your degree won't be worth the paper it's printed on." She took a quick, deep breath. "I will help you research this, but I think this is a wonderful way to turn your scar into a star."

Mom went through a list of dos and don'ts that she knew of in regard to the pokey. She had been teaching in the Hamilton County jail for years by now and had gotten a very good sense of some of the unwritten rules her students lived by, with me and Hester in mind. Never borrow anything from anyone, especially money; never owe anyone anything, especially money; don't get involved with anyone, especially staff; don't trust anyone, including staff; stay away from drugs and troublemakers; exercise regularly; do not eat too many carbohydrates; don't nap; eat all your vegetables whenever you get them; make sure the staff know you come from a good family, but don't let other inmates know this; and stay out of everyone's business. As it turned out, that was astonishingly good advice.

I made the same promise to call home as soon as I could. She told me not to panic if it took a little while before I could make any phone calls. She told me that if that happened, to know that my mother and father were praying for me every night. "As a matter of fact, let's pray together every night. We go to bed at eleven o'clock. Let's all say a Hail Mary together then."

"Okay. I like that idea. You guys can tuck me in every night." I laughed at the idea of my mother coming to prison to tuck in her forty-year-old daughter, the drug smuggler. She asked me how I was getting there, who was taking me, was there gas in the car, and what I was bringing with me, and finally, we were done. When the call was over, I really did feel ready.

I called all my friends one last time, telling them Julie would give them my address and information about visiting me as soon as we had it. I called my best friend, Natalie, and made arrangements for her to pick us up the following morning. Julie didn't have her driver's license and originally Natalie was going to drive us in my car and park it at her house in Oakland until my friend Steve could come get it. He was going to sell it for me and put the money on my account at Dublin. The account is what I would use to buy things like hygiene products, snacks, notepaper, and pens.

Miss Kitty and I finally went for our last late-night walk, but I took a little more time than usual. It was warm for January and it had rained a little. Everything looked new and shiny, and the streets were quiet. I sat down on the stairs in front of the main entrance to Grace Cathedral and prayed I would one day return there with Miss Kitty. Worst-case scenario, I would be back in November of 2010. Best-case scenario, my sentence would be overturned and I would come home sooner. I had no idea how that might happen, but I prayed for it anyway.

I looked out over the twinkling city and tried to imagine the day I would come back to San Francisco. It would be such a celebration. I looked forward to returning to the halfway house on Turk and Taylor Streets, but this time on my way out, not at the beginning of this long journey. I could see myself coming back, getting back to work in software. I might be close to forty-seven by then, but I would still have some good years left in me. My whole life wasn't wasted. Maybe I could even write a book about the whole ordeal and save someone foolish from making my mistakes.

By 9:30 in the morning Julie was up and showered, and though we did not need to and had not planned on leaving the house for another hour, I decided I wanted to get it over with and go, so I called Natalie to pull the hearse up. I threw my jacket on, grabbed my bag, and went to the window seat where Miss Kitty was napping in the morning sun.

"Well, kiddo, this is it. I have to leave you now for a little while. Please stay out of traffic and stay healthy. It's going to be a long time until we can play again. Until then, be a good girl for Julie."

"You love that cat more than you ever loved me." Julie laughed. "You don't hold a candle to Miss Kitty either." Then she smugly tossed her bag over her shoulder. I was lucky to have found a friend like her. I hoped she was going to be okay. Somehow, though, I knew she and Miss Kitty would bounce back. She had promised to wait for me, and I wanted to believe it was possible. But I knew I was probably seeing her for the last time. I knew the same was true for Miss Kitty, even though it broke my heart to admit it.

When we arrived in Dublin, it was a little disorienting. I pictured FCI Dublin being out in a vast area of mountain-size rolling hills of gold, covered with windmills and with weird little trees dotting the hillsides. As we finally approached the area where the facility was, I could see the windmills in the distance and I realized it wasn't the first time I had seen the place. When the marshals had dropped me at Santa Rita Jail seven years before, we had come from the opposite direction. We arrived at the entrance to a military base, where we had to show our IDs to a man in a booth before being allowed to pass.

We drove by a long fence that surrounded a big open field. The buildings there were like the military barracks or housing I had seen in the Presidio, but more dilapidated, and an area full of rusty old gym equipment sat out in the middle of the field. I spotted a couple of women in tan-colored jackets and blue uniforms, wearing work boots, and figured they were personnel or something. At the end of the fence, the road we were on intersected with where we had to turn to get to the facility.

Julie spotted the flag we had been given as a landmark. It was on the opposite side of the road as the dilapidated buildings we had passed. We turned up a long, windy driveway, which ended in a circle, and at the edge of the circle there was a trailer. It was the kind you see at a big construction site, the place where architects and planners hang out or where some fat guy watches a clock everyone punches in.

"*Welcome to the Hotel California . . .*" Natalie and Julie started singing this as we approached the trailer. I joined in, lit up my last cigarette, and took my last Vicodin. It wasn't the last I had; I still had about sixty of them in a bottle. But I would have to turn those over when I checked in, and I didn't know how long it would be before I got another one. I seriously doubted they would let me continue my ten-pills-a-day habit, but a girl could dream.

We still had about forty-five minutes to kill before I had to walk into the creepy trailer. I could see the fences surrounding the grounds of the place where I was headed. Two layers of fencing sat about twelve feet apart and each was topped with a big role of razor wire. I joined back in on the song. "*. . . You can check in any time you like, but you can never leave.*" And Julie made the weird guitar riff that came after. I could see beyond the fence, but I couldn't really get a view of any women inside. I asked Julie to turn around and told her I thought we could see inside if we pulled off to the right and went to the north side of the parking lot.

A white pickup truck pulled alongside her and the uniformed driver cautioned her against doing anything but dropping me at the trailer and leaving. I suppose attempting a little reconnaissance on the exterior of a federal prison was frowned upon. Having an open beer in your hand might also be pooh-poohed. Julie had the tendency to get a little bit belligerent when she drank and I realized I should send my friend on her way, before she was offered a room at the lovely hotel.

"Okay. That's it. I'm going in." I hopped out of the car. Julie hopped out and gave me a big hug and told me she would come see me as soon as she was allowed. Natalie gave me a big hug, then stepped away. I think she thought I would want to spend my last minutes with Julie. But I got out of there as fast as I could. I did not want to walk into the place bawling. "It's not a place to cry," Mom had said seven years ago.

A muscled man in a uniform came down a walkway and entered the trailer from the other side, the side inside the fence. He looked mean as hell and mad. I looked at my watch. It was 11:30.

"What?" He barked at me loudly from the trailer door like he had no idea why I was there. Surely, they knew I was coming.

"I am supposed to self-surrender here today by noon."

15 Con Air

What is it . . . not fast enough for you? . . . You think this is all my fault? What the hell are you up to? Why do you still look so fucking . . . ? I was thinking.

"Hey! Step up!" the ugly grunt yelled at me and gave me a prod toward the podium in front of her. I stepped up and stood still while she snapped the ankle cuffs, attached my chain, then adjusted the long chain wrapped around my waist, so there wasn't any excess hanging down between my feet. She gave me another prod, and the next fat grunt held on to my elbow while I carefully stepped down and got back in line. Hester had advanced a few spots in line in front of me. Her grunt had been much faster than mine, trussing her up.

We had both advanced past Piper in the line. She had been several people ahead, like she was in a race to get somewhere first. She was still on one of the podiums. The cuffs were too large for her wrists and they were trying to find a set that would work on her delicate frame. I had worried she was trying to beat us, be first, that she might try to object to one of these assholes about her being put on the same flight as Hester and me. If she did anything that caused Hester to get black-boxed, that would be it. I would lose my fucking mind and kill her.

For days Hester had been telling me to stop worrying about it, stop worrying about Piper, what she thought, or what she might be saying. But Hester was naïve; she hadn't been here before. Stupid shit like that could get us booted off this flight. I had worried all week that we would get put in the hole or I would get my face smashed to smithereens by some psychotic bitch with a grudge. Almost everyone here had co-defendants they would like to see dead. But not everyone here was a happy camper. Some of these women were violent and would act on their crazy impulses in a heartbeat. Hester or I would make great substitutes to direct their rage at.

The marshals are not supposed to put co-defendants together for this reason and I knew Piper had been complaining to the women around her. One of them had given me a look that suggested whatever Piper had said about me had not been nice. I think they were in the same cell and she looked like a DC chick. I had heard the DC chicks were nuts. If Piper was stupid enough to make alliances with those crazy bitches, it was anyone's guess what other stupid bullshit she might pull. They finished shackling her and she stepped down and into line, right behind me. *Fucking lovely!* Hester looked back at me and turned away. I thought she was actually about to crack up laughing. This took the prize on running into ex-lovers.

What a strange place the Oklahoma City Federal Transfer Center was. It was like a parody of O'Hare or LaGuardia, a hub for prisoners on the move. If you were able to cut open the entire American federal criminal justice system, peel its fatty tissue back to expose its guts, this facility is what you would be staring at. From what I could tell from inside its stomach, the building was an octagonal, five- or six-storied labyrinth of cells, elevators, ramps, and hallways. Most of its fourteen hundred inhabitants were stuck there, waiting their turn to be moved on to their next stop in the system. But every morning before dawn, hundreds of us were woken up, pulled out of our cells, and put back into the ebb and flow of this human traffic, as hundreds more arrived.

On the ground floor we were gathered in lines—mostly men, mostly black- and brown-skinned, all clad in khaki uniforms that looked like doctors' scrubs, over white tees; everyone wore blue laceless canvas slip-ons over white jock socks. I imagined from some viewpoint we might have looked like a marching band or maybe an elite military corps, without our instruments or guns. We could have been too, except that we were all in shackles and the exposed beer belly and butt crack here and there from poorly sized uniforms ruined the illusion. We stood in sleepy rows, row after row, waiting in lines to wait in line, until the lines ultimately converged in a large brightly lit white room, where a gate finally funneled us out onto the tarmac, one small group at a time, like the building was taking its daily dump.

The place was an architectural wonder. It was like the folks who had designed Disneyland to keep people from killing each other in line, the lady who'd done the documentary on the beef industry practices regarding cows on their way to slaughter, the Pinball Wizard, Franz Kafka, and George Orwell had all got together and created this place. This was their brainchild, the federal transfer center in Oklahoma City. There were only two things going on here. We were either in a holding pattern, locked up on any one of the floors full of stalled prisoners, or we were running the gamut of lines coming into or going out of the facility; getting fingerprinted, shackled or unshackled, poked and prodded, for hours before we either entered or exited the facility via the labyrinth. We were all moving across the country from one facility to another in the care of the U.S. Marshals Service and this was their LaGuardia.

When we were finally walked out into the icy cold morning in groups and told to stop when we got near the plane, the sun had come up but done nothing to warm the planet. We stayed in our groups of five and in single file, freezing our butts off, waiting our turn to get felt up for the last time by some jackbooted oaf, his M16 armed comrades at his back. All so we could board a Con Air plane.

Piper was shivering. I was not. I think it pleased me in some absurd way. Piper had not spoken to me since she'd gotten to Oklahoma. It was clear she blamed me for her conviction, whatever she had ended up agreeing to.

I didn't worry anymore about myself surviving this ordeal. I had been through much worse than this already. I'd been treated to diesel therapy before, which is what they called it when we were shipped from one prison to another across the United States by the marshals. I had not just come from a cozy little camp either. I'd come from a higher security federal correctional institution than Piper and my sister. FCIs are where the really bad girls go, not federal prison camps—FPCs—where you can romp and play outside all day and night if you choose, or so I had heard. It didn't matter where we had come from though, not at this point. FCI or FPC, either way, diesel therapy made the place you were doing your time in seem like home, a home I yearned to return to. You know life is bad when you miss your prison.

Truth is, I hated seeing anyone I loved, or once loved, go through this shit—actually anyone, even if I don't know you. This is not something anyone wants to see a person suffer through, so nobody really looks at each other. It's humiliating and degrading, and hard enough to have strangers witness it. Watching my little sister being subjected to this nightmare made me sick to my stomach and I knew it didn't give her a warm and fuzzy feeling watching me submit to my captors. But Piper was another story. She did her best to make this all worse. I hated what she was doing to herself with her stupid pride, guilt, misplaced anger, or whatever it was.

I knew why my sister would blame me but didn't. I should have gotten out, closed the door, and never looked back on the drug-smuggling world, like she had, and long before I actually did. We might not have been in Oklahoma, waiting to get on Con Air together, if I had made different choices. Piper's attitude was a little more confounding. I guess she would never have gotten into this predicament had she not gone slumming and befriended someone so far beneath her social ranking so many years ago. But she had.

She'd wanted the same thing we all had. She'd wanted to travel. She'd wanted adventure. She'd wanted a shortcut.

I hated her pompous narcissism and firm belief that she was somehow better than any of us. Years ago it hadn't been such a pronounced characteristic. She'd been a fresh Smith graduate back then and had believed it made her special. That hadn't changed; it had gotten worse. She walked around now like she thought she might actually be royalty. Hester and I had already been down two years of our sentences. I can't speak for my sister, but I know my own false belief that I was somehow better than everyone around me, an exception to the rule, a fish out of water, had withered and died. The arrogance in Piper's mannerisms looked clown-like to me now. It was hard to believe that after two years down, she hadn't let go of that fantasy. Of course, I was operating under the assumption she was doing the thirty-six-month sentence that had been listed in the sentencing report we'd seen in 2002.

Our class, color, or credit limit had no meaning here; we didn't have social or economic classes in this hell we lived in. Piper's stiff posture, refusal to acknowledge either me or my sister, and nose pointed at the sky bugged the shit out of me every time she passed by in Oklahoma. We had so much unfinished business and this made it so much worse.

I couldn't tell what of the many options was the true source of her raw and naked hatred. Was it that I'd not come to San Francisco then, never ended our relationship properly? Was it that I hadn't lied to the investigators and said she had nothing to do with us when they'd already known that was not true? Did she believe I should have saved her from this mess and sacrificed my life for hers? They had threatened me with thirty years in prison if my testimony was false. One small adjustment in the already arbitrary total weight of the drugs they had believed we were all responsible for importing and my sentencing guidelines would have gone from ten years to thirty. I knew she had gone through the same prosecutorial grinder that we all had; surely by now she knew I wouldn't have had the option to exclude her from my plea agreement, any more than she could have done the same for me. It would have been pointless. Did she actually think they hadn't already known who was sitting next to me on all those flights when they'd arrested me so many years ago, or that our co-defendants would've kept her out of this too and risked their plea agreements?

In any case, two weeks in holding had not done the trick. She still wasn't speaking. It had been over eleven years since we'd parted ways in Brussels. If I closed my eyes, I could still see her taxi pulling away.

January in Oklahoma City was cold and windy this early in the morning. It didn't bother me as much as Piper, partly because, unlike her, I had actually aged since we'd last seen each other so many years ago. I had a little body fat helping me out and my skin was certainly a little thicker, whereas her still perfect and beautiful bones had no protection from the wind. Our pleasant tour guides didn't give a shit about their livestock's comfort, and Piper's poor-me smile would get her nowhere with U.S. marshals. They wouldn't even see it.

Nope, on this trip we would all freeze every time we landed somewhere and had to get out of the plane. She would shiver and I would fiendishly enjoy her discomfort a little, but try to ignore the same from my baby sister. I'm not a mean asshole, but her fucking bullshit was needlessly cruel. Considering our circumstances, it was unconscionable to actually want to make this worse for someone else. While we were all clad in nothing but our scrubs and T-shirts, with our little blue fairy shoes, which had no soles to speak of, our captors wore gloves and big puffy, warm coats, so they took their time boarding us onto the plane while we froze. They were, however, quick when patting us down since they had to remove their gloves for this.

Hester was in front of us. She lifted her long auburn hair so they could see she wasn't hiding any machine guns in there, then she opened her mouth and stuck her tongue out to confirm she hadn't cheeked a grenade. The lady patting her down had this look of utter disgust every time she had to touch one of us. I wondered if they trained that into them or if the job drew people like that to it. People who can hate strangers so completely without cause.

I almost laughed when Piper and I got seated together. We couldn't object, though I saw Piper's hesitation to step up next to me when prodded like a cow to do so. We finally got buckled in the plane and Piper stared straight ahead. Her hair was still blond—not the same blond she had achieved in Bali. It hung down limply, not pulled back the way she'd always worn it, but that was compliance, not fashion. Rubber bands and hair ties were forbidden on Con Air. I'm not sure what deadly threat they thought could be made with a rubber band, but they weren't having it, whatever it was.

Her forearms and hands were pale and still freckled. I dared not look right at her. I feared she might bite. Nonetheless, sitting this close to someone I'd once known so very well inspired my curiosity no end. I looked over at my sister and she was smiling a very nervous smile. It was going to be a long day for her, worrying about what explosion might occur between Piper and her sister.

But then the day got brighter. I saw my sister smiling from ear to ear, and I realized it was directed at an old friend of ours. A co-defendant and former member of our little old smuggling clique was boarding the plane. He smiled back and said, "See you in Chicago." Bradley was shackled and doing the awkward shuffle to make his way down the aisle, followed by a long line of men doing the same funny dance, and he was looking no worse for the wear. The marshals barked at him to shut up. He smiled and passed by us. I wondered if we'd have more surprise reunions in store for us in Chicago, like Phillip. I wondered what he looked like now. I hadn't seen him in nine years.

We sat there on the tarmac for what felt like an eternity. I was anxious to get going and fly to whatever was next for us. It was still possible that we were going to be miraculously set free in Chicago. Mom and Dad had hired a special attorney to meet us. Tom Dawson had cleaned them out, but it was money well spent if he could magically use this trial as a vehicle to get some time off our sentences.

We had to testify, tell the court what they already knew—it was part of our plea agreements to do so. I had no choice in the matter; neither did Piper, Hester, Bradley, or the rest of our co-defendants. But to do so, we would be again in front of the same judge who had sentenced us. It certainly couldn't hurt to have a lawyer like Tom Dawson, who specialized in post-conviction appeals and sentence reduction, there. Maybe this was our Hail Mary pass. We would miraculously be found innocent but stupid and sent home. Not likely.

We were all on our way to Chicago because Henry was actually taking his case to trial. We all might not have understood this ten years earlier, but we all knew better by now. There's no fighting the feds; once you are on their radar, you are dinner. Period. Fighting it is pointless, expensive, and increases the time they give you. It also puts more people in jeopardy. Remember, while you are fighting the feds, you are contagious. I had met my share of the family members of people like Henry in prison. Parents and siblings who had paid the price for their own Henry and his or her stubborn refusal to take responsibility for his or her own shit.

One of my roommates in Dublin got six years in prison for money laundering. She had made the mistake of using her son's cash to retain a lawyer for him when he was arrested. They then arrested her for handling his dirty money. This created the leverage they hoped would push her stubborn son into a confession and toward testifying against those that they really wanted. If he did that, the charges against his mom would be dropped. She was so proud of her son for not crumbling. Unfortunately, this sweet little old lady was not an anomaly. There were other innocent mothers, sisters, and girlfriends in prison with me. My mother would have disowned me for letting her go to jail, not applauded it. But, then again, if as many Irish Catholic bodies littered the borders and freeways near Mexico as the poor souls caught in Mexican cartel disputes, she might applaud my silence too, even if it did land her in jail. Henry was either still afraid, even after all those years, or he was the bravest person I'll ever know and thought he might win at trial. Whatever the cause was, Henry's trial is what we were on our way to Chicago for.

I kept singing my own rendition of a song stuck in my head— *Fools to the left of me, jokers to the right, here I am, stuck in the middle with you*—over and over, hoping my sister would pick the tune up telepathically and join in. God knows we couldn't actually sing it out loud; we'd probably get shot. But it had become our theme song at some point, many moons ago, and it always made her laugh to sing it. I couldn't remember the lines in the song past *I'm so scared*. So I stopped singing in my head and gave up on my telepathic sing-along.

I realized the last time I had been sitting next to Piper on a plane we had been headed from Bali to Paris, Paris to New York, or was it Chicago? I think we'd had first-class seats. We'd had champagne for certain.

"Not exactly like the last time we traveled together?" I asked in my crackly voice. It crackled again when I tried to giggle; not because I was broken up or nervous about speaking, just because my throat was dry and scratchy.

"Hmm" was all she replied, devoid of any indication in her intonation as to the meaning of "hmm."

Three marshals were talking among themselves over the head of a mammoth bald man, who probably would have been forced to buy two seats if he were flying commercially. I couldn't see the poor little fellow they had put between the big man and the window— he'd probably been squashed under the guys elbow—but I could see the guy's ass, who had been seated on his other side, hanging out into the aisle. The grumpy older marshal kept roughly jabbing his butt and barking in his ear to clear the aisle. Were it not for his incessant barking, I might have drifted off to sleep. But then a rare thing, a female marshal, spat back at the grumpy old marshal, "Shut the fuck up! Where you want him, up his ass?" Finally giving words to what I'm sure a few shackled folk wanted to say but couldn't. The marshals laughed at themselves. The guy whose ass was hanging off the edge of his seat grumbled under his breath, and the lady marshal gave him a frozen glare with her bloodshot eyes that shut him down.

I could smell stale alcohol and something like barbecue sauce lingering in her wake when she passed by. I had once heard an expression used to describe someone a little rough around the edges: "rode hard and put away wet." It described this lady well. She had wrinkles in the wrinkles of her orange-tinted leathery skin, dark circles under her eyes, and dead hair teased, sprayed, and locked into something unnatural. The hair was big and stiff; it looked like a helmet when she moved and it didn't. She must've found her look in Texas in the eighties. It's a funny thing when people become a look instead of just wearing it.

I looked over at my sister; her head was tilted forward. She was asleep or praying. Piper still sat perfectly rigid next to me, staring forward. She was a lousy travel companion, but life could be much worse. I imagined how uncomfortable my comrades, stuffed in their seats next to Big Foot, would be after about twelve more hours in their positions. There was no telling how long we might be on one of these flights. They flew all over the country, stopping in weird airfields, picking up and dropping off prisoners. From what I had learned on my first trip with Con Air and what I had been able to glean from the women I'd traveled with and stayed with in the Oklahoma facility, there were at least three big planes like this one and three general routes they took into and out of Oklahoma City, one going north, one east, and one west. I had now been on each. We were on the plane for however long it took them to land wherever we were being dropped off.

There was a logo still painted on the plane's cabin partition wall: TRAVEL PLANET. We were flying on a decommissioned old 747 from a defunct charter airline company. The seats were worn and dingy, but there were still little signs of the life the plane once had. Sharp edges around a dug-out hole were all that remained of the ashtray that used to be embedded in my seat's armrest; frayed stitches lined where there had once been the magazine and barf bag pocket in the seatbacks; and now doorless luggage bins gaped empty overhead.

I couldn't sit up and turn my head to look at all my other travel companions or to imagine the former inhabitants of this plane, not without getting a black box. Nobody wanted that, so they used the threat of wearing one to keep all two hundred or so convicts docile. That's the weird little metal contraption left over from the Spanish Inquisition I got to wear once. So far, no one on this flight was wearing one.

I didn't want to be the first, so I sat still, closed my eyes, and tried to slip off to sleep. One benefit to having such a rich life was that when I dreamed, I had a lot of material to work with. It would be kind of weird to have a dream about the Piper I used to know while sitting next to the ice princess she had become. I was amusing the hell out of myself. I thought about all the stuff that had happened after she and I had gone our separate ways in Brussels, looked at the statue sitting next to me, and remembered the last thing she had said to me in Brussels about hurrying home. *Sorry, I got held up.*

16 One Flew Over the Cuckoo's Nest

Metropolitan Correctional Center (MCC), Chicago
March 2005

THE MCC IS SMACK DAB IN THE CENTER of downtown Chicago. It's a triangle-shaped building, tall and thin. We approached it from the ninety-degree corner of the building and pulled up to a big garage door at its base, so we didn't know about its odd shape until later. The marshals ran into a problem when we arrived and attempted to get the facility to open the big metal doors. They were late and the wizard on their walkie-talkies announced it was too close to the facility's four o'clock count time to open the gates to Oz. There were frantic negotiations under way to try to get the facility to accept their delivery and not make the marshals sit with us for two hours before allowing us to enter.

There were only two white vans in our little caravan. One for the men and one for the women. Piper, Hester, and I were the only women, so we had plenty of room, but Bradley was in a van packed full of men. We could see him when the van pulled up alongside us. I couldn't help but wonder if any of the men with him were here to testify for the same trial, and if they were, for which side. My quandary was answered when the marshals loudly complained to the wizard about the risks of making them sit on the street like sitting ducks with four witnesses in a big drug case. Poor dears. It hadn't even occurred to me they might get a bullet intended for one of us.

I had forgotten completely about the potential hazards of Chicago and the multitudes of Alajeh's associates there. Since there were only three of us in our van, the guys would know at least one of them was a snitch. I felt sorry for Bradley being stuck in the van with all those guys. It is my understanding that male prisoners are much more violent and prone to acting out just for shits and grins, and the marshals had given them just cause. Fortunately, the wizard agreed with the marshals' concerns for their safety and the massive doors lifted, permitting our entry.

This entry led to an underground garage and a heavy metal doorway, whose locks were also controlled by the wizard. This doorway led to an area surrounded by holding cells, with bulletproof glass half walls instead of bars. In the center, there was a command control room, also encased in bulletproof glass. The officers looked like they were operating in a dirty fishbowl and the wizard looked like a fat blowfish. Once we were locked inside one of the several holding cells, the men were all paraded in and unshackled. We could see Bradley had been placed in a cell on the opposite side of the fishbowl, but communicating with him was impossible.

Once they got us all squared away in the holding cells, all the officers except the blowfish wizard left the area, presumably to go count the inmates residing in the facility. We could rely on being in our holding cell for at least two hours. That was how long we would have been on the street waiting to enter had the wizard not been concerned with the safety of the marshals. How much longer than that would depend on whether they processed the men into the facility before us or we were first.

Hester was the one who finally broke the ice with Piper. I love my sister so much. She brokered our détente in two minutes. It was so fast I can't even remember how she did it or what magic words ended the cold silence between all of us. But she did it.

It was so strange when we started talking again. I had not seen her since October of 1993 in Brussels, when she told me she was going back to California and wanted nothing to do with my smuggling activities. I realized that we had never even officially broken up. Our relationship had gone from steamy hot, about to be married, to no contact without a single discussion about our relationship. She had called me once, shortly after Phillip and Garrett had had a very ill-fated trip, and told me it was over and that she had told someone—a lawyer, I think—about us. Before that call, I had intended to go to San Francisco, explain away why I had been held up for so long, and hopefully start over with her. But after Phillip's friend had been busted and everything else that had occurred after that, even without her call, I would never have made it to San Francisco until I was forced to go there on Con Air.

I knew she was aware of my testimony at the grand jury that had indicted her. What I hadn't expected was that she held me singly accountable for her fate. I had read a prepared statement to the grand jury, a statement prepared almost two years after my arrest. It was a very accurate accounting of my role and everyone else's roles in the conspiracy, but it was a much richer account than my proffer in the post office in Vermont had been. By then, I'd had no choice left but to read that statement, and my not doing so would have violated my plea agreement. When we first started talking, I had to take on a weird role in our little trio, Hester, Piper, and me. The tables had turned so completely from Hester being my baby sister to the wise creature she had become. I hadn't seen Hester either in almost three years, but she had changed. At first, it was a very cordial conversation between the three of us. When we finally arrived at the women's floor where we would be staying, it was clear we probably wouldn't have much to talk about with the other women in the facility.

All the women looked in our direction, and when the door to our unit opened up, a hush fell over the room like aliens had landed. I'm only guessing about the hush; I couldn't possibly hear it over the volume blasting from dueling television shows or the smoke alarm going off from popcorn someone had burned in the microwave. It was a small space for all the women they housed. My first impression of our new digs was "insane asylum."

Piper and I had an opportunity to talk through much of what had caused her reaction to me in the transfer center in Oklahoma. The conversation started as sarcastic threats to drown me in the toilet for ratting her out blurted out in jest during a marathon game of Rummy 5000. There was nothing to do in the small quarters at the MCC but read, watch television, play cards, sleep, and eat. Access to the library, recreation, and fresh air required an escort for the women—a trip on the elevator to some other floor in the facility—and that did not happen frequently. Then one day we were taking our once-a-week hour of outdoor recreation on the roof of the MCC, adjusting to the sudden increase in oxygen and the frigid wind and looking out toward Lake Michigan, and I saw the sign for the Congress Plaza Hotel at the edge of the city.

"Is that the Congress Hotel?" Piper asked me, this with a hint of astonishment in her intonation, at the very same moment I was trying to focus my eyes on the same sign.

"It is." I had stayed there for my sentencing, so I did not have the untainted memory of good times associated with the hotel anymore. I suppose she did.

"Is the Blackstone to the left or the right?" she asked, and we both looked for another huge sign but couldn't find one. We were several miles away, in the heart of downtown Chicago, so it would have to be a big flashy sign for us to see it.

"Doesn't it seem like that was in a different lifetime?" I asked.

"It does. I can't believe how stupid we were."

We—you mean me.

A few days later, in one of our rare hours of rec time at the gymnasium, we talked. I had finished riding the elliptical bike and she was in the middle of the gymnasium finishing up her yoga. I sat down on the floor nearby and just came right out and asked her if she thought I was responsible for her conviction. She did. She had every right to her anger at my grand jury testimony, but I felt she was blaming me for too much of her situation, as if she were not at all responsible for her predicament. We talked about our other co-defendants briefly—but she only knew a couple of them aside from Donald, Phillip, and Hester—comparing what we knew about the fate of each, which was not much.

I still don't know how they got to me and I no longer care. But when being asked to shoulder the entire blame, instead of letting her have this, I deflected blame. I pointed my finger at Phillip, positing he must have led the feds to me, since the guy in Chicago who was the first to get caught and cooperate did not know me from Eve. Like I said, I was still not quite finished assigning and accepting blame myself. I regret that. I stole from her a priceless opportunity to forgive me and retarded a healing process we both desperately needed. Aside from that, Phillip did the right thing and neither he nor any of my friends owned the blame for anyone else's fate but their own. The only one who didn't sign a plea agreement and cooperate with the government was Henry. He risked everything for that brand of moral clarity and he lost. He was found guilty and sentenced to ten years.

We all blame someone for the things we do that go wrong; I'm certain of it, even if it's only for a second. But unless you want to play the victim for your whole life, you have to come around sooner or later and face yourself. I made a much easier target for that blame than for her to look at her own role in it. But I have no room to judge, as I did the same thing. It took me longer than it took Piper to stop being a victim, and I still have to work at it. I blamed everything from A to Z for my circumstances, but not me.

I blamed Alajeh for scaring me and my society for its barbaric drug laws. Prohibition does not work; it just increases the value of the thing being banned, and that amplifies the problem and creates a whole new set of them, much uglier. Drugs like alcohol should be regulated, not barred. Addicts should be treated, not jailed. The drug wars have failed; we have more people dying from heroin overdoses than ever before in history. We also have the highest prison population of any country in the world, most from first-offense drug crimes.

I blamed the whole justice system for being so flawed and Opie for his unintended deception. I chose to believe that Opie really had wanted to help me. I understood why Piper was still so freshly full of angst when I found out she had only been down a year. It had taken me two years to make peace with my punishment and accept that I had earned it myself, all myself.

———— • ————

The trip back to Dublin was the beginning of my karmic retribution for testifying against Henry, I was sure of it. When we got back to the MCC after our part in the trial was over, Piper, Hester, and I had put together a nice dinner in the MCC microwave, the night before we were certain we would be picked up by the marshals to begin our trips back. We would be returned to the Oklahoma transfer facility, and we longed to get that far. At least that place was clean and quiet. That is like saying at least it's just the frying pan, not the fire. But it was an improvement, and being in Oklahoma would mean we were on our way back to our respective facilities—home.

In the morning, my sister and I got called to pack out. Piper was not on the list. We felt so awful leaving her behind in that godforsaken hole. The place was horrible, made up of mostly lunatics and women in a very different place than we were, with absolutely nothing to do but read, play cards, and watch TV or the soap operas going on in the lives around them. But at least we'd had each other. Even in a place that small, it helps to have your own people. Now we were going to have to abandon her to contend all alone with the lunatics, whom we had joined forces against. I had managed to piss a couple of the women off by being assigned to a bunk they wanted. Piper and Hester had saved me from the crafty, crazy old ladies trying to get rid of me. Leaving Piper there with them felt awful.

I was worried for Piper, as was Hester. Hester cried for her on the way to our waiting plane, but there was absolutely nothing we could do about it. Piper would have to survive in the loony bin there all alone. The next Con Air flight to Oklahoma was not for two whole weeks.

Hester probably should have reserved a few of her prayers for us. Our first stop was in a snow-covered airport in Minnesota somewhere. When the plane landed, everyone clapped, then the electricity went out.

Hester and I had missed the decision-making process that had preceded our boarding the plane in Chicago, and we had been so consumed in our own little world, we hadn't noticed everyone white-knuckling the whole ride to Minnesota or how quiet our shackled companions had been all the way there.

The marshals were now cursing themselves for not doing some necessary repair to the plane in Chicago. The part that they now needed for the plane was days away.

They talked about having everyone on the plane taken to local county jails but found that there was not enough room for all of us. In Chicago, they could have easily dropped everyone in Cook County for a few days.

It was thirty below zero outside. The mechanic did some kind of jerry-rigging to the part that had failed, the same trick he had used to keep the plane powered and in the air for the last leg of the journey, and four hours after landing, the electricity came back on and we took off. This time, though, we were acutely aware of our plane's potential to fall out of the sky. The marshals were apparently quite accustomed to the risks of their job and thought of themselves as modern-day cowboys, calling anyone who complained pansies. They didn't mind flying a plane the FAA would have grounded; of course, they were paid volunteers, not in shackles.

When we landed in Oklahoma, Hester and I looked at each other and laughed nervously. We waited patiently for our turn to exit the plane and once again enter the transfer center's gauntlet of lines. The long and boring procession from one line to another was the last obstacle to having a cigarette. We had made it back to Oklahoma. We would once again breathe fresh air and be able to smoke.

These were the two things we had missed most the five or six weeks we had been cooped up in the cuckoo's nest in Chicago.

When the marshals got to our section and were about to unload us, they called out a list of names of who was to remain seated; these were the poor bastards who had arbitrarily been chosen to do their layover in Oklahoma at a county jail. This happened whenever the FTC was overbooked. The marshals paid local jails to handle their overflow.

I was on the list. Hester reluctantly got out of her seat and left me behind. She turned around before exiting the plane in her shackles. She looked like she was about to burst into tears, but she managed to mouth the words "Shackle Shuffle."

Piper, Hester, and I had choreographed a little dance we would all do when we got to Oklahoma, or as our victory dance one day when we met again in the free world. It would be like our little secret handshake, since no one else would know what the hell we were doing or what we had been through together. My little sister was saying goodbye to me and I knew it would be years before I saw her face again. Rumor had it that getting farmed out from the FTC like this was bad luck, or in my case, a payment on the karmic debt for testifying against Henry.

A handful of women, including myself, were loaded into a white van and driven somewhere about an hour from the Oklahoma City FTC. I knew I was in trouble when one of the escorts, the older of the two guys, gave us all three cigarettes to share among the nine of us. This was payment for a titty show the teenage girl in the front row of the van had negotiated. The girl had apparently done this before. The fact that he knew he would get away with this, in spite of the grumpy and offended nonsmokers on board, did not speak well of what lay ahead.

When we pulled into the gravel parking lot and I saw the sign out front, my hopes died. We had ended up at the Grady County Jail. This place was well known among federal prisoners at the FTC. I had heard of it there. But I had heard Shady Grady had lost its contract with the feds for too many violations.

I spent two weeks in the Grady County Jail annex for women, without a change of underwear, without a shower, and without heat or air-conditioning, both of which would have been nice on different occasions. This place was deplorable. The tap water stank to high heaven and was the color of mud. They barely fed us—a biscuit and some gravy for breakfast, a baloney sandwich with one slice of baloney for lunch, and a rotation of absolutely inedible goulash for dinner. The women who had been there for a while subsisted on food that family members were allowed to drop off once a month.

The women who would have otherwise been on psychiatric medication were regularly denied their meds if they were unfortunate enough to run out of the supply the marshals brought along with them, and the women who should have been on heart and seizure medication didn't get that either. The place was contracted by the U.S. Marshals Service, and they had just gotten their lucrative, but canceled, contract back. Apparently, the refusal to provide humane conditions or comply with federal policies was considered a breach of said contract. How they had gotten the contract reinstated was beyond my imagination.

I got back to Dublin on March 10th. I wanted to kiss the ground when I arrived. It was absolutely surreal returning to the place I had once thought of as a prison. The flowers were all blooming, the grass was green, and the birds were singing. After my first shower in two weeks, I thought I had died and gone to heaven. Home sweet home.

17 Tatiana

Federal Prison Camp, Dublin, California
August 2005

MY TRANSFER OUT OF the FCI to the FPC came as a huge surprise to me. The FCI is a higher security facility with more officers lording over inmates all the time. It is behind razor wire, with armed perimeter trucks circling it. There are fourteen hundred women there, compared to fewer than three hundred women across the street in the FPC. In the FCI, we were locked down most of the day in either the housing units or facilities buildings and permitted a few minutes to move from one building to another only once an hour. The prison in Dublin also housed a much broader spectrum of criminal than the camp in Dublin.

There were cold-blooded murderers in this prison, famous felons, terrorists, rival gangs from the streets, the insane, and a huge immigrant population from all over the world. We had more Hispanic or Latina women than any other ethnicity, from an array of Latin American countries. I think the disproportionately large immigrant population there were primarily women who had been caught one too many times crossing the U.S. border from Mexico. I never took a poll to figure out exactly why the Latinas were so over-represented in Dublin. I had no desire to know exactly how many Griselda Blancos were among us. Griselda Blanco was the God-mother of the Medellín cartel. She had ordered hundreds of executions in her reign over the Miami cocaine industry.

Griselda, the Godmother of Cocaine, was no longer a resident in Dublin when I arrived. I did not want to know how many of her contemporaries were still among us in Dublin, so I never asked any of the Latina ladies why they were there. Surely, you have seen how brutally the drug wars have played out in the countries to our south. It was better to focus on being very careful not to piss off anyone I didn't know well. The weapon and attack of choice in Dublin was a padlock in the end of a tube sock, swung at your sleepy head on a pillow.

Whatever the cause for so many Latinas, the bright side was the fantastic food the Mexican mommies could create in a microwave, and our Cinco de Mayo celebrations were as big as the Fourth of July, sans the fireworks. I also learned to salsa, assuming you would even categorize my attempt at this as a dance.

The prison was not always as overcrowded as it was during my stay. Some of the old-timers who had been serving life sentences now shared rooms with three other women, rooms that they had, twenty years ago, had to themselves. Overcrowding and familiarity breed contempt, so violence, even among the gentler gender of our species, was common, brutal, and sometimes lethal. I managed to make it out of there without incident. I stayed out of people's business, for the most part, except for teaching in the computer lab. That was a difficult adjustment. I am naturally curious about everyone, perhaps nosy, but in the prison, if I saw something interesting brewing, I didn't want to know about it, not even with my close friends.

The guards and staff at the prison had also been harder to deal with than at the camp. I had gotten used to the lack of human decency there, like guards refusing to be bothered to call the nurse for a woman dying from a heart attack and threatening her bunkie with the SHU—the "special housing unit"—if she didn't calm down and go back to her room. The SHU is where bad girls are sent for solitary confinement. One officer had given a woman a shot—an incident report—for refusing to work instead of sending her to Medical as she had requested. I guess the officer had thought she was faking her headache and throwing up. She died from an aneurism that night. Ironically, she died before the incident report had been picked up by her counselor.

That was how incident reports worked. If we were given a shot, it was sent to our counselor and to the lieutenant on duty. If it was serious in nature, like a fight or women having sex, the lieutenant would come get us, put handcuffs on us, and take us to the SHU. The irony I mentioned was if the woman had just hauled off and punched the CO who wouldn't let her see the nurse, she might have lived. That is a big maybe, but who knows? At first, I was aghast by incidents like this when they occurred; they ate at me and quietly filled me with rage.

Most of the lack of human decency was subtler than these horrific examples; it was in the way they always just stood over this one girl, who was severely epileptic, and watched her bang her head on the floor over and over again while they chatted. My brother is epileptic and this drove me out of my mind. I wanted to leap from the balcony and lunge at one of those officers. The first time it happened, it was at count time, and the girl lived in my unit's wing. So we all got to watch this occur, quietly, or go to the SHU. Interrupting count time is a big no-no, an SHU offense, so is leaping from balconies and lunging at officers, so none of the 150 women watching said a peep, and I stayed in my room.

Then, of course, the daily dose of smaller indecencies add up, things like the male guards who overtly squeezed our breasts on the way out of the kitchen when they pat us down. They were in search of chicken wings. Seriously, on chicken-wing day they would pat us down and molest anyone with boobs. You might be thinking, *Cleary, could chicken bones be used as a weapon?* The plastic sporks we used every day would surely work better if that was what we were after. No, it was the delicious chicken wings they were worried about. Those could be packed in ice, hidden in the back of a toilet, and sold on non-chicken-wing days. Even certain members of the staff, normally nice people, sometimes failed the test of being a decent human. One teacher wouldn't let an old lady go to the bathroom ten feet away from his classroom. She peed her pants. Was that necessary?

The one thing it took me a long time to adapt to was my utter invisibility to most of the staff. I was an inmate, that's all, subhuman, and some staff would literally watch me die in front of them rather than get up off a chair and help me. I am a friendly person. I used to always smile when I passed by people on the street. But if I smiled at a staff member who did not know me, they looked straight through me like I wasn't even there. If every employee of the BOP were like this, it would be intolerable and our prison system would make China's record for human rights look like a good report card in comparison. Fortunately, for every one monster there, there were several perfectly wonderful human beings, like my bosses in the computer lab. But it would be the monsters that made a more lasting impression on me.

I very recently saw a YouTube video of a bunch of American fishermen on a fancy yacht using five-week-old kittens as live bait. These men were drinking beer and laughing at the pathetic mews from the precious creatures they tortured. One kitten shook and squirmed, trying to get away from the hook in its back. It was lowered on a fishing line into the ocean, where it desperately swam in circles, crying out. It was gobbled up by something big in the water, then the video showed the guy pulling a huge fish into the boat, falling over on it, and humping it.

These men in the video made me think of some of the correctional officers in the FCI, who used to jokingly kick at the stray cats that lived on the grounds, chase the geese and their goslings, stomping while they ran to scare them, and otherwise harass every smaller and defenseless creature that crossed their paths. These are people completely stripped of any normal impulses and lacking even the most miniscule ounce of empathy for any creature, let alone a human being. The video triggered me; it upset me in the same way watching the correctional officers in the FCI did once. By the time I was transferred to the camp, though, I was blind to these people in my world. These monsters were invisible to me. I didn't smile as I passed by them anymore. I just pretended they did not exist. The only people I focused on were the nice ones, and that includes both inmates and staff.

I had to survive though. I didn't want to go mad, and dwelling on all that was wrong with my little world would have no other result. After dinner, we had open movement on the compound until around nine o'clock at night. On Saturdays and Sundays we had open movement all day except for a couple of hours around the ten A.M. count, when we all returned to our units and rooms to be counted, then again at four P.M. I found a niche, a routine, a way to avoid most of what was ugly or unbearable in the FCI and see only what was good: I stayed at work during weekdays, while there was no open movement, and out of the living unit at all other times, when I could be out of the units and roam around the yard freely. I spent this time at the tennis courts; in the rec field, lying out in the sun; at the weight pile, working out; at movie nights in the gymnasium; taking paper-making classes, legal-research classes, pottery classes, and crochet classes; looking for places to hide with my lover to try to steal a kiss without getting caught; having picnics in the rec field with my friends; or with my friends on picture days, when we were allowed to get our pictures taken together.

At night, when we were once again locked in the units and my lover was back in her unit, I had mail call to look forward to: letters from Mom and Dad, aka Catherine and Eugene Wolters. Just like in the free world, there were shows I watched regularly with my friends: *Nip/Tuck* and *Rescue Me* nights, etc. My routine kept me in motion, and being in motion made time fly. Then it all came to an abrupt halt, and there was not a thing I could do about it.

The timing of my transfer to camp sucked. I had been in the FCI for two and a half years, and it felt like my sentence was going by so quickly. I had earned the right to be pretty much left alone by the staff. Some of them even liked me and spoke freely about their disdain for the same staff that inmates hated, so I knew there were humans among them; just like anyplace else, there were normal people, nice people, and complete assholes. I was in the last days of my second prison love affair and at the beginning of a big computer lab project for the regional director of education for the Bureau of Prisons. Tatiana, my beautiful friend, worked with me in the computer lab. We were both tutors for all the computer classes offered to other inmates and we worked on special assignments not normally entrusted to inmates, like creating a movie incorporating pictures and footage from the prison's history with cheesy special effects for a thirtieth anniversary party for the BOP staff. It featured personal photos of old wardens and pictures of the staff outside of their roles in the pokey, in street clothes, mixed in with some of the more notorious residents and happenings in Dublin. People like Griselda Blanco, the Godmother; Heidi Fleiss, the Hollywood Madame; Marilyn Buck, the white Black Panther; and Stella, the Tylenol Killer (actually a copycat who used Excedrin, but they still called her the Tylenol lady).

Of all the work assignments I could have gotten, the computer lab was the best. My knowledge of programming and networking should have been cause to ban me from even visiting the computer lab. The Bureau of Prisons (BOP for short) is very nervous about inmate access to technology. But "institutional need," the trump card invoked to bypass BOP policies, was used because I could provide a needed service. I had been put there to replace an inmate who had just been released after nine years. She had been a systems administrator in the real world and had kept the computer lab hardware and software functioning. The lab's equipment was about as outdated as her knowledge of information technology.

I was first introduced to Tatiana at a Hacky Sack game in front of my unit. I had seen her floating across the commons on many occasions, but she didn't land within my social reach prior to a certain Sunday afternoon's game. Prior to this introduction, I was also still with Sissy, my first love in prison. Sissy had recently been released and so I had been nursing a broken heart when my friends started dragging me out of the unit to participate in life again as a remedy for my blues.

Watching Tatiana play Hacky Sack was like watching a Cirque du Soleil act. Tatiana is an extraordinarily graceful being; she played Hacky Sack as if it were an elegant dance. I think the sack even slowed itself in midair to keep her from having to jerk awkwardly like we humans do when playing the silly game. Of course, I know that can't happen, but as someone who plays Hacky Sack like she's being stung by red ants, I needed to believe in magic in order to keep playing in the presence of such magnificence.

At first glance, Tatiana consisted almost entirely of legs—long, slender, creamy white, athletic legs. She didn't have a hint of cellulite. She wasn't bony though, more like a classic Roman statue. Imagine the graceful, winged, and headless statue Victory of Samothrace hopping up and playing a little Hacky. No, scratch that, that's just plain weird. Tatiana was slightly above average height. She had long straight black hair, green eyes, red lips, and flawless pale white skin. She was exotic and had learned to speak English in London, so she had a scrumptious accent. I was mesmerized and she was straight.

Tatiana enrolled in one of the classes I taught and I discovered she was also intelligent, really intelligent, and that was it for me. For a while, I turned beet red and stammered whenever she simply asked a question in the class. The other students thought it was funny, except one. Sara Jane Moore, the failed assassin of Gerald Ford, didn't think my distraction was funny at all. She lodged a formal complaint against me for being a lousy tutor and paying too much attention to Tatiana. I had to defend my behavior to the computer lab boss, with Tatiana present. He was only following the required protocol for the complaint. It was his intention to resolve the problem informally, not to embarrass me or sanction me for my crush on Tatiana.

His informal resolution was that I convincingly apologize to Sara

Jane Moore and give her more focused attention for a little while. In my defense, I told my boss how smart Tatiana was and that she would be a great tutor in the lab. That was why I was so invested in her success. When Tatiana and Sara Jane Moore left his office, he sarcastically agreed with my assessment of her potential as a tutor in the computer lab.

Tatiana was pulled from one of the grunt crews to work in the lab shortly after that. The "institutional need" she fulfilled probably had more to do with her appearance than her background. She was hired right after one of the underskilled clerks, who looked a lot like Tatiana, went home. Tatiana and I became quick friends after all that and my crush on her became a topic she teased me with. I didn't deny my attraction to her but told her not to worry about it, no one could ever replace Sissy, who had gone home to Seattle. At the time, I thought I was going to move to Seattle and live happily ever after with Sissy when I got out.

Tatiana and I started playing tennis together regularly, then going to lunch, then dinner. I got to know one of her relatives, who was also a resident in FCI Dublin. I learned of the horrific details of her family's long tragedy and how they eventually had been granted asylum in the United States. But they'd ended up in a nonsensical drama that had resulted in much of her family being sent to federal prison for a conspiracy to help illegal aliens get to and stay in the United States.

I started hanging out with Tatiana's friends, a group of eastern Slavic women from various countries once part of the Soviet Union. They were referred to as the KGB by others. Tatiana taught me to speak and write their common language, Russian—well, tried anyway. One day we were having a heated debate on whether or not homosexuality was an abomination, a perversion, and completely unnatural, as she believed, or a natural and genetically assigned tendency, as I believed. Somehow we got on the topic of what this abnormal sex was like.

"What do lesbians do?" she asked.

"Oh my God! Tatiana, use your imagination." She had made

herself blush by asking the question and that amused me. But not enough to give her a *Joy of Sex* introduction to lesbian positions. Her curiosity grew and then focused on me.

This was a particularly tricky relationship to conduct. Not only did we have to keep it secret and hidden from the prison staff. Sex in federal prison is a 200-series infraction, a 205 specifically, which is of the same severity as rioting or assault. Getting caught would result in going to the SHU, losing the great computer lab jobs, getting sent back to an A and O room (that is "arrival and orientation"), and an A and O job in the kitchen and in the garbage. But we also had to worry about the KGB. Tatiana did not want anyone to find out what we were doing.

As Tatiana's release date approached, the status of her asylum was in jeopardy because of her possible status as a convicted felon. Her five-year sentence was nearly completed, but due to a series of continuances, her family's appeal for wrongful conviction was still stalled in the Appellate Court. After the fruits of prosecutorial misconduct were removed from a potential new trial, if a new and fair trial were granted, she said there would be no case or conviction for her or her family members. Her husband would be released from prison the same day as Tatiana.

Tatiana and I were together for only a year by then and I was still in that madly in love phase when we had to split up. We had spent all of our time playing tennis, teaching in the computer lab, working on special projects for the facility, or *doing inventory* in the storage closet in the lab. While it's not as easy to do as fictional fantasies about women and sex in prison suggest, it is possible to have a lover. The one thing you cannot do is determine when and how your relationship will end. It comes with an expiration date; someone gets to go home first.

Our relationship was originally scheduled to end on her release date. This is a traumatic time for lovers in prison. It's one lover's release day, the happy day you wait and pray for years you will make it to. But with a lover, it's also the end of a love affair. Somebody has to leave somebody behind, which puts a bit of a damper on what would otherwise be an amazing day. Being left behind is excruciating; I had gone through that happy event once already with Sissy. But with Tatiana, it was all the more confusing because I didn't know if she would be all right when she left. It all depended on whether she and her husband lost their asylum and had to find someplace else on the planet to run to for safety.

Our goodbye was cut extremely short. About a week before her release date, I went back to my unit for the four P.M. count and she went to hers. I found out I was going to be transferred to the camp, and by dinner I was gone. I was only across the street, but it might as well have been in another universe, hundreds of light-years away. My unplanned departure was probably a heavenly intervention. Tatiana would also be leaving some of her family behind. God had wanted Tatiana and her family to spend that last week together, not us.

I spent the first week at the camp bored out of my mind, sitting on a picnic table across the street and staring at the FCI entrance, hoping to get one more glimpse of Tatiana before she left my universe. I worried about her too. Because of the questionable state of her asylum, there was a good chance she would be picked up by Immigration and taken to a county jail being used for immigration holdovers when she walked out the front gates of the prison.

I had prayed, done voodoo dances, and made chocolate cupcake offerings to the squirrel gods for the whole week prior to her release for her unimpeded passage to Los Angeles. Being over in the camp, I couldn't find out how it all turned out until her release day. Her husband was getting out of his prison on the same day from a facility somewhere in Texas. If she came out of the FCI, got into a waiting car, and no Immigration van pulled up to intercept her, all was well. If not, I had mailed her contact information to my father and he promised to find out what had happened to her and her husband and make sure they had the legal representation they needed. Dad was my hero.

If nothing went wrong, Tatiana and her husband would both be safely at home by nightfall. I had already gotten her sister's phone number in Los Angeles added to my approved list, and so I could call there with my PAC (phone access code). We were only able to dial out to a preapproved list of telephone numbers on the phone systems in prison, and Tatiana and my calls would be monitored, so I would have to be careful about what we said when we spoke, if we spoke. I would also have to make sure her sister's number made it onto my list in time.

There is a form I had to fill out and hand in to my counselor to get a new number added to this list. The counselor would then type the number into another computer-based form if she approved it. The electronic addition is instant, but my counselor was not so quick to make the entry, unless I brought the form to her in person and urged her to add the number then and there.

I hadn't tried to expedite the process by personally delivering the form and sitting with my counselor until she added it, lest she get curious and figure out the number belonged to Tatiana's sister and not a former coworker from the free world. But I found the number added to my list two days after I'd submitted it and in plenty of time for Tatiana's release day. All that was left to happen, so that I could talk to my Tatiana at least one more time, was that she not be picked up by Immigration and booted out of the country.

My dad was sending a note to both Tatiana and her husband at the sister's house in Los Angeles. He'd told me this was the best way he could think of to let her know I was happy for both of them, for her whole little family. He knew I had been her lover for a year and had told me he thought her husband would understand. He cautioned me, though, that if she never told him, to be her friend and keep her secret safe. She'd been through enough already.

On Tatiana's release day, I followed a bunch of campers who did landscaping work across the street to the front of the FCI and pretended to be sweeping the parking lot near the entrance while the rest of the group of campers spread out to do their real work, mowing, pruning, watering, and planting. The parking lot near the entrance to the FCI was way past the yellow line we were not to cross without permission, but a friend, a former FCI inhabitant and now camper, had gotten me added to her landscaping team to be a sweeper for the day. My plan, if I got caught out of bounds, was to play dumb, like I had not understood I was to sweep only the camp parking lot and not the neighboring area in front of the FCI.

Tatiana came out of the FCI entrance dressed in black. I was shocked to see her in a different color than khaki, when that and gray sweats were the only colors I had ever seen her dressed in. Her hair had been styled, and she was all made up. She was absolutely stunning. She saw me milling about in the parking lot with a broom in hand, trying to pretend I was sweeping and not lurking around the entrance to the FCI. I was wearing my new colors. Camp residents wore light blue, not khaki. She waved and smiled at me and then waved at her friends in the waiting car and yelled something to them in her language. She couldn't come to me, but I could tell how happy she was to see me, and how happy she was to be free after five years in prison. She yelled to me that it felt funny walking out of the prison and she kept looking up at the sky, like something might drop from it and crush her. I laughed loudly.

I had never understood the weird reactions some women had on their release days, until I had walked out the front gate of the FCI myself after thirty months. Shit, one lady had even turned around and wanted to come back in. The phenomenon is strange, because you are not going from being locked indoors to suddenly seeing the sky above you for the first time in however long. You are just walking through a building; on one side you are free, on the other you are not. Even so, something subtle feels off, like when you get off a boat and it feels like the ground is fluid. I had gotten the odd sensation of being untethered when I had walked out a week earlier, and all I had been doing was walking across the street to the camp unescorted.

"I don't know what I am doing!" She laughed at herself and the strange reaction she had to walking out the front door of the FCI. "I love you!" She yelled this to me right in front of her friends in the car and it surprised me. Tatiana's crew of Russian friends inside were big homophobes. "I will see you again in London!"

"I love you too. Be safe!" We had made plans to meet in London when we could travel again, but we both knew it was fantasy. I stared right through the car with her in it for a moment, imagining what it must feel like to be sitting down in the air-conditioned car, about to drive away as she was, instead of standing in the hot sun, pushing a broom, with so much time left to do, as was my fate. Her friend jumped out of the car and put her bag into the trunk. He was tall and beefy and probably had no idea who I was or that he was driving away with my lover. He waved to me, almost dismissively, and got back into the car.

I could see Tatiana, sitting in the passenger seat, light up a cigarette and she made sure I saw this. Smoking had been banned from federal facilities in January while I had been away in Chicago. We had paid twenty dollars in commissary for one cigarette when I'd gotten back, then we'd quit. But now she took a big puff of her pink Nat Sherman, the brand she'd smoked on the streets. We'd only had access to cheap generic brands when they had sold them legally inside, then stale tobacco rolled up in paper from tampon and toilet paper wrappers after smoking had been banned.

I saw the taillights flash once and heard the Volvo's engine, then it pulled forward and circled the same roundabout I had been dropped at thirty months earlier. As the Volvo made its way around the big circle, they came closer to where I was standing with my broom and slowed down a little. Tatiana smiled at me. She stretched her arms out wide, like a bird, and when the car accelerated, she flew away.

18 Patches

Federal Prison Camp, Dublin, California
August 2005 to October 2008

THE VOLVO TATIANA WAS IN disappeared around the corner of the perimeter fence at the end of Eighth Street and vanished. On the other side of that fence was the free world. It was so close all the time I was inside the FCI but invisible until now. Eighth Street was used only by cars and service vehicles entering and exiting there to go to either the federal prison camp (FPC) on the left, the federal correctional institution (FCI) for women, the federal detention center (FDC) for men on the right, or the warehouses and staff housing farther up the road. That road intersected with Eighth Street, about an eighth of a mile beyond where the FPC and FCI entrances faced each other.

There was a yellow line at the edge of the parking lot in the camp. The line crossed the paved entryway, which was just past the last building in a row of five identical buildings that made up the camp. If you were not assigned to landscaping, to the warehouses, or to some duty that required you to cross that line, it was out-of-bounds. I was approximately fifty yards beyond that yellow line, out-of-bounds and trying to look busy, as if I had a reason to be there. The campers roamed all over the area I have just described, and we all wore blue uniforms; there were no special outfits for newcomers. So I knew I was as invisible as the ground squirrels to most of the staff passing by me, but there was always the chance someone like my old computer lab boss from the FCI might take notice that it was me in the blue they were accustomed to ignoring on their way into work.

I had to make a quick dash across the parking lot, Eighth Street, and back into the camp without getting an incident report for being out of bounds. Mr. Green, the boss at CMS, which I think stood for Contracting Maintenance Service, didn't write me up when he'd caught me lurking near the FCI's entrance earlier that week. I was still accustomed to the more militant posturing from the guards inside the razor wire at the FCI. So I had been certain I was in for a good dose of humiliation and a shot when Mr. Green caught me over there the first time, but nothing had happened. He had just laughed, asked me if I was lost, turned around, and buzzed away across the parking lot on his golf cart.

It would have sucked to start out my stay at the camp with commissary or phone restriction for thirty days, especially since my parents were coming to visit me the following week. I had not seen them in over two years and changing their plans would have been impossible this late in the game. They were visiting me on their way to Hawaii. Besides, I didn't want to do anything to cancel their annual visit. It meant so much to me and I couldn't wait to see them. They would be so happy too, to visit me in the camp where we could sit at picnic tables in the beautiful green outdoors—so much nicer than their visit was inside FCI the year before.

When I reached the edge of the FCI parking lot, I dashed back across Eighth Street and over to the smaller camp parking lot, stopping every so often to look busy, like I had actually been sent out there to work with the landscaping crew I had tagged along with. I swept random swaths of clean blacktop or sidewalk with such purpose you would have thought I was competing, except that I was all alone. Still being an A and O, though, sweeping and raking leaves was what I should have been doing all morning, just not across the street. That made me nervous, the closer I got to camp. Though I was an A and O again—which stands for "arrival and orientation" or "Please humiliate and torture me; I am new"—all the camp staff knew me already from the FCI. Therefore, with exception to my living arrangement, I was spared the normal routine abuses for newcomers, like being stalked around the compound and harassed or belittled until you were humbled enough to willingly accept your newly acquired, subhuman stature. But this familiarity meant they would know I had no business being as far out as I had gone.

The camp was made up of five long two-story buildings, like giant train cars set side by side. Between each of the buildings, there was a walkway and two or three entrances to the buildings on either side. The buildings were labeled C1, C2, C3, and C4. It had taken all of about five minutes to get the lay of the land there. C1 and C2 were permanent housing. The rooms were about twice the size of those in the FCI. I wasn't yet fortunate enough to have one of these rooms, but I would soon. In these units, each prisoner shared a room with four others, but there was plenty of space to move around; they were like college dorm rooms.

The dining room, kitchen, and a room big enough for two desks, which served as the law library, were on the first floor of C1. Education classrooms and the computer lab were on the first floor of C2. The administrative offices, commissary, medical services, and a rec room with a few stationary bikes and old funky gym equipment were in C3.

Unlike the FCI, where a toilet and sink were inside each tiny cell, the toilets and sinks at the camp were in a bathroom where they belonged. The one and only guard or officer in charge (OIC), as they were called at the camp, was stationed on the first floor of C2. That was a big adjustment, not having an officer everywhere I looked. The OIC was different every shift, but the same three covered the camp for at least a quarter of the year before a new set were condemned to the camp from one of the other facilities.

C4 was the zoo and where I lived. This is what they called "temporary housing." It was where I was sent to live first or where I would be sent back to if I lost my nice permanent room as punishment for getting into trouble. There was no privacy, just big open areas filled with bunk bed after bunk bed, county jail style. Illusory room sections were created by the arrangement of beds and lockers, each section containing three or four bunk beds arranged around a tower of stacked lockers in the middle. These bed-and-locker configurations ran along the length of the unit on either side of an aisle the guards could walk down unimpeded.

There was a shared bathroom in the middle of the first and second floors. But these amenities were identical to those in the other units. But in C4 they were shared by twice as many women as in C1 and C2. This was not a peaceful space. But as soon as someone in permanent housing got released or tossed in the SHU, someone in C4 would take her place. That only took about one hundred and eighty sleepless nights.

The staff was funny at the camp. There were a bunch of camp residents who had started at the FCI. We had been sent from the FCI to the camp as a reward for good behavior, but the staff considered being sent to work at the camp for a quarter a hardship or a punishment. It was boring there, and for the first time, I actually had something obvious in common with the staff and officers. They had congratulated me for making it to camp, and we'd both had to try not to laugh. Either that or they would've had to simply welcome me to the slums.

At camp, being an A and O meant I could be sent anywhere to work, to do anything. More often than not, though, this meant I got garbage duty in the kitchen, or sweeping or raking leaves in the yard at the crack of dawn. Mr. Green was my boss the day Tatiana left. He was a nice guy, but he was not the only staff member I had to worry about, and the closer I got to camp, the easier it would be for the other staff to recognize me coming back from the FCI.

The first one to watch out for was the OIC. Our OIC that day was Ms. Presley, a truly psychotic bitch. She was supposedly working in the camp because she was not allowed to work inside the FCI for a period of time. She was allegedly being punished for some misdeed. Officers rotated all posts among the three facilities on a quarterly basis and the OIC post in the camp was the short straw. Most of them hated it; Ms. Presley did, and if she was miserable, so were we. We all prayed Ms. Presley would only be in the camp as our OIC for one quarter.

As I crossed the yellow line and back into the safe zone, Ms. Presley came busting out of the door of C2, the building that held the officers' station, an itty-bitty air-conditioned room with a glass partition. I started sweeping and did not look up, but I could hear her big clodhopper boots and jangling keys and chain coming toward me. Then she passed right by me and hopped into a perimeter truck that had pulled up, which had also worried me, and rode away.

I took a deep breath, relieved I was not the focus of Ms. Presley's attention. I walked over and sat down on the stairs of the porch in front of C4, my new home. Mission accomplished.

Theresa, a fellow lesbian who had transferred from the FCI months earlier and was still pining for the lover she had left inside the FCI, was walking out of C4, carrying a ladder. "Did you get to see her?"

"I did. Tatiana's on her way, and I got to see her. Thanks."

"You okay?"

"I am." I tried to make a big smile, but I think I was actually making the same face you do when you have really bad gas.

"Yeah, great. I can tell." Theresa was being sarcastic and she laughed as she walked away with her ladder. She was all too familiar with how I felt at the moment—sort of anyway. "One door closes, another opens!" She yelled over her shoulder as Kara, an absolutely scrumptious girl, walked by, too young for either of us. Theresa probably didn't realize how tactless she'd sounded. Everyone dealt with expiration/release dates differently, and while I had gone almost directly from Sissy to Tatiana, it had not been my intention. I wondered if Sissy would write me back if I tried to write her again. Getting letters out of the camp that I didn't want read by the mail monitors was much easier than it had been from inside the FCI.

When Theresa disappeared into C5, the CMS building, it got very quiet. I listened to the leaves rustle in the big trees overhead and it reminded me of home. Not Vermont or Northampton; the sound made me think of my parents' house in the woods outside Cincinnati, where I grew up. I used to sit on the porch in the backyard there, on this huge stump of a tree that had been cut down years earlier, or lie for hours on a big rock up on our hill with my cat, just listening to the birds and the leaves rustle, when I wanted to be alone. I had been one of those teenagers who want a lot of alone time. As I sat there in front of C4, I realized it had been years since I had been alone like this, sitting in the quiet outdoors.

Lunchtime would roll around soon though, and that would be the end of my temporary solace. But for the moment, I had no place else to be and no real work assignment. As far as I could tell, there was nothing other than work to keep me busy at the camp.

There was a camp cat named Patches that lived on the porch. When I had first come over to the camp, she sat on my lap while I had a good cry over Tatiana, and Miss Kitty, and Dum Dum, and Edith, and my sister, and everything under the sun. I had gotten my period the next day after my arrival. Apparently, my biological clock had reset itself to the cycle of the women at the camp in an instant. I briefly turn into an emotional basket case once a month for about ten minutes, usually over something totally innocuous, like a piece of paper on the floor or a bird eating a worm. I would have known my period was going to make a surprise visit a week early had I not had so many real issues on my plate at the time.

Patches was sweet and she reminded me of all my little black girls, for some reason, even though she was a calico and drooled when you pet her. I had thought my crying binge over everything was triggered by that or by my first realization that I would be bored out of my mind for the next three years, not by my pointless biological clock. Really, why do lesbians have to have periods anyway, and why do women's monthly cycles get synchronized with other women and not by the presence of men?

I asked Patches the cat what she was up to, even though that was obvious. She was currently sleeping on the rail of the porch, looking as though she might be about to fall off it. She opened her eyes and looked at me. She seemed to be a little bit grumpy and unresponsive to my kissing noises. She twitched her ears each time I made the noise, like she was being bothered by a fly. She finally got up and gave me a look that said, *Okay! I'm coming. Shut up already.* But before she made her way down to me, one of my old bosses pulled up in front of the camp and honked his horn at me.

It took me a minute to register the horn honk was for me and that I knew the driver of the beat-up old car. I had never seen any of my computer lab bosses outside of the computer lab and in street clothes instead of his gray uniform. It was weird, all this semi-freedom. Mr. Wonka had been on a two-week vacation when my transfer happened, so he had missed it and missed Tatiana's departure date too, though he'd known that was coming. He had been pissed, not at me, but for the fact that no one had given him or any of the computer lab supervisors a heads-up. With Tatiana's release and my unexpected departure, he had been left pretty short-handed.

"Please get me transferred back!" As I said this, I wondered if that was what I really wanted.

"Man, I wish I could. Shit like that doesn't look right though, Wolters."

"What about institutional need?" I asked. Nobody would think I was sleeping with the computer lab boss. He knew that. I hoped he knew that. I knew the staff in education knew I was gay; it was just never openly discussed, since sex is prohibited. But the real prison staff in education didn't care about my sexuality and a couple of them definitely turned a blind eye to Tatiana's and my obsession with inventory in the storage room in the lab.

I think they were actually a little uncomfortable with the idea of punishing a gay person for being gay. Unlike some of the other guards and correctional officers, they had enough intellect to have an intellectual conflict. On the one hand, prison was for punishment and they couldn't allow inmates to turn a prison stay into an orgiastic feast or all of the lonely gays in San Francisco would be lining up to rob banks. On the other hand, they all lived in the Bay Area, so persecuting homosexuality probably felt a little off.

I decided then to take advantage of my old boss's short-handed situation to make my time at camp a little better. Mr. Wonka wasn't really worried about not having tutors; they could be trained. There were a few women working in the lab already who had gotten to be pretty effective tutors in the Microsoft Office products and had done well with the Total Training CDs for Adobe products. What he didn't have was someone he could trust and who had already been proven trustworthy to the warden to do the warden's pet projects. The camp really didn't have a computer lab to speak of. It had a small room no bigger than a walk-in closet with a few clunky old computers that barely functioned and a set of self-paced instruction books. I wasn't sure exactly what was at stake with the project that he had wanted me to work on, which I could not work on, because I had been transferred to the camp where there were no computers or programs up to the task. But six months after my arrival at the camp, he had a whole lab built with sixteen new workstations and new software, there were new classes for the women, and I had a new work assignment. I was also able to complete the project I had had to abandon when transferred from the FCI to the camp.

Things were a little more laid back at the camp. Not all the guards were maniacs like Ms. Presley, we had no razor wire, and there were no murderers, assassins, or terrorists. Fights were more of a seasonal event than a daily occurrence, but they still happened, and over stupid things like what television shows to watch, petty theft, cigarettes, and cutting in line for the microwave, phones, or showers.

The camp was made up of mostly recovering drug addicts, women related to the drug world by marriage or blood, and participants, like myself, in drug trafficking. The rest were white-collar criminals—people who had fudged bank papers, evaded taxes, and committed crimes that required a degree. My bunkies were people like Carol, the ex-mayor of a prestigious town in Connecticut; Lang, a diplomat from the U.S. embassy in South Korea; and Lisa, a deposed billionaire cosmetics queen. One of the tennis court royalty (a group of women who looked like they belonged in a country club and played tennis really well) from the FCI had been moved over to the camp too. The dark-haired goddess Elaine was at camp with me. Her claim to fame was that she was Heidi Fleiss's ex-prison-lover. Elaine's crime was drug related; she was a first-time drug offender who'd had the misfortune of being arrested at the height of the drug war hype. She was wrapping up a twenty-year sentence she had done more than sixteen years of. I had started to consider myself lucky for getting only ninety-four months. Drug sentences were so arbitrary. Some women got almost no time for doing much worse, others got more time for doing less. Elaine's sentence made me feel very blessed.

Elaine and I spent a lot of time together, complaining about the decrepit state of our new home, searching for cigarettes to buy, and smoking them. Cigarettes were only forty dollars a pack in the camp; they were easier to get into the camp. Elaine was a hot shit with a brilliant, dry wit and was entertaining as hell. She had long brown hair and brown eyes, and she carried herself like she might really believe she was royalty. Being her friend was like a promotion to the clique of "cool" girls.

We tried to play tennis, and tried, and tried. The so-called tennis court fit the style and ambiance of the place perfectly. Instead of the well-lit, country club grade courts we had enjoyed inside the FCI, the camp called a crumpling bit of asphalt and a sagging net their tennis courts, more like the courts in public parks. Even in the rare event I could hit the balls to Elaine, as soon as they hit the ground, it was anyone's guess where they would bounce. The rackets were questionably shaped, like they had been used as bats, and there was nothing but a sticky residue where the grips kept getting stolen. The balls looked as though a dog had donated them to Goodwill after they'd lost their chewiness. There was no fence around the court, so ball chasing took up most of our time. The ground sloped and the cracks made puckers in the smooth surface everywhere. Injury-free face-planting was a necessary skill neither of us had acquired, so we gave up on tennis before it got ugly.

Time slowed to a crawl at the camp in spite of my new job. I spent most of my time working in the computer lab in C2 or in the law library writing; I decided it was high time I finished a novel I had started writing in the FCI. If I was not in either of these two places, I was sitting on the C4 porch with Patches. We had been inseparable ever since the day we'd met. I guess you could say Patches was my new girlfriend.

She followed me everywhere, just like a dog might. When I walked the track, she walked with me, round and round, looking up at me occasionally with a quizzical little expression that said, *What the hell are we doing?* When I worked out, she would sit on the bench and watch, looking at me like I was crazy. When I was finally moved from the C4 zoo into a room in C1, Patches followed me. She moved from the C4 porch to the backside of C1, sleeping directly under my window or on the fire-escape stairs.

I woke one night to find her in my bunk. It was a warm night and the fire-escape door had been propped open to let the breeze through the hallway. She had come up the back stairs, found my room, my bed, and gotten in. I was on the upper bunk, so that was an impressive route for a cat to navigate. Carol, the former mayor, started grooming Patches regularly and even going so far as to brush her teeth daily. Carol was typical of the white-collar campers. She had been convicted in a scam to convert apartments to condominiums using forged documents of some kind to expedite the process.

For an outdoor cat, Patches was becoming quite domesticated and spoiled. She was a smart little shit too. She knew she was not supposed to be inside the housing unit. When the guards came around to count us at night, she would either crawl under my blanket or jump down and hide behind the curtain in our window. This astounded me.

Patches had an old blue cat carrier she had apparently been delivered in nine years earlier, or so the myth went. We moved it over to

C1 when she decided she wanted to live in our building. Everyone who liked her regularly scouted for new bed linens to make her little mobile home comfy. Patches had fewer places for shelter behind and under C1 than she did back at C4, but she insisted on staying near me. When the weather got bad—cold or rainy—I felt awful, since I was the reason she had moved and didn't have as many places to seek shelter. I got garbage bags and carefully wrapped her carrier, so that the rain and wind could not get in, but there was no danger of her suffocating.

I had acquired a treasure at one point, a pack of Camel Wides. My plan was to go see my counselor, Ms. Hosen; I had paperwork I had to fill out with her and didn't want to walk into her office after smoking. I didn't want to make myself a target for locker tossing, which is exactly what would happen if Ms. Hosen smelled cigarette smoke on me. Instead, I would go to smoke after that was done, and I hid my treasure in Patches's blue carrier. I would find a better hiding place later, after I finished my visit to the counselor's office.

As I sat, filling out the paperwork with Ms. Hosen, I saw the two other counselors walking behind the buildings. This probably meant surprise inspections were under way. When I heard women running down the halls to their rooms in C2, then the counselors yelling "Inspection!" my suspicions were confirmed.

Failing an inspection for being messy or possessing contraband like chicken wings could cost an inmate her room. She would get put back into the C4 zoo and once again be placed on the first-come, first-served list for a real room. They did these inspections once a week. My room was always spotless, and I didn't have any worthwhile contraband, so I wasn't worried about losing my bed and getting popped back into C4 to live. But when they came back out of C2 and headed to C1, they paused at Patches's carrier and my heart stopped. I saw one counselor, the lady I didn't like from the FCI, hold up a pack of Camels, and the guy she was with, the nice counselor, grabbed Patches's home and carried it back toward where I was with my counselor, in C3.

I heard the counselor I disliked, Ms. Bright, hoot and holler, all excited by her big bust. I could hear the noisy wooden stairs, hanging off the back of C3, creak and rumble as they made their way up to the second floor and in through the back door. Then the two counselors piled back into the office with Patches's home and bedding still in their possession.

"Jesus, this cat's got half of Laundry here." Laundry Services is where we were issued our one sheet, one blanket, and one pillow slip allotment.

Mr. Dansler, the other counselor, looked over at me and blushed. He hadn't realized that I was the inmate sitting in the office with Ms. Hosen. He and Ms. Bright knew Patches was my buddy.

"One of your friends just screwed your little cat, Wolters," Ms. Bright commented, as though every woman in the camp was my friend. She took the pack of Camels and taped them to the air-conditioning unit behind her desk, but only after opening the pack's lid up and pulling one cigarette slightly out of the pack. That way when she started her interrogations, which I figured she would be getting started with soon, whoever was seated where I was would be looking right at the delicious pack of cigarettes on display.

"You're punishing Patches? I can tell you for certain she does not smoke! She doesn't sell cigarettes either or she'd be as fat as her house. Christ! How much tuna that pack of cigarettes would buy." I said this, not sure I understood how far Ms. Bright was willing to go with whatever she had up her evil sleeves, but I wanted to remind her that Patches was a cat being sheltered, not an inmate allegedly being punished. Since my arrival in Dublin, there had been rumors of the cats, all the cats, being removed from both facilities and put to sleep. It was a rumor perpetuated by a couple of officers who hated the cats. But I had a dear friend in San Francisco, Carol Mooreland, ready to come collect Patches if those rumors actually ever turned out to be true or if I thought another inmate posed a serious threat to her.

If Ms. Bright assumed that the cigarettes were mine, why not just come out and say it? If she didn't think they were mine, were they seriously going to take away Patches's shelter on a cold day when it was about to rain? But threatening to torture my sweet little kitty in their power games was exactly what the counselors had proposed as the plan. I just needed to make sure they understood that— maybe if I made them say it out loud again, they would really hear what they were saying. If they didn't think those were my cigarettes, what the hell did they think I could do.

"No! We are not punishing the cat." She said this as though it was crazy to think she would do such a thing. "She'll get her house back the instant the owner of these cigarettes mans up." That was her favorite phrase. "Man up" is an odd phrase for a women's camp, but I knew what she meant. Someone had to step up and confess to being the owner of the cigarettes before Patches would get her house back.

"Patches will go under the building to sleep. She will be fine." Mr. Dansler slapped his bony knees and sat up. "Don't worry about your cat." They didn't think the Camels were mine; what he'd said made no sense if they did. But that was worse—at least if they thought they were my cigarettes, this was all a ploy to get me to 'fess up.

"But you took her house?" I was responding to Ms. Bright's claim they were not punishing my cat, not Mr. Dansler's claim she would be fine. It was only sprinkling outside, but the sky was gray; sprinkles could change to a downpour in a heartbeat. Mr. Dansler shrugged his shoulders and Ms. Bright picked up the phone and dialed up the numbers that would put her on the intercom for the camp.

"Oh well!" Ms. Bright's response to my observation was condescending, curt, and rude. I felt around in my pocket and my fingers touched the cigarette I had planned on taking over to C4 to smoke. She put the phone to her ear and practically yelled into it, as if she was talking to someone hard of hearing. She always did that and I knew that instead of being able to hear what she was saying in the camp, all anyone would hear was "Wah-wah-wah cat-wah wah-wah Camels wah, come see me," broadcast intolerably loud, all over the camp.

"Give me that." Mr. Dansler stood up, leaned across her desk, and took the phone receiver from her, held his hand over the mouth-piece, and remarked, "Fifteen years and you still don't know how to use this?" He'd said this as if he was joking, but of course, he and Ms. Hosen knew he was serious.

"Fuck you, Bob," Ms. Bright snapped back at him and laughed. She was always so cheerful when she was being cruel or engaged in a hunt. I could totally see these guys out at night together, the three counselors. They probably drank like fish. A couple of them lived in the staff housing up the hill. The girls from landscaping always reported on interesting developments in the staff housing area, where they mowed and watered the lawns or raked leaves depending on the season.

Ms. Hosen put a paper in front of me to sign and we were done with what I had actually come there to do. I pulled my hand out of my pocket and left the office. Ms. Bright's lovely crooning flooded the camp for another hour. I couldn't now smoke the cigarette burning a hole in my pocket. Everyone would know I was the idiot who had cost Patches her home. Besides that, with Ms. Bright on her rampage, nobody would dare smoke in the C4 bathroom until she went home for the day. Instead, I searched for something to make into a temporary home for Patches, until I could figure out what to do. From outside, I heard everyone complaining about Ms. Bright's intercom noise every time she repeated the unintelligible terms for giving the cat her house back.

Then someone inside C1, who apparently understood what she was saying, said they knew how to shut the counselor up. "I'm killing that fucking cat. Bright can have the fucking rodent's house." Then someone else laughed, arguing that Cleary would go batshit crazy.

I put the box down that I had found and picked Patches up, giving her a quick hug and kiss. "You stay away from these fuckers, Patchy-poo." I walked back over to the counselors' office, walked in, and sat down across from Ms. Bright. Ms. Hosen and Mr. Dansler looked at me like I had lost my mind. We didn't just walk right into the counselors' office and sit down. We were supposed to knock and wait in the hallway until you were beckoned. I pointed at her trophy, the package of cigarettes taped to the air-conditioner. "They are mine."

"Oh fuck, Wolters!" Ms. Bright didn't believe me. I am pretty certain she was about to start laughing. Because if she had believed me, she would have already exploded or been on the phone telling the lieutenant to come get me.

"You can't do this. You know how crazy these women are. Someone just said they would kill the cat . . . that it would shut you up." I did a quick gasp. I was so angry, I was about to cry. Nope, it was happening. I was crying.

"Aw shit." Mr. Dansler stood up. "She's right." He started to walk out of the office, as if by doing so it would be assumed he had no part in what they had done.

"Who said it?" Ms. Bright was genuinely furious now, though not with me. But, oh boy, if she only knew, she probably would have leapt across her desk and stabbed me with her index finger. Either that or peed herself laughing. I could never tell if her whole rage thing was an act or not. Something deep down told me it was a put-on and that if I had met her in the real world, she might be a friend. She was almost exactly my age, a slightly heavyset blonde, smart, with an infectious laugh and twisted sense of humor. But as the target of her potential rage, it was better to assume the worst and be cautious.

"I have no clue who said it! I heard it through the windows, while I was outside trying to make a temporary house for my poor cat. It's raining and the ground under the building floods when it rains." I looked at Mr. Dansler. He was still trying to escape the office but trapped in his corner by Ms. Hosen's seat. Ms. Hosen was apparently frozen in her seat, so he was stuck standing there. I think she was frightened that something bad was about to happen, and if she stayed perfectly still, it would pass her over, whatever it was. Dansler was the one who had suggested Patches sleep under the building.

"She's not your cat, Wolters. She's not a house cat. She's fine." Ms. Bright offered this bit of wisdom up as a solution. I guess she thought if she cleared that up, I would shut up and quit my bellyaching, and stop my ridiculous confession and attempt to save Patches. But I could hear the fun draining out of her voice.

"Tell Patches that!" I laughed a little, because I didn't know what else to do and couldn't quite figure out where this was all going to go. "What does that matter anyway? The cigarettes are mine, so give the cat her home back and take me to the SHU." I put my hands out in front of me and held my wrists together. This was too much, I guess. Ms. Bright turned red and started laughing so hard, I know she peed herself a little, and I know she didn't believe me.

None of them believed me, but my confession totally fucked up their fun game. Ms. Bright didn't like having to back down from threats she had made to the whole camp, and she had told the camp at least a hundred times that the cat wasn't getting her house back until someone claimed the cigarettes. It was no secret how much I loved Patches and it would not remain secret that I had complied with her demands. If she didn't give the cat its house back, she would look like an unreasonable beast. If she punished me, she would look worse. Everyone would say I confessed to save Patches even though that was not the case. Mr. Dansler told me to get out of the office, to wait in the hall, so they could speak. So I did. I waited, trying to eavesdrop on their conversation, and listening for the jangling keys of a fetched lieutenant.

A couple of minutes later, Mr. Dansler came out and called me back in. "You're not going to the SHU. We're writing a shot. Two weeks' commissary and phone restriction, and extra duty. We're giving the house back, but your extra duty is to build her a real house." Ms. Bright sat quietly, content, while Dansler handed down my judgment.

Everyone would think she was an asshole. They would think I had fessed up to something I hadn't done just to save Patches and she had punished me anyway. But she could lift the sanctions off Patches without losing face. Ms. Bright added, "Get Barnes. Go with her to CMS Monday morning and she will show you how the houses are made. I'll clear it with Mr. Smith. Happy?"

"Happy." I was so grateful. I knew exactly how lucky I was, so the fact that they had punished me for something they thought I hadn't done didn't bother me one bit. I had a funny feeling Ms. Bright did know what had just happened and had saved my ass. It's weird. I had started out in the FCI hating her almost as much as she terrified me. But now, when I saw her breaking in women who had just arrived at the camp from the street, the same way she had me, her vitriol actually made sense. It didn't bother me to hear it anymore. She was a Band-Aid ripper, that's all. Instead of timidly peeling it off slowly, trying to help an inmate avoid her inevitable pain, she made it clear you were an inmate, nobody gave a shit who you were or how you felt, and you had nothing coming, period. The sooner you accepted this, the easier your time would be.

"Good. Now get the fuck out of my face." *Rip!* I could have sworn she was trying not to smile. The idea that she might know she had just saved my ass was kind of endearing. If it were true, she was both apologizing for the cat-house thing and confirming she knew her coworkers were idiots. I just had to do my part now and whine to everyone about my unjust punishment.

My phone restriction bothered me more than I thought it would, certainly more than the commissary ban. I hadn't realized that my weekly call home played such an important role in my well-being until I couldn't make it.

19 Four Incident Reports and a Funeral

A T SIX YEARS OLD, my grasp of death was totally spot-on. When I had returned from my grandfather's funeral, my weepy grandmother, concerned with my emotional state, had asked me if I understood what was happening. I had told her, "We drove all over town looking for a hole to put Gramps in."

My real belief about life and death remained fairly simple and it has not changed much since my grandmother died when I was eleven years old. I'm told that when she died, I insisted on knowing the exact time of her death. I was afraid she had seen me do something of which she would not have approved. On January 22, 2007, I prayed my dad wasn't observing me, not at the moment.

"What are you looking at?" A darling young girl, who had either mixed the wrong drugs or missed a few doses of something she should have been on, asked me as she crawled across our cement bench toward me, kind of like a cross-eyed cat. I tried to scoot another inch or two away from her, but I had already backed myself up into the corner. I really didn't want any trouble and these can be such unpredictable folks. She had already claimed she loved me and was going to kill me, and I hadn't even spoken to her yet.

Fortunately, her arresting officer walked in front of the glass partition that separated the temporary holding cell we were in from him, and he stopped. Distracted, she flew from the bench to the glass and started making love to it. The officer outside the glass laughed, told her to settle down, and acknowledged her as a regular visitor. From his side of the glass it was probably quite a show; she was mashing her bare breasts against the glass, grinding, and French-kissing her reflection. Not for long though. She spun around, fell flat on her face, and started crying. It's unusual that anyone can cycle through emotions this quickly.

"Am I being moved?" I asked the officer, but he ignored me and walked back out the door that kept the sound in our wing from interrupting the business being conducted in the intake area.

The young lady, still on the floor, had violated a restraining order that her ex-boyfriend had taken out on her, and she found that ridiculous. She was the one, she believed, who had put a restraining order on his restraining order. She seemed fairly convinced, too, that she was not in the wrong and that showing up at his work in her current state and kicking his scrawny ass was perfectly acceptable behavior. He had cheated on her and slept with his wife.

I had been sitting in the holding cell for about five hours. It didn't take long to figure out I was in the drunk tank. Aside from the glass-licking loon, there were three other nice ladies in the cell with me, but they were sound asleep now. One was on the cement floor, curled around the base of the nasty metal toilet bowl with her dress up around her ears and an obscenely large black bush where I wished her panties were. The other two were passed out on the cement bench opposite me. One of them kept rolling over and stopping herself just short of falling face-first onto the dirty cement floor.

I patiently waited for my nice hosts at the Hamilton County jail to find me a bunk to sleep in. Ms. Bright would retrieve me in the morning and take me to my father's funeral. But it was beginning to look like I would not be getting any sleep or a place to do that before then. This was the same jail my mother had taught adult basic education classes in for so many years. Mom had been retired for a few years, but I had foolishly hoped that someone who processed me into the facility for the night might remember her and know about Dad's passing, and that might translate into a little compassion— maybe a cell with a door, a blanket, and some quiet. We have the same name, remember, so even if they didn't recognize me personally, surely they would know the name on the paperwork and get curious. In any case, they knew that whoever I was, I was here for my father's funeral. Ms. Bright had told the lady she had dropped me off with that much.

Unfortunately, they forgot me altogether. I know this because Ms. Bright was pissed off and told me so when she finally got me out of there the next morning. They apparently had a little trouble finding me, which had freaked her out. I had spent the night sitting in a cold block of cement, trying to avoid the rage, affection, and vomit of a drunk crackhead, and it had cost my brother his entire savings to get me there. It had probably taken him ten years to save up the money. I wondered if I could sue for the fee we'd had to pay for their hospitality.

The night's stay in the Hamilton County jail was only one part of the expense for the trip. We had to have at least four thousand dollars in my commissary account to cover the plane fare for both myself and Ms. Bright, her overtime pay for escorting me, her hotel and meals, and my lovely accommodations. Ironically, my security level should probably have already been dropped. If it had, I would have been given a furlough like Hester and been permitted to stay at my parent's house and get myself to the funeral and back to camp unescorted.

Hester's and my efforts to get furloughed had started out as a request for a bedside visit. That is what it's called when you are granted a forty-eight-hour furlough to go to see someone whose death is imminent and validated by their doctor in triplicate. As long as this someone is your parent, child, or spouse, you can request to be furloughed to go to their bedside and say goodbye, in case they really do die. If you have to be escorted, very few of those forty-eight hours are actually spent with the relative.

Getting a doctor to put it in writing that they are losing a patient is no easy piece of work, but my aunt Jane and my mother succeeded in doing so. At that point, Hester got her furlough and my counselor dropped the bomb that my commissary account needed to have the funds required to cover expenses in it before she could submit my request for an escorted furlough to the warden. I suspected they hadn't told us about the money from the get-go because either they thought we wouldn't be able to get the necessary documentation from the hospital or they thought my father wasn't as sick as I claimed—inmates being so full of shit and all.

In any case, by the time we got that little bit of added information, my mother couldn't leave my father's side to go do banking, so my brother stepped in with his savings and sent the money via Western Union. Once my counselor, Ms. Hosen, could verify the funds had been sent, they disclosed the next obstacle to my furlough: everyone needed to make it happen was on vacation. I all but gave up. But Ms. Bright and Ms. Hosen jumped through hoops to get my trip approved, and Ms. Bright volunteered to escort me.

Before I knew that was happening, though, I went to work that Monday in the computer lab and told my boss what had happened over the weekend. I had been called to the chapel from work on the preceding Friday, right before the four o'clock count, so my boss knew something had happened over the weekend, just not what. Hearing my name over the intercom followed by "Report to the chaplain's office" meant bad news. I knew it was going to be about my father but hoped otherwise. He had been fighting Merkyl cell carcinoma, a rare but largely curable form of cancer.

We had two chaplains sort of available to us in the camp, but we shared them with the FCI, so it had taken some persistence on my mother's part to get one of them to come over to the camp that

Friday to talk to me. The Asian female chaplain was the one who
finally came over, if for no other reason than to get my mother to
stop calling. Once we were in the chaplain's office, she dialed the
hospital and was connected to my father's room. Mother answered
the phone, and I braced myself for the news. Dad had fallen the
preceding Sunday. His heart had stopped. They'd had to give him
a pacemaker to keep his heart beating, and he had already had five
blood transfusions. He was stabilized, but they were having diffi-
culty keeping his red blood cell count up. Mother told me I needed
to come home.

All I heard was "He's stabilized." Mother asking me to come home
sounded exactly like something she would say, something crazy. I
was in jail. I couldn't come home. I can't recall the rest of the conversation, other than she'd thought she had lost him. My aunt Jane
was on her way to Cincinnati and my dad's other brothers and sisters were coming behind Jane. That relieved me. Knowing Mom
would have them there to help her deal with my father's hospital-
ization made all the difference in the world.

We hung up and I broke down in tears. I was about to ask the
chaplain why it had taken five days for them to get this information
to me. But the chaplain warned me not to get too emotional, as it
was her responsibility to put me in the SHU if she thought I could
not handle the news I had just received.

I left the chaplain's office and went into the chapel. She followed
me and stood with her arms crossed at the back of the room, watching me pray. There is very little more absurd than a prison chaplain
wielding their power. I had to stay with her until the four P.M. count
was over. I closed my eyes, pretended I was alone, and prayed for
my father's quick recovery and the strength I needed not to kick the
chaplain's ass out of the second-story window.

When I heard "Clear!" I knew it was safe to move about. I left the
building, walking slowly and calmly past the chaplain. She was still
watching me, trying to determine if she should have me tossed in
the hole.

My close friends were already outside C3 when I stepped through the door. Kara and Misty hugged me and I started sobbing again. That was not a phone call I had ever expected to get. The idea that Mom, Hester, Gene, and I had come so close to losing my father freaked me out. Hester was going to be released in March. We were almost there, almost to the end of our decadelong nightmare. It had never occurred to me that one of us wouldn't be there when it was all finally over. My family was always there, no matter what. If that vanished, I would be lost.

I could not reach anyone on my approved phone list through the weekend. On Monday, my boss let me call my father's hospital room from his office in the computer lab. Mom answered and told me he was still too weak to hold the phone, but he could talk a little. I asked her to stop trying to tell him what I was saying and hold the phone up to his ear for me; I wanted to talk to him. She did so. "Dad. Dad! It's me, Cleary."

"I waw-waw-walk." I couldn't make out what he was trying to say. Mom told me he had just had the breathing tubes removed from his throat and his mouth was so dry he couldn't speak well yet. They were only letting him suck on ice cubes, so far. I told her to put the phone back up to his ear.

"Dad. I love you! I'm coming home to see you, okay?" I yelled into the phone.

"Wa-wo." It almost sounded like he'd said "Uh-oh," and this made me laugh, him too. It was a pathetic, sad little laugh, but still a laugh.

"Stop trying to talk. Your tongue might break off!" I heard him laugh again and then try to say something.

"A-uhb-ewe. Aw-etting-etter." He stopped talking and made an awful noise, like he couldn't breathe. Then he was quiet again, and I could hear his slow, steady breath.

"I love you too." I think he had also said he was getting better. He had repeated this like a mantra, every time I had called home for the last three months. "I know. You are getting better. You sure scared the bejesus out of me though."

"Awry." Dad's reply had been either "All right" or "Sorry." It couldn't be easy for him to try to speak, so I kept talking.

I remembered something special. "Dad, one of the times I was being a big baby, you told me 'Let the arms of Morpheus hold you now and take you to your dreams.'" I had been in Santa Rita Jail, crying, begging him to get me out of that hellhole, when he'd said this to me. It was so long ago. It had just popped into my head while I was trying to keep talking. Dad had lots of these little nuggets from his stage and seminary days. He could pull the most obscure but perfectly timed tidbits out of his hat.

I remembered him and the Fonze spontaneously busting out in Shakespeare one Saturday afternoon at Playhouse in the Park. This was just before Henry Winkler had joined the cast of *Happy Days*. At the time, though, he had been just the cute guy who watched me and bought me Cokes in a glass bottle when Dad was on stage rehearsing. Dad's friends had been theater people or work people, not both. Our Christmas parties had been fancy and stuffy; his cast parties had not.

I remembered when he got his first bell-bottom hip-huggers: my birthday in 1973. They were red, white, and blue striped; mine were a smaller version of the same. I remembered speeding down Columbia Parkway in his red Fiat and thinking I had the coolest, most handsome dad in the world. I remembered him imitating Julia Child, looking for his pastry bag, and I remembered his man purse. In 1985, he wore it to the Tea Dance at the Boatslip in Provincetown and one of Hester's gay friends had had an instant crush on him. He was sure the man purse had meant there was hope.

"You can do that too, you know. You don't have to stay awake and take care of anyone." I understood now that he had been lying to me every time he'd said he was getting better. He hadn't wanted me to worry. "Be a baby and let Morpheus take you. Mom says they're giving you a morphine drip. It would be such a shame to waste that." He laughed again. His laugh was so warm. I couldn't believe this was happening, why he had to be so sick when I couldn't be there for him. "Dad, close your eyes and go to sleep. I'll be there Tuesday and Hester will be there when you wake up." I had to make that happen, no matter what it took. I couldn't just give up.

Dad died that night, before Hester arrived. Aunt Jane said he went peacefully, and with a smile. Hester missed him by just a few hours, but she only had a forty-eight-hour furlough, so she had to leave before the wake and the funeral, before all of our family gathered.

Instead, she said goodbye in private. She wrote him a letter and tucked it into his breast pocket. They read this at the funeral mass. The funeral home prepared Dad's body early. T. P. White and Sons arranged a private viewing; just Dad, Hester, and her husband, Matt.

The official wake was held on Tuesday night at the T. P. White home, a beautiful old Victorian in Mount Washington. It had started snowing when Ms. Bright and I landed in Cincinnati and our plane was a little late getting in, so we arrived at the funeral home two hours after the wake had started. It doesn't snow in San Francisco or Dublin. It was so beautiful when we walked up to the entry of the funeral home. I had a feeling Dad had arranged the snow; it was too perfect a scene.

The place was packed. The casket was set up at one end of the living room. Someone with very expensive taste and a love for antiquities had decorated the house. It felt warm and inviting, like you were walking into someone's holiday party. Dad had a lot of friends and a huge family. He was the oldest son and the first of their brood to pass. His brothers and sisters knew about Hester's and my situation; so did many of the friends there. So when I did walk in, everyone turned in my direction. I was once again like a bloody car crash: everyone had to get a peek at the poor daughter who had come from prison. They knew how hard I had tried to get there before he died and that Hester had barely missed him. They knew she'd had to go back before the funeral. I guess they expected a mess.

I made my way through the crowd in the living room, toward Dad. As I approached him, the people parted and there he was. Mom was cool as a cucumber, standing at the head of his casket, accepting condolences. My brother was at the foot, bawling his eyes out, and I finally saw for myself, my dad was dead. I'm not sure what it is I had thought prior to that moment, but it hit me like a fucking freight train. I fell to my knees on the pew alongside him and looked at his peaceful face.

"You sleeping?" I whispered to his corpse and waited for a response I knew would never come. I held his cold, waxy hand, saying nothing, just being still, the same way we would be doing if he were alive. He couldn't put his arm around me anymore. My bawling brother knelt down next to me. "Cleary, I love you. He knows you tried." And that was it. The floodgates opened and I was a mess of snot and tears. Mom tapped on my shoulder and handed me a bunch of tissue.

She put her hand under my elbow. "Pull yourself together, honey." She stared at me with an utterly blank gaze. Then her pupils flashed at me, like a cat's eyes do in the dark, but Mom's pupils were white. I freaked out and stood right the fuck up. Dad had insisted my mother have eye surgery six months before. She had lens implants and this was the first time I was seeing them. They caught the light and reflected it back. Until I could get used to them, it was quite freaky looking, like horror-movie weird. She was like a stranger. A vacancy sign hanging around her neck would have been a better accessory accompanying her alien and glassy stare than her special-occasion jewelry. Mom, the normally inconsolable basket case, was completely shut down, devoid of all emotion and personality. I could barely feel my mother's presence, even though she was in front of my face. She told my brother to take me outside for some air, and when I tried to hug her, she said, "No," and turned away.

It was right after this that Ms. Bright took me to the Hamilton County jail to spend the night. My dad's family was taking Gene and Mom to Smokey Bones for dinner and drinks, but Ms. Bright didn't want to get to the jail too late; she wanted to make sure they got me into a bed. So we passed on the dinner part of my father's wake and my chance to try to comfort my mom. She was a train wreck. I had never seen her so devoid of any emotion and it scared me a little.

The next day we went to the house I had grown up in. It's a beautiful home. When I'd lived there, it had been canary yellow with white trim. They had changed the color scheme to dusty rose with cinnabar trim. This was probably as close to pink as Mom would let Dad get. When we pulled into my parents' private drive and made our way up the long wooded lane, Ms. Bright blurted out, "I knew it!"

It was a bizarre twist of fate that this lady was the one accompanying me from prison to the home I had grown up in. Of all the people who could have escorted me, Ms. Bright was someone I had considered to be such a perfect evil archetype in my incarceration that I had turned her into the villainous antagonist in one of my novels. I guessed she had just pegged me for a spoiled brat.

We parked next to the hundred-year-old oak trees, and I stared at the house and snow-covered woods I used to play in. It looked like an enchanted scene from a movie I had once watched, but it wasn't; it was my real life. We got out of the car and Ms. Bright asked me if I was okay. I had forgotten for a split second why we were there. I needed to change into clothes appropriate for a funeral. We made our way to the door and went inside. My aunts and uncles were all there with Mom. She was sitting in front of the fireplace with a blanket over her lap but otherwise ready to go to the cathedral.

I borrowed a black dress, coat, and heels from my mother, put on some makeup, and wandered around upstairs. Hester and I had had this whole floor to ourselves when growing up. I felt like I was in a museum looking through the artifacts of someone else's life when my tour was interrupted. My brother had ordered my favorite pizza from Mio's, just for me, and my aunt Jane yelled to me upstairs to come get a slice. This was my first food from the real world in four years. I stood in my father's gourmet kitchen and savored every bite of my slice, as if it were one of the gourmet delicacies my father used to prepare in this space. Gourmet cooking had been my dad's other hobby.

We went to Saint Peter in Chains Cathedral, where Dad had a full house. Then we all drove around Cincinnati, looking for a hole to put my dad in. We found one, and once he was in the ground, I went back to the car. I changed from my black funeral clothes back into the sweatpants and sweatshirt I had traveled in. I gave my aunt Jane the clothes, coat, and shoes, kissed my mother goodbye, and went back to jail—it didn't feel like going home this time.

The last eighteen months of my sentence went by quickly. I stayed busy and stopped giving a shit about anything. The illusive boundary between "us" and "them" had been irreparably violated and the magic spell broken; staff and officers didn't scare me anymore. They were just people, and miserable ones, for the most part. I started smoking again, got busted for possession of tobacco, and went to the SHU on Christmas Day 2007. On New Year's Eve, I called my sister at home from the SHU. That was the best Christmas present ever: she was at home, her home.

I was alone and in the SHU on the anniversary of Dad's death. It had been my first holiday without him and probably the best place for me to be. I called Mom and Gene every day I was in there, just to make sure Mom was doing all right. If I had not been in the SHU, I would have been so busy trying not to focus on the holidays, I might not have been there for her.

Patches, my sidekick and partner in crime, came over to the SHU and slept right outside the long, thin window I couldn't see anything out of the whole time I was in there. She would hop up onto the small exterior sill, where I could see colors up against the frosted glass while she was sunning, and I could hear her meow a few times at night.

On October 4, 2008, Saint Francis of Assisi's feast day and eleven days before my release date, I went to the SHU again. This time it was for releasing a baby skunk from one of the traps that had been set at the camp to catch the raccoons. Someone had fucked up a few days earlier and called Animal Control instead of Noah's Ark to come deal with the baby skunk's mother, who had accidentally been trapped. They killed the mother skunk in front of everyone in C4 during count time, then tossed her body into the garbage bin. You have to remember that the women considered these creatures their pets, their children, even the skunks. It was the baby skunk that had next been accidentally trapped and that I released a few days later.

The morning of this jail break, Patches was frantically trying to get me to go behind the C4 building, out of bounds. This is where I discovered the little baby skunk—who by then had been adopted by the crazy cat Angel—stuck in a trap. I made a skunk-spray protective suit from garbage bags and freed it. I got put in the SHU for tampering with prison security devices. *Huh?* I was threatened with a 200-series shot. A shot this severe meant I would lose my release date and could be facing a new charge, or so the guards in the SHU told me.

On October 10, 2008, my original release date, my mother needed me and didn't know it. My brother knew it and he was scared. Alzheimer's was setting in. She would have that glass of wine she loved, forget about it, have another, and repeat. She crashed her poor Cadillac nine times that year and kept forgetting to pay her bills and take her medications. You get the picture. After the skunk episode came to a happy conclusion, I was released on *my date* to a halfway house. But I did not go back to San Francisco as I had always planned. I went home to Cincinnati and took Patches, the prison kitty, with me. She got to go straight to Mom's. I had one more obstacle to get through: the halfway house.

Halfway houses are supposed to be where people without support networks or family can get their bearings and get a little help and guidance getting themselves prepared to reenter the world as a responsible and employed human being. In reality, the people with the least support are the most likely to fail the gauntlet of meaningless and sometimes insurmountable obstacles a halfway house presents to reentry. Those poor people just get ground up and spit back into the prison system, pronto.

The other type of people not going to benefit from this environment are professionals. For example, a research scientist from Columbus placed in a Cincinnati halfway house (a hundred miles away) was encouraged to take a job at McDonald's rather than attempt getting a job in her field. The rationale was that since the United States was on the verge of an economic collapse, she had better take the job or risk finding nothing else and being sent back.

Her case manager told her, she said, she also thought it might help curb her arrogance.

I knew getting back on my feet in Cincinnati would require a Herculean effort. Without the personal and professional connections I had established and maintained in San Francisco, and the felony conviction hanging around my neck, it was going to be a challenge. It took me almost two years to finally get a job in software again. I even worked for nothing on a couple of projects in California just to keep my skills honed. But in the meantime, being employed was a requirement of the place I had been sent to.

The Cincinnati halfway house had a whole array of rules that didn't exist or had been deemed obsolete or unenforceable in the San Francisco halfway house. These would make my job hunt harder. For example, while there, I was forbidden from accessing the Internet or owning a cell phone. That ruled out returning to work for a software company or even finding one that was hiring. I had very little time to find a job before they would start threatening to send me back. It became clear very fast that it wasn't yet time to really go back to work.

In order to go job hunting I had to submit a request to go to a specific address and get it approved—that meant filling out an application. If I were granted this privilege, I had to call when I arrived at said address, then call again before I left said address, all without a cell phone. I learned there were very few pay phones left in Cincinnati, I guess since everyone has cell phones. That meant I had to ask to use the phone wherever I went to fill out an application so that I could call in, twice. I was not allowed to get rides from family members or friends to go to these places. I had to take the city busses. When I got past all this and found someone who would hire an ex-felon living in a halfway house, they also had to accept frequent unannounced visits at work from my case manager.

I was happier than I should have been when I found a job. I washed dishes at Uno Pizzeria about a mile from Mom's until I got out of the halfway house. There was a bitter kind of irony to scrubbing the original Chicago deep-dish pizza crust from three hundred pans a night. Chicago was where it had all started. But four weeks after returning to Cincinnati and depositing Patches at Mom's, I finally got to go home for a four-hour pass. Patches had adjusted well to her new surroundings. She had already trained the dog and had made peace with Dad's surviving cats, Buddy and Kitty Kat. But Patches was not allowed to go outside yet, and that made her angry. I was afraid she wouldn't come back in though, and winter was coming.

Hester and I ended up with the same very rigid probation officer. It made no difference to us; we weren't trying to do anything they wouldn't have approved of. But there were a few notable exceptions.

We couldn't travel outside of the state without written permission. Cincinnati sits on the Ohio River, and on the other side is Kentucky. The best route to downtown Cincinnati from my mother's house is south on 275 to 471 through Kentucky. It's the route I had taken a million times. The first time I made the trip to town from home with Gene and Mom in the car, I wasn't thinking about the specifics of my driving direction. I got onto 275 south as I had always done and immediately freaked out. I had to reverse up the shoulder of the busy entrance ramp to avoid violating the terms of my supervised release. My poor mother actually threatened to ground me while I was backing up the ramp, she was so frightened we were going to get rear-ended.

Our first holiday season back in Cincinnati was complicated by my sister and me sharing the same mother and brother. She had to get permission to have dinner with me. I was still in the halfway house, so I didn't have to get permission from my PO yet. But the best I could do was to get a pass to go to dinner with my family, but not in Kentucky. So rather than go to the Mallecki house in Kentucky, as was a decades-old tradition for my family, we went to a restaurant. Hester got permission to see me and we settled on a new family ritual.

Only a couple of things happened while I was in the halfway house that almost pushed me over the edge. I called home one night after work. Patches snuck outside on the night of our winter's first snowstorm. She had never seen snow in her life and certainly never experienced temperatures in the teens, but she would not come back inside for my brother. I was just about to make a run for it and drive back to Mom's to get my silly cat inside before it got dark. But on my fiftieth panicked-screaming-crying call home, she had finally come back in for my brother. I made him chase her around with the phone in hand so I could talk to her. That's when the women at the halfway house decided I was nuts. When I told them where Patches had come from, they knew I was.

On another occasion my mother had dropped me off a block away from the halfway house after giving me an illegal ride home from work. She did this a couple of times just to get to see me, talk to me, and make sure I was fine and ready to come home. When I finally got through on the phone to my brother that night to make sure Patches was still in, as had become a necessary prerequisite to my sleep, I found out that Mom had not made it back home. He had just gotten home from the hospital where she had been taken. She had a nasty fall outside of a restaurant she had stopped at on her way home. It was a bad fall. But he said, "At least she hadn't been driving."

Mom was beginning to show more of the signs of Alzheimer's my brother had said I needed to come home because of, and the martinis didn't help the symptoms go away. It was after hours when I learned of her accident. She had a broken nose and road rash on her face. He said she looked like she'd been in a boxing match and told me what her blood alcohol level had been. I wanted to go to the hospital to be there when she woke up, but they wouldn't let me. It was after business hours, so no one could approve a pass for me to go.

At another time in my life, I might not have been able to stifle all the urges I had when the snarky woman at the desk said, "Sorry, I guess you should have thought of that when you broke the law." But instead of walking out the door of the halfway house, shaming her for her lack of basic decency, and running to my mother's bedside, I smiled and walked away. The snarky woman was right, of course, except that if anyone had that kind of wisdom at the time it was required, no laws would ever be broken, not even the ten she had probably broken in the last week.

Even my release from the halfway house was problematic. They released me and before I was fully unpacked at home, they called to say, *Oops!* They had screwed the date up and I had to go back for another week. But I made it home. I had never seen a cat smile before, but when I didn't get up and leave her after watching a whole season of *Dexter* from the long-absent comfort of a fluffy bed, I noticed she had a big fat cheesy smile on her face.

In the end, the thing that bothered me most was that it felt like I was being punished for my decision to come home and take care of my mother. The halfway house in California would have been a breeze. In California, if you don't "drop a dirty" (that is when you test positive for drugs), you keep your job, and you don't bother your PO, that's all it takes to get released from your federal probation after a year. But not me, not in Ohio.

I had no desire to break the rules; get drunk and fight or drive, get high, rob a bank, or do any of the obvious things everyone thinks people get violated over. Neither did Hester. We never were real criminals, whatever that is, just young and stupid. But we still wanted off paper. Almost three years into my period of supervision, I had a great job, I was helping to support my mother and brother, I had finally completed my bachelor's and my master's, and I was working on my Ph.D. Hester had also completed her bachelor's and was starting her master's. But we were both still on paper.

Hester stopped waiting for her PO to file the paperwork and paid her lawyer to file a motion with the court for early dismissal of her supervised release. The probation department and even our prosecutor recommended the judge grant it. That he would not surprised everyone. I didn't even bother trying.

My greatest remaining fear was being violated while stuck on paper for something not in my control. I'd survive even if they did send me back to Dublin. But the impact it would have on everyone who depended on me now would be cruel. My mother and brother could become prisoners too. We could not leave Mom alone anymore and she didn't want to go to a nursing home. As long as Gene and I shared the duty of keeping her company, it worked. But it wouldn't if I was violated.

It's every ex-felon's fear, to be unfairly violated; it happens too often to believe it can't happen to you. One thing I could be certain of is that the people in power are not always the ones that should be, and those were the people my fate depended on until the day I received that last piece of news, a brief letter from the Department of Justice that said I am done, paid in full. I let this fear get the best of me and ceased to exist at some point.

I didn't want anyone I worked with to know about my past—what if I was judged by that and not my abilities—so I kept to myself at work. While it's not illegal to be gay in prison, years of being hunted for practicing it twisted it for me. I was afraid that engaging in the free world might be like my gateway drug, so I didn't seek out other gay women. It felt like I had crawled back into the closet. But, between working, taking care of my mother and the house, and being in school twenty-four hours a day, seven days a week, I was safe.

I think I got a little stressed out after a while. I had a heart attack on August 8, 2012, and nearly died at forty-nine years old. Open-heart surgery, a five-way bypass, and a very handsome doctor saved my life. I felt blessed and full, but I was still hiding under a rock made of so many secrets.

Then the strangest thing happened. I was watching television and a commercial came on. This girl stepped out of a van, dressed in some familiar clothes, hugging a pillow, and said, "My name is Piper Chapman . . ."

Epilogue: Karma Continued

Cincinnati, Ohio
2013

YOU KNOW WHERE Piper and I landed at the end of all this. Hester is working with recovering addicts now. I have no idea how she does that work. We go to lunch on Fridays and on one of these occasions she expressed how it was like an out-of-body experience for her, coming face-to-face with someone she knew all too well but had long since forgotten: herself.

I was just beginning to allow myself the latitude to explore my earlier self and it had not occurred to me that in writing this all down, I would also have to face head-on how horribly my poor choices had affected persons directly in my life, much less the countless others whom I'll never know. I would have to acknowledge my part in their pain, suffering, and loss.

Addiction: I fed this dog of greed for a season, all for the sake of my own creature comforts and safety without so much as a thought to the misery I helped to traffic. I did not understand then the cost of my choices on generations of families troubled by addiction. I do now. To those whom I owe the most considered confession, generations of nameless families troubled by addiction, what remains now for me is to tell you that I am sorry, and I *am* sorry.

Piper's work inspired me to join a growing chorus illuminating a part of society in desperate need of attention. When the occasion came for me to sit down and write my record of events, I hoped it would all come together into a neat little package, that I would be able to convey it without much effort. I did not imagine the utter shame I would feel while retelling my past for the entire world to read.

Telling my story in all of its embarrassing detail, alongside so many others doing the same, might make a difference though, so I tossed my heavy shell and planted this seed. This is what finally set me free, not the piece of paper from the Department of Justice that said I'm done, time served, debt paid.

Acknowledgments

OR THE PRIVILEGE of your eyes upon these pages, so many dominoes had to be stood up, aligned just so, and then set into motion. There was a time in my life when my perspective permitted me to see only the dominoes fall, one at a time. It would be years before I was graced with the wisdom, distance, and perspective that allowed me to view the intelligent design behind it all. If your faith in God has ever been shaken, these pages are a proof of life, my beauty for ashes.

I want to thank my father for lighting my way, and both my mother and father for holding my hand and never letting it go. I thank my big brother, Gene, for being my port in a storm, and Hester for being my touchstone—no matter how crazy I get she is always there to pull me back. I am grateful to her husband, Matt, for being the light in my sister's eyes and the song in my sister's heart. Thank you all for your wisdom, beauty, strength, and forgiveness.

Without the encouragement, work, and bravery of Piper Kerman no one would even care about my real life or the lives of the many incarcerated men and women who benefit from her efforts to right so many wrongs. Thank you for your precious coattails and your astounding integrity.

Without the following people these pages would not have come to life and found you:

Sue Carswell interviewed me for *Vanity Fair Online,* never allowing the interest in my story to override her patience and the ethical manner in which she respected my need to remain quiet for so long. Sue helped me select, from an infinite number of possibilities, the small number of salient points from which to best tell my story, and then she gave me the confidence to do so.

I cannot forget my friend and unbelievably great literary agent, Claudia Cross at Folio Literary Management, for her unmovable albeit questionable faith in my ability to write my own story, for convincing me of the importance of my voice's addition to the choir, and for finding the best home for my story: HarperOne.

Out of Orange was placed in the care of Nancy Hancock. She is, with the exception of my father, the finest and most brilliant editor in the universe. She became my friend, my navigator, my confessor, and my conscience, and then she introduced me and my work to another astonishing editor, Hilary Lawson. If you think I write well, trust me, it's all their doing. They got me to the finish line, along with Elissa Cohen, Mark Tauber, Claudia Boutote, Laina Adler, Terri Leonard, and Suzanne Quist. Thank you.

I would like to offer my sincere gratitude to my lawyer and old friend Alan Dressler for his contributions to this story and to my life. I thank him for his generosity and his desire for justice and for his faith twenty years ago that this young broke moron was worth saving.

I would like to thank my employer, Reed Elsevier, for giving me the chance to prove myself in spite of my past and for their continued support even after my unexpected infamy.

I would like to thank Jenji Kohan and Laura Prepon for creating Alex Vause and making me tall.

Last but not least, I want to thank God's little creatures, the precious strays that find themselves in prison consoling broken people, teaching some to care for something other than themselves, and

dodging the monsters. But most of all, Patches, whose uncondi-
tional love and companionship all these many years, saved me.
Patches died of cancer on December 17, 2014, at nineteen years old
(that is almost 140 in human years). She died peacefully. She fell fast
asleep in my arms and went home to God, Dad, catnip clouds, and
a bunch of little winged mice eager to play.